A PEOPLE'S HISTORY
OF CIVILIZATION

feralhouse.com

A PEOPLE'S HISTORY OF CIVILIZATION
John Zerzan

A People's History of Civilization

ISBN 978-1-62-731059-8

Feral House
1240 W. Sims Way
Suite 124
Port Townsend, WA 98368

10 9 8 7 6 5 4 3 2 1

Design: designSimple

TABLE OF CONTENTS

INTRODUCTION

A People's History of Civilization could have been titled *Contributions Toward a History of Civilization in the West—mainly Europe—From an Anti-Civilization Perspective*. But that would not be as snappy a title.

The fifteen essays in this book are my more strictly historical ones. Chapter 1 (agriculture and domestication) dates from the 1980s, as does Chapter 14 (World War I). Other essays are much more recent. Arranged chronologically, with updates and revisions, they provide an episodic but coherent narrative. A narrative informed by a critique of civilization.

Oswald Spengler, Arnold Toynbee, and their predecessors have written histories of world civilization from varying viewpoints. None has dwelt on civilization's logic. That is, the WHY behind the demise of every civilization so far. Ironically, contemporary historian Felipe Fernández-Armesto (*Civilizations*) seems to favor cultures that have especially emphasized domination of nature, although that commitment hastened their end. Few historians have paid serious attention to social crises or transition points as potentially fatal to the project of civilization itself.

There is now only one, totalizing civilization. It is time to recognize its death throes and vulnerabilities. Historians have always written about the past in awareness of their own lives and times. This is still true, and never more pressingly so. It's time to look at the course of history in relation to where, so precariously, we stand now.

1

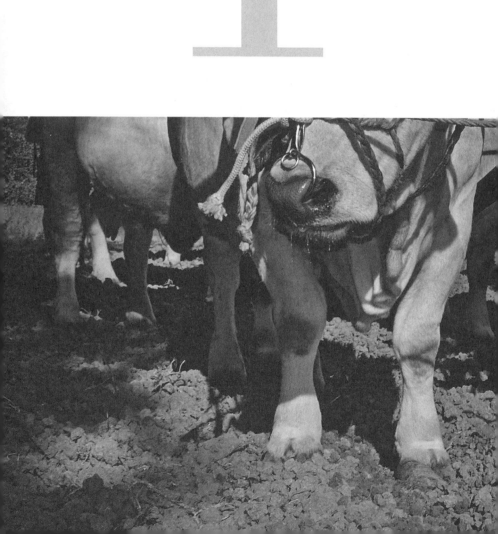

AGRICULTURE/DOMESTICATION: CORNERSTONE OF CIVILIZATION

THE MOVE from forager to farmer, the move to do-mestication of plants and animals—and ourselves—was the most deeply qualitative shift in the history of our spe-cies. It changed everything and continues to do so. Control emerged as the defining principle, the inner logic that links farming to nanotechnology, genetic engineering, and total surveillance. Domestication and agriculture bring ruin to every civilization, including our own now-global version.

Agriculture is the birth of production, complete with its essential features and deformation of life and consciousness. The land itself becomes an instrument of production and the planet's species its objects. Wild or tame, weeds or crops

speak of that duality that cripples the soul of our being, ushering in, relatively quickly, the despotism, war and impoverishment that is high civilization over the great length of that earlier oneness with nature. The forced march of civilization, which Adorno recognized in the "assumption of an irrational catastrophe at the beginning of history," which Freud felt as "something imposed on a resisting majority," of which Stanley Diamond found only "conscripts, not volunteers," was dictated by agriculture. And Mircea Eliade was correct to assess its coming as having "provoked upheavals and spiritual breakdowns" whose magnitude the modern mind cannot imagine.

"To level off, to standardize the human landscape, to efface its irregularities and banish its surprises," these words of E.M. Cioran apply perfectly to the logic of agriculture, the end of life as mainly sensuous activity, the embodiment and generator of separated life. Artificiality and work have steadily increased since its inception and are known as culture: in domesticating animals and plants man necessarily domesticated himself.

Historical time, like agriculture, is not inherent in social reality but an imposition on it. The dimension of time or history is a function of repression, whose foundation is production or agriculture. Hunter-gatherer life was anti-time in its simultaneous and spontaneous openness; farming life generates a sense of time by its successive-task narrowness, its directed routine. As the non-closure and variety of Paleolithic living gave way to the literal enclosure of agriculture, time assumed power and came to take on the character of an enclosed space. Formalized temporal reference points—ceremonies with fixed dates, the naming of days, etc.—are crucial to the ordering of the world of production; as a schedule of production, the calendar is integral to civilization. Conversely, not only would industrial society be impossible without time schedules, the end of agriculture (basis of all production) would be the end of historical time.

Representation begins with language, a means of reining in desire. By displacing autonomous images with verbal symbols, life is reduced and brought under strict control; all direct, unmediated experience is subsumed by that supreme mode of symbolic expression. Language cuts up and organizes reality, as Benjamin Whorf put it, and this segmentation of nature, an aspect of grammar, sets the stage for agriculture. Julian Jaynes, in fact, concluded that the new linguistic mentality led very directly to agriculture. Unquestionably, the crystallization of language into writing, called forth mainly by the need for record-keeping of agricultural transactions, is the signal that civilization has definitively begun.

In the non-commodified, egalitarian hunter-gatherer ethos, the basis of which (as has so often been remarked) was sharing, number was not wanted. There was no ground for the urge to quantify, no reason to divide what was whole. Not until the domestication of animals and plants did this cultural concept fully emerge. Two of number's seminal figures testify clearly to its alliance with separateness and property: Pythagoras, center of a highly influential religious cult of number, and Euclid, father of mathematics and science, whose geometry originated to measure fields for reasons of ownership, taxation and slave labor. One of civilization's early forms, chieftainship, entails a linear rank order in which each member is assigned an exact numerical place. Soon, following the anti-natural linearity of plow culture, the inflexible 90-degree gridiron plan of even earliest cities appeared. Their insistent regularity constitutes in itself a repressive ideology. Culture, now numberized, becomes more firmly bounded and lifeless.

Art, too, in its relationship to agriculture, highlights both institutions. It begins as a means to interpret and subdue reality, to rationalize nature, and conforms to the great turning point which is agriculture in its basic features. The pre-Neolithic cave paintings, for example, are vivid and bold, a dynamic exaltation of animal grace and freedom. The Neolithic art of farmers and pastoralists, however, stiffens into stylized forms; Franz Borkenau typified its pottery as a "narrow, timid botching of materials and forms." With agriculture, art lost its variety and became standardized into geometric designs that tended to degenerate into dull, repetitive patterns, a perfect reflection of standardized, confined, rule-patterned life. And where there had been no representation in Paleolithic art of men killing men, an obsession with depicting confrontation between people advanced with the Neolithic period, scenes of battles becoming common.

Time, language, number, art and all the rest of culture, which predates and leads to agriculture, rests on symbolization. Just as autonomy preceded domestication and self-domestication, the rational and the social precede the symbolic.

Food production, it is eternally and gratefully acknowledged, "permitted the cultural potentiality of the human species to develop." But what is this tendency toward the symbolic, toward the elaboration and imposition of arbitrary forms? It is a growing capacity for objectification, by which what is living becomes reified, thing-like. Symbols are more than the basic units of culture; they are screening devices to distance us from our experiences. They classify and reduce, "to do away with," in Leakey and Lewin's remarkable phrase, "the otherwise almost intolerable burden of relating one experience to another."

Thus culture is governed by the imperative of reforming and subordinating nature. The artificial environment which is agriculture accomplished this pivotal mediation, with the symbolism of objects manipulated in the construction of relations of dominance. For it is not only external nature that is subjugated: the face-to-face quality of pre-agricultural life in itself severely limited domination, while culture extends and legitimizes it.

It is likely that already during the Paleolithic era certain forms or names were attached to objects or ideas, in a symbolizing manner but in a shifting, impermanent, perhaps playful sense. The will to sameness and security found in agriculture means that the symbols became as static and constant as farming life. Regularization, rule patterning, and technological differentiation, under the sign of division of labor, interact to ground and advance symbolization. Agriculture completes the symbolic shift and the virus of alienation has overcome authentic, free life. It is the victory of cultural control; as anthropologist Marshall Sahlins puts it, "The amount of work per capita increases with the evolution of culture and the amount of leisure per capita decreases."

Price and Bar-Yosef saw that "most ethnographically known societies of hunter-gatherers exhibit evolved mechanisms for dampening dominance behavior in favor of the sharing of food and property, caring of kin, and egalitarian relationships." They contrasted this to "the coterminous appearance of agriculture and hierarchy."

Today, the few surviving hunter-gatherers occupy the least "economically interesting" areas of the world where agriculture has not penetrated, such as the snows of the Inuit or desert of the Australian aborigines. And yet the refusal of farming drudgery, even in adverse settings, bears its own rewards. The Hazda of Tanzania, Filipino Tasaday, !Kung of Botswana, or the Kalahari Desert !Kung San—who were seen by Richard Lee as easily surviving a serious, several years' drought while neighboring farmers starved—also testify to Hole and Flannery's summary that "No group on earth has more leisure time than hunters and gatherers, who spend it primarily on games, conversation and relaxing." Service rightly attributed this condition to "the very simplicity of the technology and lack of control over the environment" of such groups. And yet simple Paleolithic methods were, in their own way, "advanced." Consider a basic cooking technique like steaming foods by heating stones in a covered pit; this is immemorially older than any pottery, kettles or baskets (in fact, is anti-container in its non-surplus, non-exchange orientation) and is the most nutritionally sound way to cook, far healthier than boiling food in water, for example. Or consider the fashioning of such stone tools as the long and exceptionally thin "laurel leaf" knives, delicately chipped but strong, which modern industrial techniques cannot duplicate.

The hunting and gathering lifestyle represents the most successful and enduring adaptation ever achieved by humankind. In occasional pre-agriculture phenomena like the intensive collection of food or the systematic hunting of a single species can be seen signs of impending breakdown of a pleasurable mode that remained so static for so long precisely because it was pleasurable. The "penury and day-long grind" of agriculture, in Clark's words, is the vehicle of culture, "rational" only in its perpetual disequilibrium and its logical progression toward ever-greater destruction, as will be outlined below.

Although the term hunter-gatherer should be reversed (and has been by not a few current anthropologists) because it is recognized that gathering constitutes by far the larger survival component, the nature of hunting provides salient contrast to domestication. The relationship of the hunter to the hunted animal, which is sovereign, free and even considered equal, is obviously qualitatively different from that of the farmer or herdsman to the enslaved chattels over which he rules absolutely.

Evidence of the urge to impose order or subjugate is found in the coercive rites and uncleanness taboos of incipient religion. The eventual subduing of the world that is agriculture has at least some of its basis where ambiguous behavior is ruled out, purity and defilement defined and enforced. Mark Aldenderfer is one of many who noted the role of ritual in the birth and extension of hierarchy and inequality. The people who emerge in charge of ritual begin to embody this negative development.

Lévi-Strauss defined religion as the anthropomorphism of nature; earlier spirituality was participatory with nature, not imposing cultural values or traits upon it. The sacred means that which is separated, and ritual and formalization, increasingly removed from the ongoing activities of daily life and in the control of such specialists as shamans and priests, are closely linked with hierarchy and institutionalized power. Religion emerges to ground and legitimize culture, by means of a "higher" order of reality; it is especially required, in this function of maintaining the solidarity of society, by the unnatural demands of agriculture.

In the Neolithic village of Catal Hüyük in Turkish Anatolia, one of every three rooms was used for ritual purposes. Plowing and sowing can be seen as ritual renunciations, according to Burkert, a form of systematic repression accompanied by a sacrificial element. Speaking of sacrifice, which is the killing of domesticated animals (or even humans) for ritual purposes, it is pervasive in agricultural societies and found only there.

Some of the major Neolithic religions often attempted a symbolic healing of the agricultural rupture with nature through the mythology of the earth mother, which needless to say does nothing to restore the lost unity. Fertility myths are also central: the Egyptian Osiris, the Greek Persephone, Baal of the Canaanites, and the New Testament Jesus, gods whose death and resurrection testify to the perseverance of the soil, not to mention the human soul. The first temples signified the rise of domestication or barnyard, which in turn serves to justify the suppression of human autonomy. Whereas precivilized society was, as Redfield put it, "held together by largely undeclared but continually realized ethical conceptions," religion developed as a way of creating citizens, placing the moral order under public management.

Domestication involved the initiation of production, vastly increased division of labor, and the completed foundations of social stratification. This amounted to an epochal mutation both in the character of human existence and its development, clouding the latter with ever more violence and work. Contrary to the myth of hunter-gatherers as violent and aggressive, by the way, recent evidence shows that existing non-farmers, such as the Mbuti ("pygmies") studied by Turnbull, apparently do what killing they do without any aggressive spirit, even with a sort of regret. Warfare and the formation of every civilization or state, on the other hand, are inseparably linked.

Primal peoples did not fight over areas in which separate groups might converge in their gathering and hunting. At least "territorial" struggles are not part of the ethnographic literature and they would seem even less likely to have occurred in pre-history when resources were greater and contact with civilization nonexistent.

Indeed, these peoples had no conception of private property, and Rousseau's figurative judgment, that divided society was founded by the man who first sowed a piece of ground, saying "This land is mine," and found others to believe him, is essentially valid. "Mine and thine, the seeds of all mischief, have no place with them," reads Pietro's 1511 account of the natives encountered on Columbus' second voyage. Centuries later, surviving Native Americans asked, "Sell the Earth? Why not sell the air, the clouds, the great sea?" Agriculture creates and elevates possessions; consider the *longing* root of *belongings*, as if they ever make up for the loss.

Work, as a distinct category of life, likewise did not exist until agriculture. The human capacity of being shackled to crops and herds, devolved rather quickly. Food production overcame the common absence or paucity of ritual and hierarchy in society and introduced civilized activities like the forced labor of temple-building. Here is the real "Cartesian split" between inner and outer reality, the separation whereby nature became merely something to be "worked." On this capacity for a sedentary and servile existence rests the entire superstructure of civilization with its increasing weight of repression.

Male violence toward women originated with agriculture, which transmuted women into beasts of burden and breeders of children. Before farming, the egalitarianism of foraging life "applied as fully to women as to men," judged Eleanor Leacock, owing to the autonomy of tasks and the fact that decisions were made by those who carried them out. In the absence of production and with no drudge work suitable for child labor such as weeding, women were not consigned to onerous chores or the constant supply of babies.

Along with the curse of perpetual work, via agriculture, in the expulsion from Eden, God told woman, "I will greatly multiply thy sorrow and thy conception; in sorrow thou shalt bring forth children; and that desire shall be to thy husband, and he shall rule over thee." Similarly, the first known codified laws, those of the Sumerian king Ur-Namu, prescribed death to any woman satisfying desires outside of marriage. Thus Whyte referred to the ground women "lost relative to men when humans first abandoned a simple hunting and gathering way of life," and Simone de Beauvoir saw in the cultural equation of plow and phallus a fitting symbol of the oppression of women.

As wild animals are converted into sluggish meat-making machines, the concept of becoming "cultivated" is a virtue enforced on people, meaning the weeding out of freedom from one's nature, in the service of domestication and exploitation. As Rice points out, in Sumer, the first civilization, the earliest cities had factories with their characteristic high organization and refraction of skills. Civilization from this point exacts human labor and the mass production of food, buildings, war and authority.

To the Greeks, work was a curse and nothing else. Their name for it—*ponos*—has the same root as the Latin *poena*, sorrow. The famous Old Testament curse on agriculture as the expulsion from Paradise (Genesis 3:17–18) reminds us of the origin of work. As Mumford put it, "Conformity, repetition, patience were the keys to this [Neolithic] culture...the patient capacity for work." In this monotony and passivity of tending and waiting is born, according to Paul Shepard, the peasant's "deep, latent resentments, crude mixtures of rectitude and heaviness, and absence of humor." One might also add a stoic insensitivity and lack of imagination inseparable from religious faith, sullenness, and suspicion among traits widely attributed to the domesticated life of farming.

Although food production by its nature includes a latent readiness for political domination and although civilizing culture was from the beginning its own propaganda machine, the changeover involved a monumental struggle. Fredy Perlman's *Against Leviathan! Against His-Story!* is unrivaled on this, vastly enriching Toynbee's attention to the "internal" and "external proletariats," discontents within and without civilization. Nonetheless, along the axis from digging stick farming to plow agriculture to fully differentiated irrigation systems, an almost total genocide of gatherers and hunters was necessarily effected.

The formation and storage of surpluses are part of the domesticating will to control and make static, an aspect of the tendency to symbolize. A bulwark against the flow of nature, surplus takes the forms of herd animals and granaries. Stored grain was the earliest medium of equivalence, the oldest form of capital. Only with the appearance of wealth in the shape of storable grains do the gradations of labor and social classes proceed. While there were certainly wild grains before all this (and wild wheat, by the way, is 24 percent protein compared to 12 percent for domesticated wheat), the bias of culture makes every difference. Civilization and its cities rested as much on granaries as on symbolization.

The mystery of agriculture's origin seems even more impenetrable in light of the recent reversal of long-standing notions that the previous era was one of hostility to nature and an absence of leisure. "One could no longer assume," wrote Arme, "that early man domesticated plants and animals to escape drudgery and starvation. If anything, the contrary appeared true, and the advent of farming saw the end of innocence." For a long time, the question was "Why wasn't agriculture adopted much earlier in human evolution?" More recently, we know that agriculture, in Cohen's words, "is not easier than hunting and gathering and does not provide a higher quality, more palatable, or more secure food base." Thus the consensus question now is, "Why was it adopted at all?"

Rik Smits, in 2016, wrote: "The only possible explanation is that the necessary mental machinery was not yet available." It is ludicrous that this opinion survives and is published. There is zero support for it in the literature of any discipline. To the contrary: studies are constantly indicating that human intelligence was equal to our own, hundreds of thousands of years ago.

Many more cogent theories have been advanced, none convincingly. Childe and others argue that population increase pushed human societies into more intimate contact with other species, leading to domestication and the need to produce in order to feed the additional people. But it has been shown rather conclusively that population increase did not precede agriculture but was caused by it. "I don't see any evidence anywhere in the world," concluded Flannery, "that suggests that population pressure was responsible for the beginning of agriculture." Jacques Cauvin determined that "the rich landscape of the Near East would have been able to accommodate the human population for a long time yet." Another theory has it that major climatic changes occurred at the end of the Pleistocene, about 11,000 years ago, that upset the old hunter-gatherer life-world and led directly to the cultivation of certain surviving staples. Recent dating methods have helped demolish this approach; no such climatic shift happened that could have forced the new mode into existence. Besides, there are scores of examples of agriculture being adopted—or refused—in every type of climate. Another major hypothesis is that agriculture was introduced via a chance discovery or invention as if it had never occurred to the species before a certain moment that, for example, food grows from sprouted seeds. It seems certain that Paleolithic humanity had a virtually inexhaustible knowledge of flora and fauna for many thousands of years before the cultivation of plants began, which renders this theory especially weak.

Agreement with Carl Sauer's summation that "Agriculture did not originate from a growing or chronic shortage of food" is sufficient, in fact, to dismiss virtually all originary theories that have been advanced. A remaining idea, presented by Hahn, Isaac and others, holds that food production began at base as a religious activity. This hypothesis has plausibility. As Gebauer and Price put it, "Rather than the result of external forces and stress, the adoption of domesticates may well have been an internally motivated process."

Sheep and goats, the first animals to be domesticated, are known to have been widely used in religious ceremonies, and to have been raised in enclosed meadows for sacrificial purposes. Before they were domesticated, moreover, sheep had no wool suitable for textile purposes. The main use of the hen in southeastern Asia and the eastern Mediterranean—the earliest centers of civilization—"seems to have been," according to Darby, "sacrificial or divinatory rather than alimentary." Sauer adds that the "egg laying and meat producing qualities" of tamed fowl "are relatively late consequences of their domestication." Wild cattle were fierce and dangerous; neither the docility of oxen nor the modified meat texture of such castrates could have been foreseen. Cattle were not milked until centuries after their initial captivity, and representations indicate that their first known harnessing was to wagons in religious processions. Brian Hayden points out that "early domesticates appear to have been highly labor intensive and could only compete with the returns of wild foods after hundreds or thousands of years of genetic manipulation."

Plants, next to be controlled, exhibit similar backgrounds so far as is known. Consider the New World examples of squash and pumpkin, used originally as ceremonial rattles. Johannessen discussed the religious and mystical motives connected with the domestication of maize, Mexico's most important crop and center of its native Neolithic religion. Likewise, Anderson investigated the selection and development of distinctive types of various cultivated plants because of their magical significance. The shamans, I should add, were well-placed in positions of power to introduce agriculture via the taming and planting involved in ritual and religion, sketchily referred to above.

Though the religious explanation of the origins of agriculture has been somewhat overlooked, it brings us, in my opinion, to the very doorstep of the real explanation of the birth of production: that non-rational, cultural force of alienation which spread, in the forms of time, language, number and art, to ultimately colonize material and psychic life in agriculture. "Religion" is too narrow a conceptualization of this infection and its growth. Domination is too weighty, too all-encompassing to have been solely conveyed by the pathology that is religion.

But the cultural values of control and uniformity that are part of religion are certainly part of agriculture, and from the beginning. Noting that strains of corn cross-pollinate very easily, Anderson studied the very primitive agriculturalists of Assam, the Naga tribe, and their variety of corn that exhibited no differences from plant to plant. True to culture, showing that it is complete from the beginning of production, the Naga kept their varieties so pure "only by a fanatical adherence to an ideal type." This exemplifies the marriage of culture and production in domestication, and its inevitable progeny, repression and work.

The scrupulous tending of strains of plants finds its parallel in the domesticating of animals, which also defies natural selection and re-establishes the controllable organic world at a debased, artificial level. Like plants, animals are mere things to be manipulated; a cow, for instance, is seen as a kind of machine for converting grass to milk. Transmuted from a state of freedom to that of helpless parasites, these animals become completely dependent on man for survival. In domestic mammals, as a rule, the size of the brain becomes relatively smaller as specimens are produced that devote more energy to growth and less to activity. Placid, infantilized, typified perhaps by the sheep, most domesticated of herd animals; the remarkable intelligence of wild sheep is completely lost in their tamed counterparts. The social relationships among domestic animals are reduced to the crudest essentials. Non-reproductive parts of the life cycle are minimized, courtship is curtailed, and the animal's very capacity to recognize its own species is impaired.

Farming also created the potential for rapid environmental destruction, and the domination over nature soon began to turn the green mantle that covered the birthplaces of civilization into barren and lifeless areas. "Vast regions have changed their aspect completely," estimates Zeuner, "always to quasi-drier condition, since the beginnings of the Neolithic." Deserts now occupy most of the areas where the high civilizations once flourished, and there is much historical evidence that these early formations inevitably ruined their environments.

Throughout the Mediterranean Basin and in the adjoining Near East and Asia, agriculture turned lush and hospitable lands into depleted, dry, and rocky terrain. In *Critias*, Plato described Attica as "a skeleton wasted by disease," referring to the deforestation of Greece and contrasting it to its earlier richness. Grazing by goats and sheep, the first domesticated ruminants, was a major factor in the denuding of Greece, Lebanon, and North Africa, and the desertification of the Roman and Mesopotamian empires.

Another, more immediate impact of agriculture, brought to light increasingly in recent years, involved the physical well-being of its subjects. Lee and Devore's researches show that "the diet of gathering peoples was far better than that of cultivators, that starvation is rare, that their health status was generally superior, and that there is a lower incidence of chronic disease." Conversely, Farb summarized, "Production provides an inferior diet based on a limited number of foods, is much less reliable because of blights and the vagaries of weather, and is much more costly in terms of human labor expended."

The new field of paleopathology has reached even more emphatic conclusions, stressing, as does Angel, the "sharp decline in growth and nutrition caused by the changeover from food gathering to food production. Earlier conclusions about life span have also been revised. Although eyewitness Spanish accounts of the sixteenth century tell of Florida Indian fathers seeing their fifth generation before passing away, it was long believed that primitive people died in their 30s and 40s. Robson, Boyden and others have dispelled the confusion of longevity with life expectancy and discovered that current hunter-gatherers, barring injury and severe infection, often outlive their civilized contemporaries. During the industrial age only fairly recently did life span lengthen for the species, and it is now widely recognized that in Paleolithic times humans were long-lived animals, once certain risks were passed. DeVries is correct in his judgment that duration of life dropped sharply upon contact with civilization.

"Tuberculosis and diarrheal disease had to await the rise of farming, measles and bubonic plague the appearance of large cities," wrote Jared Diamond. Malaria, probably the single greatest killer of humanity, and nearly all other infectious diseases are the heritage of agriculture. Nutritional and degenerative diseases in general appear with the reign of domestication and culture. Cancer, coronary thrombosis, anemia, dental caries, and mental disorders are but a few of the hallmarks of agriculture; previously women gave birth with no difficulty and little or no pain.

People were far more alive in all their senses. !Kung San, reported R.H. Post, have heard a single-engine plane while it was still seventy miles away, and many of them can see four moons of Jupiter with the naked eye. The summary judgment of Harris and Ross, as to "an overall decline in the quality—and probably in the length—of human life among farmers as compared with earlier hunter-gatherer groups," is understated. It is also true that resistance often persevered. For instance, Baltic peoples held to their traditional lifeway for more than a thousand years after their neighbors to the southeast had become farmers.

One of the most persistent and universal ideas is that there was once a Golden Age of innocence before history began. Hesiod, for instance, referred to the "life-sustaining soil, which yielded its copious fruits unbribed by toil." Eden was clearly the home of the hunter-gatherers, and the yearning expressed by the historical images of paradise must have been that of disillusioned tillers of the soil for a lost life of freedom and relative ease.

The history of civilization shows the increasing displacement of nature from human experience, characterized in part by a narrowing of food choices. According to Rooney, prehistoric peoples found sustenance in over 1,500 species of wild plants, whereas "All civilizations," Wenke reminds us," have been based on the cultivation of one or more of just six plant species: wheat, barley, millet, rice, maize, and potatoes."

It is a striking truth that over the centuries "the number of different edible foods which are actually eaten," Pyke points out, "has steadily dwindled." The world's population now depends for most of its subsistence on only about twenty genera of plants while their natural strains are replaced by artificial hybrids and the genetic pool of these plants becomes far less varied.

The diversity of food tends to disappear or flatten out as the proportion of manufactured foods increases. Today the very same articles of diet are distributed worldwide, so that an Inuit Eskimo and an African may soon be eating powdered milk manufactured in Wisconsin or frozen fish sticks from a single factory in Sweden. A few big multinationals such as Unilever, the world's biggest food production company, preside over a highly integrated service system in which the object is not to nourish or even to feed, but to force an ever-increasing consumption of fabricated, processed products upon the world.

When Descartes enunciated the principle that the fullest exploitation of matter to *any* use is the whole duty of man, our separation from nature was virtually complete and the stage was set for the Industrial Revolution. Three hundred and fifty years later this spirit lingered in the person of Jean Vorst, curator of France's Museum of Natural History, who pronounced that our species, "because of intellect," can no longer re-cross a certain threshold of civilization and once again become part of a natural habitat. He further stated, expressing perfectly the original and persevering imperialism of agriculture, "As the earth in its primitive state is not adopted to our expansion, man must shackle it to fulfill human destiny."

The early factories literally mimicked the agricultural model, indicating again that at base all mass production is farming. The natural world is to be broken and forced to work. One thinks of the mid-American prairies where settlers had to yoke six oxen to plow in order to cut through the soil for the first time. Or a scene from the 1870s in *The Octopus* by Frank Norris, in which gang-plows were driven like "a great column of field artillery" across the San Joaquin Valley, cutting 175 furrows at once.

Today the organic, what is left of it, is fully mechanized under the aegis of a few petrochemical corporations. Their artificial fertilizers, pesticides, herbicides and near-monopoly of the world's seed stock define a total environment that integrates food production from planting to consumption. Although Lévi-Strauss is right that "Civilization manufactures monoculture like sugar beets," only since World War II has a completely synthetic orientation begun to dominate.

Agriculture takes more organic matter out of the soil than it puts back, and soil erosion is basic to the monoculture of annuals. Regarding the latter, some are promoted with devastating results to the land; along with cotton and soybeans, corn, which in its present domesticated state is totally dependent on agriculture for its existence, is especially bad. J. Russell Smith called it "the killer of continents...and one of the worst enemies of the human future." The erosion cost of one bushel of Iowa corn is two bushels of topsoil, highlighting the more general large-scale industrial destruction of farmland. The continuous tillage of huge monocultures, with massive use of chemicals and no application of manure or humus, obviously raises soil deterioration and soil loss to much higher levels.

The dominant agricultural mode has it that soil needs massive infusions of chemicals, supervised by technicians whose overriding goal is to maximize production. Artificial fertilizers and all the rest from this outlook eliminate the need for the complex life of the soil and indeed convert it into a mere instrument of production. The promise of technology is total control, a completely contrived environment that simply supersedes the natural balance of the biosphere.

But more and more energy is expended to purchase great monocultural yields that are beginning to decline, never mind the toxic contamination of the soil, groundwater and food. The U.S. Department of Agriculture says that cropland erosion is occurring in this country at a rate of two billion tons of soil a year. The National Academy of Sciences estimates that over one-third of topsoil is already gone forever. The ecological imbalance caused by monocropping and synthetic fertilizers causes enormous increases in pests and crop diseases; since World War II, crop loss due to insects has actually doubled. Technology responds, of course, with spiraling applications of more synthetic fertilizers, and "weed" and "pest" killers, accelerating the crime against nature.

Another postwar phenomenon was the Green Revolution, billed as the salvation of the impoverished Third World by American capital and technology. But rather than feeding the hungry, the Green Revolution drove millions of poor people from farmlands in Asia, Latin America and Africa as victims of the program that fosters large corporate farms. It amounted to an enormous technological colonization creating dependency on capital-intensive agribusiness, destroying older agrarian communalism, requiring massive fossil fuel consumption and assaulting nature on an unprecedented scale.

Desertification, or loss of soil due to agriculture, has been steadily increasing. Each year, a total area equivalent to more than two Belgiums is being converted to desert worldwide. The fate of the world's tropical rainforests is a factor in the acceleration of this desiccation: half of them have been erased in the past thirty years. In Botswana, the last wilderness region of Africa has disappeared like much of the Amazon jungle and almost half of the rainforests of Central America, primarily to raise cattle for the hamburger markets in the U.S. and Europe. The few areas safe from deforestation are where agriculture doesn't want to go; the destruction of the land is proceeding in the U.S. over a greater land area than was encompassed by the original thirteen colonies, just as it was at the heart of the severe African famine of the mid-1980s and the extinction of one species of wild animal and plant after another.

Returning to animals, one is reminded of the words of Genesis in which God said to Noah, "And the fear of you and the dread of you shall be upon every fowl of the air, upon all that moveth upon the earth, and upon all the fishes of the sea; into your hands are they delivered." When newly discovered territory was first visited by the advance guard of production, as a wide descriptive literature shows, the wild mammals and birds showed no fear whatsoever of the explorers. The agriculturalized mentality, however, so aptly foretold in the biblical passage, projects an exaggerated belief in the fierceness of wild creatures, which follows from progressive estrangement and loss of contact with the animal world, plus the need to maintain dominance over it.

The fate of domestic animals is defined by the fact that agricultural technologists continually look to factories as models of how to refine their own production systems. Nature is banished from these systems as, increasingly, farm animals are kept largely immobile throughout their deformed lives, maintained in high-density, wholly artificial environments. Billions of chickens, pigs, and veal calves, for example, no longer even see the light of day much less roam the fields, fields growing more silent as more and more pastures are plowed up to grow feed for these hideously confined beings.

The high-tech chickens, whose beak ends have been clipped off to reduce death from stress-induced fighting, often exist four or even five to a 12" by 18" cage and are periodically deprived of food and water for up to ten days to regulate their egg-laying cycles. Pigs live on concrete floors with no bedding; foot-rot, tail-biting and cannibalism are endemic because of physical conditions and stress. Sows nurse their piglets separated by metal grates, mother and offspring barred from natural contact. Veal calves are often raised in darkness, chained to stalls so narrow as to disallow turning around or other normal posture adjustment. These animals are generally under regimens of constant medication due to the tortures involved and their heightened susceptibility to diseases; automated animal production relies upon hormones and antibiotics. Such systematic cruelty, not to mention the kind of food that results, brings to mind the fact that captivity itself and every form of enslavement has agriculture as its progenitor or model.

Food has been one of our most direct contacts with the natural environment, but we are rendered increasingly dependent on a technological production system in which finally even our senses have become redundant; taste, once vital for judging a food's value or safety, is no longer experienced, but rather certified by a label. Overall, the healthfulness of what we consume declines, and land once cultivated for food now produces coffee, tobacco, grains for alcohol, marijuana, and other drugs, creating the context for famine. Even the non-processed foods like fruits and vegetables are now grown to be tasteless and uniform because the demands of handling, transport and storage, not nutrition or pleasure, are the highest considerations.

Total war borrowed from agriculture to defoliate millions of acres in Southeast Asia during the Vietnam War, but the plundering of the biosphere proceeds even more lethally in its daily, global forms. Food as a function of production has also failed miserably on the most obvious level: half of the world, as everyone knows, suffers from malnourishment ranging to starvation itself, even as obesity rates rise.

Meanwhile, the "diseases of civilization," as discussed by Eaton and Konner in the January 31, 1985 *New England Journal of Medicine* and contrasted with the healthful pre-farming diets, underline the joyless, sickly world of chronic maladjustment we inhabit as prey of the manufacturers of medicine, cosmetics, and fabricated food. Domestication reaches new heights of the pathological in genetic food engineering, with new types of animals in the offing as well as contrived microorganisms and plants. Logically, humanity itself will also become a domesticate of this order as the world of production processes us as much as it degrades and deforms every other natural system.

The project of subduing nature, begun and carried through by agriculture, has assumed gigantic proportions. The "success" of civilization's progress, a success earlier humanity never wanted, tastes more and more like ashes. James Serpell summed it up this way: "In short we appear to have reached the end of the line. We cannot expand; we seem unable to intensify production without wreaking further havoc, and the planet is fast becoming a wasteland."

Awareness of the consequences of civilization and its history seems to be making itself felt in the twenty-first century. This awareness may even come to rival the overall sense of civilization's inevitability. It is showing up in the academic literature, for example. In the journal *Nature* (07 January 2016), S. Kathleen Lyons et al. point out that plant and animal communities were stable and healthy for 300 million years, before they were disrupted 6,000 years ago by the spread of agriculture. John R. Schramski et al. (*Nature*,

04 May 2015) describe the earth reaching an end point, a battery running out of dischargeable energy. Research by Anthony D. Barnosky et al. (*Nature*, 04 May 2012) contemplates collapse, a global ecosystem approaching a tipping point.

Jared Diamond termed the initiation of agriculture "a catastrophe from which we have never recovered." Agriculture has been and remains a "catastrophe" at all levels, the one which underpins the entire material and spiritual culture of alienation now destroying us. Liberation is impossible without its dissolution.

Author's note: This chapter was written for a publication that did not want endnotes.

2

CIVILIZATION *IS* PATRIARCHY

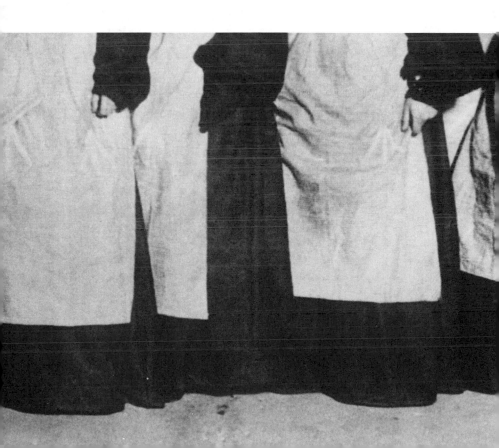

CIVILIZATION, VERY fundamentally, is the history of the domination of nature and of women. Patriarchy means rule over women and nature. Are the two institutions at base synonymous?

Philosophy has mainly ignored the vast realm of suffering that has unfolded since it began, in division of labor, its long course. Hélène Cixous calls the history of philosophy a "chain of fathers." Women are as absent from it as suffering, and are certainly the closest of kin.

Camille Paglia, anti-feminist literary theorist, meditates thusly on civilization and women:

When I see a giant crane passing on a flatbed truck, I pause in awe and reverence, as one would for a church procession. What power of conception: what grandiosity: these cranes tie us to ancient Egypt, where monumental architecture was first imagined and achieved. If civilization has been left in female hands, we would still be living in grass huts.[1]

The "glories" of civilization and women's disinterest in them. To some of us the "grass huts" represent not taking the

---

1   Camille Paglia, *Sexual Personae: Art and Decadence from Nefertiti to Emily Dickinson* (New Haven: Yale University Press, 1990), p. 38.

wrong path, that of oppression and destructiveness. In light of the globally metastasizing death drive of technological civilization, if *only* we still lived in grass huts!

Women and nature are universally devalued by the dominant paradigm and who cannot see what this has wrought? Ursula Le Guin gives us a healthy corrective to Paglia's dismissal of both:

> Civilized Man says: I am Self, I am Master, all the rest is other—outside, below, underneath, subservient. I own, I use, I explore, I exploit, I control. What I do is what matters. What I want is what matter is for. I am that I am, and the rest is women and wilderness, to be used as I see fit.[2]

There are certainly many who believe that early civilizations existed that were matriarchal. But no anthropologists or archaeologists, feminists included, have found evidence of such societies. "The search for a genuinely egalitarian, let along matriarchal, culture has proved fruitless," concludes Sherry Ortner.[3] The evidence, according to Cynthia Eller, supports neither the existence of matriarchy nor a patriarchal revolution that overturned any such matriarchies.[4]

There was, however, a long span of time when women were generally less subject to men, before male-defined culture became fixed or universal. Since the 1970s anthropologists such as Adrienne Zihlman, Nancy Tanner and Frances

---

2   Ursula Le Guin, "Women/Wildness," in Judith Plant, ed., *Healing the Wounds* (Philadelphia: New Society, 1989), p. 45.

3   Sherry B. Ortner, *Making Gender: The Politics and Erotics of Culture* (Boston: Beacon Press, 1996), p. 24.

4   Cynthia Eller, *The Myth of Matriarchal Prehistory: Why an Invented Past Won't Give Women a Future* (Boston: Beacon Press, 2000), pp. 13, 179. See also her *Gentlemen and Amazons* (Berkeley: University of California Press, 2011) for nineteenth-century origins of the matriarchal myth.

Dahlberg[5] have corrected the earlier focus or stereotype of prehistoric "Man the Hunter" to that of "Woman the Gatherer." Key here is the datum that as a general average, pre-agricultural band societies received about 80 percent of their sustenance from gathering and 20 percent from hunting. It is possible to overstate the hunting/gathering distinction and to overlook those groups in which, to significant degrees, women have hunted and men have gathered.[6] But women's autonomy in foraging societies is rooted in the fact that material resources for subsistence are equally available to women and men in their respective spheres of activity.

In the context of the generally egalitarian ethos of hunter-gatherer or foraging societies, anthropologists like Eleanor Leacock, Patricia Draper and Mina Caulfield have described a generally equal relationship between men and women.[7] In such settings where the person who procures something also distributes it and where women procure about 80 percent of the sustenance, it is largely women who determine band society movements and camp locations. Similarly, evidence indicates that both women and men made the stone tools used by pre-agricultural peoples.[8]

---

5   For example, Adrienne L. Zihlman and Nancy Tanner, "Gathering and Hominid Adaptation," in Lionel Tiger and Heather Fowler, eds., *Female Hierarchies* (Chicago: Beresford, 1978); Adrienne L. Zihlman, "Women in Evolution," *Signs* 4 (1978); Frances Dahlberg, *Woman the Gatherer* (New Haven: Yale University Press, 1981); Elizabeth Fisher, *Woman's Creation: Sexual Evolution and the Shaping of Society* (Garden City, NY: Anchor/Doubleday, 1979).

6   James Steele and Stephan Shennan, eds., *The Archaeology of Human Ancestry* (New York: Routledge, 1995), p. 349. Also, M. Kay Martin and Barbara Voorhies, *Female of the Species* (New York: Columbia University Press, 1975), pp. 210–211, for example.

7   Leacock is among the most insistent, claiming that whatever male domination exists in surviving societies of this kind is due to the effects of colonial domination. See Eleanor Burke Leacock, "Women's Status in Egalitarian Society," *Current Anthropology* 19 (1978); and her *Myths of Male Dominance* (New York: Monthly Review Press, 1981). See also S. and G. Cafferty, "Powerful Women and the Myth of Male Dominance in Aztec Society," *Archaeology from Cambridge* 7 (1988).

8   Joan Gero and Margaret W. Conkey, eds., *Engendering Archaeology* (Cambridge, MA: Blackwell, 1991); C.F.M. Bird, "Woman the Toolmaker," in *Women in Archaeology* (Canberra: Research School of Pacific and Asian Studies, 1993).

With the matrilocal Pueblo, Iroquois, Crow, and other American Indian groups, women could terminate a marital relationship at any time. Overall, males and females in band society move freely and peacefully from one band to another as well as into or out of relationships.[9] According to Rosalind Miles, the men not only do not command or exploit women's labor, "they exert little or no control over women's bodies or those of their children, making no fetish of virginity or chastity, and making no demands of women's sexual exclusivity."[10] Zubeeda Banu Quraishy provides an African example: "Mbuti gender associations were characterized by harmony and cooperation."[11]

And yet, one wonders, was the situation really ever quite this rosy? Given an apparently universal devaluation of women, which varies in its forms but not in its essence, the question of when and how it was basically otherwise persists. There is a fundamental division of social existence according to gender, and an obvious hierarchy to this divide. For philosopher Jane Flax, the most deep-seated dualisms, even including those of subject-object and mind-body, are a reflection of gender disunity.[12]

Gender is not the same as the natural/physiological distinction between the sexes. It is a cultural categorization and ranking grounded in a sexual division of labor that may be the single cultural form of greatest significance. If gender introduces and legitimates inequality and domination, what

---

9   Claude Meillasoux, *Maidens, Meal and Money* (Cambridge, MA: Cambridge University Press, 1981), p. 16.

10   Rosalind Miles, *The Women's History of the World* (London: Michael Joseph, 1986), p. 16.

11   Zubeeda Banu Quraishy, "Gender Politics in the Socio-Economic Organization of Contemporary Foragers," in Ian Keen and Takako Yamada, eds., *Identity and Gender in Hunting and Gathering Societies* (Osaka: National Museum of Ethnology, 2000), p. 196.

12   Jane Flax, "Political Philosophy and the Patriarchal Unconscious," in Sandra Harding and Merrill B. Hintikka, eds., *Discovering Reality* (Dortrecht: Reidel, 1983), pp. 269–270.

could be more important to put into question? So in terms of origins—and in terms of our future—the question of human society without gender presents itself.

We know that division of labor led to domestication and civilization, and drives the globalized system of domination today. It also appears that artificially imposed sexual division of labor was its earliest form and was also, in effect, the formation of gender.

Sharing food has long been recognized as a hallmark of the foraging life-way. Sharing the responsibility for the care of offspring, too, which can still be seen among the few remaining hunter-gatherer societies, in contrast to privatized, isolated family life in civilization. What we think of as the family is not an eternal institution, any more than exclusively female mothering was inevitable in human evolution.[13]

Society is integrated via the division of labor and the family is integrated via the sexual division of labor. The need for integration bespeaks a tension, a split that calls for a basis for cohesion or solidarity. In this sense Testart is right: "Inherent in kinship is hierarchy."[14] And with their basis in division of labor, the relations of kinship become relations of production. "Gender is inherent in the very nature of kinship," as Cucchiari points out, "which could not exist without it."[15] It is in this area that the root of the domination of nature as well as of women may be explored.

As combined group foraging in band societies gave way to specialized roles, kinship structures formed the infrastructure of relationships that developed in the direction of inequality

---

13 See Patricia Elliott, *From Mastery to Analysis: Theories of Gender in Psychoanalytic Feminism* (Ithaca: Cornell University Press, 1991), e.g., p. 105.

14 Alain Testart, "Aboriginal Social Inequality and Reciprocity," *Oceania* 60 (1989), p. 5.

15 Salvatore Cucchiari, "The Gender Revolution and the Transition from Bisexual Horde to Patrilocal Band," in Sherry B. Ortner and Harriet Whitehead, eds., *Sexual Meanings: The Cultural Construction of Gender and Sexuality* (Cambridge, UK: Cambridge University Press, 1984), p. 36. This essay is of great importance.

and power differentials. Women typically became immobilized by a privatizing child care role; this pattern deepened later on, beyond the supposed requirements of that gender role. This gender-based separation and division of labor began to occur around the transition from the Middle to Upper Paleolithic eras.[16]

Gender and the kinship system are cultural constructs set over and against the biological subjects involved, "above all a symbolic organization of behavior," according to Juliet Mitchell.[17] It may be more telling to look at symbolic culture itself as required by gendered society, by "the need to mediate symbolically a severely dichotomized cosmos."[18] The which-came-first question introduces itself, and is difficult to resolve. It is clear, however, that there is no evidence of symbolic activity (e.g., cave paintings) until the gender system, based on sexual division of labor, was apparently under way.[19]

By the Upper Paleolithic, that epoch immediately prior to the Neolithic Revolution of domestication and civilization, the gender revolution had won the day. Masculine and feminine signs are present in the first cave art, about 35,000 years ago. Gender consciousness arises as an all-encompassing ensemble of dualities, a specter of divided society. In the new polarization activity becomes gender-related, gender-defined. The role of hunter, for example, develops into association with males, its requirements attributed to the male gender as desired traits.

That which had been far more unitary or generalized,

---

16 Olga Soffer, "Social Transformations at the Middle to Upper Paleolithic Transition," in Günter Brauer and Fred H. Smith, eds., *Replacement: Controversies in Homo Sapiens Evolution* (Rotterdam: A.A. Balkema, 1992), p. 254.

17 Juliet Mitchell, *Women: The Longest Revolution* (London: Virago Press, 1984), p. 83.

18 Cucchiari, *op. cit.*, p. 62.

19 Robert Briffault, *The Mothers: The Matriarchal Theory of Social Origins* (New York: Macmillan, 1931), p. 159.

such as group foraging or communal responsibility for child tending, had now become the separated spheres in which sexual jealousy and possessiveness appear. At the same time, the symbolic emerges as a separate sphere or reality. This is revealing in terms of the content of art, as well as ritual and its practice. It is hazardous to extrapolate from the present to the remote past, yet surviving non-industrialized cultures may shed some light. The Bimin-Kushusmin of Papua New Guinea, for example, experience the masculine-feminine split as fundamental and defining. The masculine "essence," called *finiik*, not only signifies powerful, warlike qualities but also those of ritual and control. The feminine "essence," or *khaapkhabuurien*, is wild, impulsive, sensuous, and ignorant of ritual.[20] Similarly, the Mansi of northwestern Siberia place severe restrictions on women's involvement in their ritual practices.[21] With band societies, it is no exaggeration to say that the presence or absence of ritual is crucial to the question of the subordination of women.[22] Gayle Rubin concludes that the "world-historical defeat of women occurred with the origins of culture and is a prerequisite of culture."[23]

The simultaneous rise of symbolic culture and gendered life is not a coincidence. Each of them involves a basic shift from non-separated, non-hierarchized life. The logic of their development and extension is a response to tensions and inequalities that they incarnate; both are dialectically interconnected to earliest, artificial division of labor.

20   Theodore Lidz and Ruth Williams Lidz, *Oedipus in the Stone Age* (Madison, CT: International Universities Press, 1988), p. 123.

21   Elena G. Fedorova, "The Role of Women in Mansi Society," in Peter P. Schweitzer, Megan Biesele and Robert K. Hitchhock, eds., *Hunters and Gatherers in the Modern World* (New York: Berghahn Books, 2000), p. 396.

22   Steven Harrall, *Human Families* (Boulder, CO: Westview Press, 1997), p. 89. "Examples of the link between ritual and inequality in forager societies are widespread," according to Stephan Shennan, "Social Inequality and the Transmission of Cultural Traditions in Forager Societies," in Steele and Shennan, *op. cit.*, p. 369.

23   Gayle Rubin, "The Traffic in Women," *Toward an Anthropology of Women* (New York: Monthly Review Press, 1979), p. 176.

On the heels, relatively speaking, of the gender/symbolic alteration came another Great Leap Forward, into agriculture and civilization. This is the definitive "rising above nature," overriding the previous two million years of non-dominating intelligence and intimacy with nature. This change was decisive as a consolidation and intensification of the division of labor. Meillasoux reminds us of its beginnings:

> Nothing in nature explains the sexual division of labor, nor such institutions as marriage, conjugality or paternal filiation. All are imposed on women by constraint, all are therefore facts of civilization which must be explained, not used as explanations.[24]

Kelkar and Nathan, for example, did not find very much gender specialization among hunter-gatherers in western India, compared to agriculturalists there.[25] The transition from foraging to food production brought similar radical changes in societies everywhere. It is instructive, to cite another example closer to the present, that the Muskogee people of the American Southeast upheld the intrinsic value of the untamed, undomesticated forest; colonial civilizers attacked this stance by trying to replace Muskogee matrilineal tradition with patrilineal relations.[26]

The locus of the transformation of the wild to the cultural is the domicile, as women become progressively limited to its horizons. Domestication is grounded here (etymologically as well, from the Latin *domus*, or household): drudge work, less robusticity than with foraging, many more children, and

---

24 Meillasoux, *op. cit.*, pp. 20–21.

25 Cited by Indra Munshi, "Women and Forest: A Study of the Warlis of Western India," in Govind Kelkar, Dev Nathan and Pierre Walter, eds., *Gender Relations in Forest Societies in Asia: Patriarchy at Odds* (New Delhi: Sage, 2003), p. 268.

26 Joel W. Martin, *Sacred Revolt: The Muskogees' Struggle for a New World* (Boston: Beacon Press, 1991), pp. 99, 143.

a lower life expectancy than males are among the features of agricultural existence for women.[27] Here another dichotomy appears, the distinction between work and non-work, which for so many, many generations did not exist. From the gendered production site and its constant extension come further foundations of our culture and mentality.

Confined, if not fully pacified, women are defined as passive. Like nature, of value as something to be made to produce; awaiting fertilization, activation from outside herself/itself. Women experience the move from autonomy and relative equality in small, mobile anarchic groups to controlled status in large, complex governed settlements.

Mythology and religion, compensations of divided society, testify to the reduced position of women. In Homer's Greece, fallow land (not domesticated by grain culture) was considered feminine, the abode of Calypso, of Circe, of the Sirens who tempted Odysseus to abandon civilization's labors. Both land and women are again subjects of domination. But this imperialism betrays traces of guilty conscience, as in the punishments for those associated with domestication and technology, in the tales of Prometheus and Sisyphus. The project of agriculture was felt, in some areas more than others, as a violation; hence, the incidence of rape in the stories of Demeter.

---

27 The production of maize, one of North America's contributions to domestication, "had a tremendous effect on women's work and women's health." Women's status "was definitely subordinate to that of males in most of the horticultural societies of [what is now] the eastern United States" by the time of first European contact. The reference is from Karen Olsen Bruhns and Karen E. Stothert, *Women in Ancient America* (Norman: University of Oklahoma Press, 1999), p. 88. Also, for example, Gilda A. Morelli, "Growing Up Female in a Farmer Community and a Forager Community," in Mary Ellen Mabeck, Alison Galloway and Adrienne Zihlman, eds., *The Evolving Female* (Princeton: Princeton University Press, 1997): "Young Efe [Zaire] forager children are growing up in a community where the relationship between men and women is far more egalitarian than is the relationship between farmer men and women" (p. 219). See also Catherine Panter-Brick and Tessa M. Pollard, "Work and Hormonal Variation in Subsistence and Industrial Contexts," in C. Panter-Brick and C.M. Worthman, eds., *Hormones, Health, and Behavior* (Cambridge, MA: Cambridge University Press, 1999), in terms of how much more work is done, compared to men, by women who farm vs. those who forage.

Over time as the losses mount, the great mother-daughter relationships of Greek myth—Demeter-Kore, Clytemnestra-Iphigenia, Jocasta-Antigone, for example—disappear.

In *Genesis*, the Bible's first book, woman is born from the body of man. The Fall from Eden represents the demise of hunter-gatherer life, the expulsion into agriculture and hard labor. It is blamed on Eve, of course, who bears the stigma of the Fall.[28] Quite an irony, in that domestication is the fear and refusal of nature and woman, while the Garden myth blames the chief victim of its scenario, in reality.

Agriculture is a conquest that fulfills what began with gender formation and development. Despite the presence of goddess figures, wedded to the touchstone of fertility, in general Neolithic culture is very concerned with virility. From the emotional dimensions of this masculinism, as Cauvin sees it, animal domestication must have been principally a male initiative.[29] The distancing and power emphasis have been with us ever since; frontier expansion, for instance, as male energy subduing female nature, one frontier after another.

This trajectory has reached overwhelming proportions, and we are told on all sides that we cannot avoid our engagement with ubiquitous technology. But patriarchy too is everywhere, and once again the inferiority of nature is presumed. Fortunately "many feminists," says Carol Stabile, hold that "a rejection of technology is fundamentally identical to a rejection of patriarchy."[30]

There are other feminists who claim a part of the technological enterprise, which posits a virtual, cyborg "escape

---

28 The Etoro people of Papua New Guinea have a very similar myth in which Nowali, known for her hunting prowess, bears responsibility for the Etoros' fall from a state of well-being. Raymond C. Kelly, *Constructing Inequality* (Ann Arbor: University of Michigan Press, 1993), p. 524.

29 Jacques Cauvin, *The Birth of the Gods and the Origins of Nature* (Cambridge, MA: Cambridge University Press, 2000), p. 133.

30 Carol A. Stabile, *Feminism and the Technological Fix* (Manchester: Manchester University Press, 1994), p. 5.

from the body" and its gendered history of subjugation. But this flight is illusory, a forgetting of the whole train and logic of oppressive institutions that make up patriarchy. The dis-embodied high-tech future can only be more of the same destructive course.

Freud considered taking one's place as a gendered subject to be foundational, both culturally and psychologically. But his theories assume an already present gendered subjectivity, and thus beg many questions. Various considerations remain unaddressed, such as gender as an expression of power relations, and the fact that we enter this world as bisexual creatures.

Carla Freeman poses a pertinent question with her essay titled "Is Local: Global as Feminine: Masculine? Rethinking the Gender of Globalization."[31]

The general crisis of modernity has its roots in the imposition of gender. Separation and inequality begin here at the period when symbolic culture itself emerges, soon becoming definitive as domestication and civilization: patriarchy. The hierarchy of gender can no more be reformed than the class system or globalization. Without a deeply radical women's liberation we are consigned to the deadly swindle and mutilation now dealing out a fearful toll everywhere. The wholeness of original genderlessness may be a prescription for our redemption.

---

31 Carla Freeman, "Is Local:Global as Feminine:Masculine? Rethinking the Gender of Globalization," *Signs* 26 (2001).

THE CITY AND ITS INMATES

AS DOMESTICATION took hold in the Neolithic, a tide of urbanism soon began to sweep the planet.

The city is a barrier between its inmates, a world of strangers. As Pierre Manent described it, the city is anything but a family or community. "In reality, it subordinates the family and the group.... It takes young men from their families living, and brings them back dead."[1]

As tools became systems of technology—that is, as social complexity developed—the city appeared. The city-machine was the earliest and biggest technological phenomenon, the

---

1   Pierre Manent, *Metamorphosis of the City* (Cambridge, MA: Harvard University Press, 2013), p. 27.

culmination of the division of labor. Or as Lewis Mumford characterized it, "the mark of the city is its purposive social complexity."[2] The two modes in this context are the same. Cities are the most complex artifacts ever contrived, just as urbanization is one of the prime measures of development.

The coming world-city perfects its war on nature, obliterating it in favor of the artificial, and reducing the countryside to mere "environs" that conform to urban priorities. All cities are antithetical to the land.

---

2   Lewis Mumford, *The Culture of Cities* (New York: Harcourt, Brace and Company, 1938), p. 6. For all of the valid historical content, Mumford can also lapse into absurdity, e.g., "the city should be an organ of love..." in *The City in History* (New York, Harcourt, Brace, 1961), p. 575.

Certeau's "Walking in the City" has rather an eerie quality, given its subject and the fact that it was written in 2000. Certeau saw the World Trade Center as "the most monumental figure" of Western urbanism and felt that "to be lifted to [its] summit is to be carried away by the city's hold."[3] The viability of the city has entered its inevitable stage of being doubted, accompanied by an anxiety heightened—but not created—on 9/11. The deep ambivalence about urban life, felt throughout civilization's reign, has become much more pronounced.

Domestication made civilization possible, and intensified domestication brought forth urban culture. Primary horticultural communities—settlements and villages—were superseded by cities as massified agriculture took hold. One enduring marker of this shift is megalithic monumentality. In early Neolithic monuments all the qualities of the city are found: sedentism, permanence, density, a visible announcement of the triumphal march of farming over foraging. The city's spectacular centralization is a major turning point in human cultural evolution, the arrival of civilization in its full, definitive sense.

There have been civilizations without cities (e.g., the early Maya civilization), but not many. More often they are a key feature and develop with a relatively sudden force, as if the energy repressed by domestication must burst forth to a new level of its control logic. The urban explosion does not escape some bad reviews, however. In the Hebrew tradition, it was Cain, murderer of Abel, who founded the first city. Similarly, such urban references as Babylon, the Tower of Babel, and Sodom and Gomorrah are wholly negative. A deep ambivalence about cities is, in fact, a constant of civilization.

By about 4000 B.P.E. the first cities appeared in Meso-

---

3   Michel de Certeau, *The Certeau Reader*, edited by Graham Ward (London: Blackwell Publishers, 2000), p. 103.

potamia and Egypt, when political means were devised to channel the surpluses created by a new agricultural ethos into the hands of a ruling minority. This development required economic input from wider and wider areas of production; large-scale, centralized, bureaucratic institutions were not long in coming. Villages were pulled into increasingly specialized maximization strategies to produce bigger surpluses flowing to the cities. Greater grain production, for example, could only be achieved with additional work and more coercion. Resistance occurred within this well-known framework, as the more primitive farming communities were forcibly converted into administered towns, such as Nineveh. Nomadic peoples of Sinai refused to mine copper for the Egyptian rulers, to cite another instance.[4] Small-holders were forced off the land into cities; this displacement is a basic part of a familiar pattern that continues today.

Urban reality is primarily about trade and commerce, with a nearly total dependence on support from external areas for continued existence. To guarantee such an artificial subsistence, city fathers turn inevitably to war, that chronic civilizational staple. "Conquest abroad and repression at home," in Stanley Diamond's words, is a defining characterization of cities from their very origins.[5] The early Sumerian city-states, for example, were constantly at war. The struggle for stability of urban market economies was an unremitting matter of survival. Armies and warfare were cardinal necessities, especially given the built-in expansionist character of the urban dynamic. Uruk, the biggest Mesopotamian city of its time (ca. 2700 B.P.E.), boasted a double-ring wall six miles long, fortified by nine hundred towers. From this early period through the Middle Ages, virtually all cities were fortified

---

4   Stanley Diamond, *In Search of the Primitive* (New Brunswick, NJ: Transaction Books, 1974), p. 7.

5   *Ibid.*, p. 1.

garrisons. Julius Caesar used the word *oppidum* (garrison) to denote every town in Gaul.

The first urban centers also consistently reveal a strong ceremonial orientation. The movement away from an immanent, earth-based spirituality to emphasis on sacred or supernatural spaces receives a further deformation with literally awe-inspiring, mighty urban temples and tombs. The elevation of a society's gods corresponded to the increasing complexity and stratification of its social structure. Religious monumentality was not only an obedience-inducing tactic by those in authority, it was also a fundamental vehicle for the spread of domestication.[6]

But the rise to dominance began not only with intensified agriculture—and the appearance of writing systems, as Childe, Lévi-Strauss and others have noted—but with metallurgy. Following the Neolithic, so in the Iron Age. According to Toynbee, "If the increase in the size of cities in the course of history is presented visually in the form of a curve, this curve will be found to have the same configuration as a curve presenting the increase in the potency of technology."[7] And with the increasingly urbanized character of social life, the city can be seen as a container. Cities, like the factories that are already present, rely on containment. Cities and factories are never at base freely chosen by the people inside them; domination keeps them there. Aristophanes put it well in his 414 B.C. creation, *The Birds*: "A city must rise, to house all birds; then you must fence in the air, the sky, the earth, and must surround it by walls, like Babylon."

States as we know them already existed by this period, and powerful cities emerged as capitals, the loci of state power. Political domination has always flowed from these urban cen-

---

6   Andrew Sherratt, *Economy and Society in Prehistoric Europe* (Princeton: Princeton University Press, 1997), p. 362.

7   Arnold Toynbee, *Cities on the Move* (New York: Oxford University Press, 1970), p. 173.

ters. Walls are the defining structures in cities. In China, walls are literally synonymous with cities; the characters for wall and city are the same. Fortified cities are a function of what cities are, their very basis. Writing about Roman emperor Constantine, Noel Lenski also saw the advancement of cities as key to authority: "Urban centers represented the nodes of civil life around which the empire constructed its networks of power."[8] Promised security from nature and outsiders, citizens soon became part of the conquest in every sense.

In this context, peasants leave behind one known and hated servitude for new, initially undisclosed forms of bondage and suffering. The city, already a site of local power and war, is an incubator of infectious diseases, including plague, and of course greatly magnifies the impacts of fire, earthquake, and other dangers.

For thousands of generations humans rose at daybreak and slept after the sun went down, basking in the glories of sunrise, sunset, and starry skies. Half a millennium ago, city bells and clocks announced an increasingly ordered and regulated daily life, the reign of urban timekeeping. With modernity, lived time disappears; time becomes a resource, an objectified materiality. Measured, reified time isolates the individual in the force field of deepening division and separation, ever diminishing wholeness. Contact with the earth ebbs, as urbanization grows; and as Hogarth depicted in his mid-eighteenth-century images of London, physical contact among people lessens dramatically. At this time Nicolas Chamfort declared, "Paris is a city of gaieties and pleasures, where four-fifths of the inhabitants die of grief."[9] In *Emile* (1762), Rousseau put it more personally: "Adieu,

---

8   Noel Lenski, *Constantine and the Cities: Imperial Authority and Civic Politics* (Philadelphia: University of Pennsylvania Press, 2016), p. 88.

9   Nicolas Chamfort, quoted in James A. Clapp, *The City, A Dictionary of Quotable Thought on Cities and Urban Life* (New Brunswick, NJ: Center for Urban Policy Research, 1984), p. 51.

Paris. We are seeking love, happiness, innocence. We shall never be far enough away from you."[10] The pervasive weight of urban existence penetrated even the most outwardly vital political phenomena, including the French Revolution. Crowds in revolutionary Paris often seemed strangely apathetic, prompting Richard Sennett to detect there the first pronounced modern signs of urban passivity.[11]

In the following century Engels, in contrary fashion, decided that it is in the city that the proletariat achieves its "fullest classic perfection."[12] But Tocqueville had already seen how individuals in cities feel "strangers to the destinies of each other."[13] Later in the nineteenth century, Durkheim noted that suicide and insanity increase with modern urbanization. In fact, a sense of dependence, loneliness, and every kind of emotional disturbance are generated, giving rise to Benjamin's perception that "Fear, revulsion, and horror were the emotions which the big-city crowd aroused in those who first observed it."[14] The technological developments in the areas of sewage and other sanitation challenges, while required in burgeoning metropoles, also enable urbanization and its further growth. Life in cities is only possible with such continual technological supports.

By 1900, Georg Simmel understood how living in cities brings about not only loneliness, but also the reserve or emotional numbness that exacerbates it. As Simmel saw, this is very closely analogous to the effects of industrial life in gener-

---

10 Jean-Jacques Rousseau, *Emile*, translated by Allan Bloom (New York: Basic Books, 1979), p. 355.

11 Richard Sennett, *Flesh and Stone: The Body and the City in Western Civilization* (New York: W.W. Norton, 1994), p. 23.

12 Friedrich Engels, *The Condition of the Working Class in England* (St. Albans: Panther Press, 1969), p. 75.

13 Alexis de Tocqueville, *Democracy in America* v. 2 (New York, Vintage, 1963), p. 141.

14 Walter Benjamin, *Illuminations*, translated by Harry Zahn (New York: Schocken Books, 1969), p. 174.

al: "Punctuality, calculability, exactness are forced upon life by the complexity and extension of metropolitan existence."[15] The urban languor and impotence expressed in T.S. Eliot's early poetry, for example, helps fill in this picture of reduced life.

The term "suburb" was used from Shakespeare and Milton onwards in very much the modern sense, but it was not until the onslaught of industrialization that the suburban phenomenon truly emerged. Thus residential development appeared on the outskirts of America's biggest cities between 1815 and 1860. Marx referred to capitalism as "the urbanization of the countryside"[16]; suburbanization really hit its stride, in its contemporary meaning, just after World War II. Refined mass production techniques created a physical conformity to match and magnify social conformity.[17] Depthless, homogenized, a hothouse of consumerism fenced in by strip malls and freeways, the suburb is the further degraded outcome of the city. As such, the differences between urban and suburban should not be exaggerated or seen as qualitative. Withdrawal, facilitated by an array of high-tech devices—iPods, cell phones, etc.—is now the order of the day, a very telling phenomenon.[18]

Civilization, as is clear from the word's original Latin meaning, is what goes on in cities.[19] More than half of the world's population now lives in cities, McDonaldizing non-places like Kuala Lumpur and Singapore that have so resolutely turned their backs on their own rich contexts. The urbanizing imperative is an ongoing characteristic of civilization.

---

15   Kurt H. Wolff, *The Sociology of Georg Simmel* (New York: The Free Press, 1950), p. 413.

16   Karl Marx, *Grundrisse* (New York, Vintage, 1973), p. 479.

17   A typical and apposite work is Richard Harris, *Creeping Conformity: How Canada Became Suburban, 1900–1960* (Toronto: University of Toronto Press, 2004).

18   Very pertinent is Michael Bull, *Sounding Out the City: Personal Stereos and the Management of Everyday Life* (New York, Oxford University Press, 2000).

19   This is not only true in the West. In Arabic civilization, for example, *madaniyya*, or civilization, comes from *madine*, which means city.

A certain perverse allure still obtains for some, and it has become so hard to escape the urban influence zone anyway. There is still a flicker of hope for community, or at least for diversion, in the metropolis. And some of us remain there in order not to lose contact with what we feel compelled to understand, so we can bring it to an end. Certainly, there are those who struggle to humanize the city, to develop public gardens and other amenities, but cities remain what they have always been. Most of their inhabitants simply accept the urban reality and try to adjust to it, with the same outward passivity they express toward the enveloping techno-world.

Some try always to reform the unreformable. Let's have "a new modernity," "a new attitude about technology," etc. etc. Julia Kristeva calls for "a cosmopolitanism of a new sort..."[20] Such orientations reveal, among other things, the conviction that what are widely considered essentials of social life will always be with us. Max Weber judged modernity and bureaucratic rationality to be "escape-proof," while Toynbee saw the Ecumenopolis, as he called the stage of gigantism succeeding the stage of the megalopolis, "inevitable."[21] Ellul referred to urbanization as that "which can only be accepted."[22]

However, given today's urban reality, and how and why cities came to be in the first place and continue to exist, what James Baldwin said of the ghetto fully applies to the city: "[It] can be improved in one way only: out of existence."[23] There is a strong consensus among urban theorists, by the way, that "cities are newly divided and polarized."[24] That

---

20 Julia Kristeva, *Strangers to Ourselves* (New York: Columbia University Press, 1991), p. 192.

21 Toynbee, *op. cit.*, p. 196.

22 Jacques Ellul, *The Political Illusion* (New York: Alfred A. Knopf, 1967), p. 43.

23 James Baldwin, *Nobody Knows My Name* (New York, The Dial Press, 1961), p. 65.

24 Peter Marcuse and Ronald van Kempen, editors, *Of States and Cities: The Partitioning of Urban Space* (New York, Oxford University Press, 2002), p. vii.

the poor and the indigenous must be urbanized is another primary facet of colonialist-imperialist ideology.

The original monumentalism is still present and underlined in today's city, with the same dwarfing and disempowering of the individual. Human scale is obliterated by high-rises, sensory deprivation deepens, and inhabitants are assailed by monotony, noise, and other pollutants. The cyberspace world is itself an urban environment, accelerating the radical decline of physical presence and connection. Urban space is the always advancing (vertically and horizontally) symbol of the defeat of nature and the death of community. What John Habberton wrote in 1889 could not be more valid now: "A great city is a great sore—a sore which can never be cured."[25] Or as Kai W. Lee replied to the question whether a transition to sustainable cities is imaginable: "The answer is no."[26]

The proportion of humanity living in cities has been growing exponentially, along with industrialization. The megalopolis is the latest form of urban "habitat," increasingly interposing itself between human life and the biosphere.

It is the dominant culture at its center, its height, its most dominant. Joseph Grange is, sadly, basically correct in saying that it is "par excellence, the place where human values come to their most concrete expression."[27] (If one pardons the pun, also sadly apt.) Of course, the word "human" receives its fully deformed meaning in the urban context, especially that of today. Everyone can see the modern "flatscape," in Norberg-Schulz's terse term (1969), the Nothing Zones of placelessness where localism and variety are steadily being

25 John Habberton, *Our Country's Future* (Philadelphia: International Publishing Company, 1889), cited in Clapp, *op. cit.*, p. 105.

26 Kai N. Lee, "Urban Sustainability and the Limits of Classical Environmentalism," in *Environment and Urbanization* 18:1 (April 2006), p. 9.

27 Joseph Grange, *The City: An Urban Cosmology* (Albany: State University of New York Press, 1999), p. xv.

diminished, if not eradicated.[28] The supermarket, the mall, the airport lounge are everywhere the same, just as office, school, apartment block, hospital, and prison are scarcely distinguishable one from another, in our own cities.[29]

The mega-cities have more in common with each other than with any other social organisms. Their citizens tend to dress the same and otherwise consume the same global culture, under a steadily more comprehensive surveillance gaze. This is the opposite of living in a particular place on the earth, with respect for its uniqueness. These days, all space is becoming urban space; there is not a spot on the planet that couldn't become at least virtually urban upon the turn of a satellite. We have been trained and equipped to mold space as if it were an object. Such an education is mandated in this Digital Age, dominated by cities and metro regions to an extent unprecedented in history.

How has this come to pass? As Weber put it, "one may find anything or everything in the city texts except the informing principle that creates the city itself."[30] But it is clear what the fundamental mechanism/dynamic/"principle" is and always has been. As Weber continued: "Every device in the city facilitating trade and industry prepares the way for further division of labor and further specialization of tasks."[31] Further massification, standardization, equivalence.

Copán, Palenque, and Tikal were rich cities of Maya civilization abandoned at their height, between 600 and 900 A.D. With similar examples from various cultures, they point a way forward for us. The literature of urbanism has only

---

28   Edward Relph, *Place and Placelessness* (London: Pion Ltd., 1976), p. 6.

29   Meanwhile, phenomena such as "Old Town" areas and historical districts distract from tedium and standardization, but also underline these defining urban characteristics. The patented superficiality of postmodern architecture underlines it as well.

30   Max Weber, *The City*, translated by Don Martindale and Gertrud Neuwirth (Glencoe, IL: The Free Press, 1958), p. 11.

31   *Ibid.*, p. 21.

grown darker and more dystopian in recent years, as terrorism and collapse cast their shadows on the most untenable products of civilization: the world's cities. Turning from the perpetual servitude and chronic sickness of urban existence, we may draw inspiration from such places as former indigenous settlements on what is now called the Los Angeles River. Places where the sphere of life is rooted in subsisting as fully skilled humans in harmony with the earth.

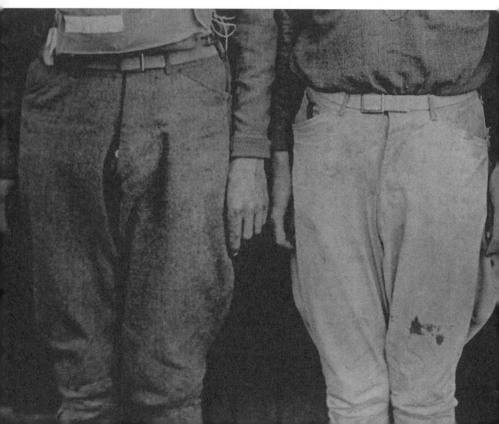

WAR ENTERS THE PICTURE

WAR IS A STAPLE of civilization. Its mass, rationalized, chronic presence has increased as civilization has
spread and deepened. Among the specific reasons it doesn't
go away is the desire to escape the horror of mass-indus-
trial life. Mass society of course finds its reflection in mass
soldiery and it has been this way from early civilization. In
the age of hyper-developing technology, war is fed by new
heights of dissociation and disembodiment. We are ever further from a grounding or leverage from which to oppose it
(while too many accept paltry, symbolic "protest" gestures).

　　How did it come to be that war is "the proper work of
man," in the words of Homer's Odysseus? We know that or-

ganized warfare advanced with early industry and complex social organization in general, but the question of origins predates even Homer's early Iron Age. The explicit archaeological/anthropological literature on the subject is surprisingly slight.

Civilization has always had a basic interest in holding its subjects captive by touting the necessity of official armed force. It is a prime ideological claim that without the state's monopoly on violence, we would be unprotected and insecure. After all, according to Hobbes, the human condition has been and will always be that of "a war of all against all." Modern voices, too, have argued that humans are innately aggressive and violent, and so need to be constrained by armed authority. Raymond Dart (e.g., *Adventures with the Missing Link*, 1959), Robert Ardrey (e.g., *African Genesis*, 1961), and Konrad Lorenz (e.g., *On Aggression*, 1966) are among the best known, but the evidence they put forth has been very largely discredited.

In the second half of the twentieth century, this pessimistic view of human nature began to shift. Based on archaeological evidence, it is now a tenet of mainstream scholarship that pre-civilization humans lived in the absence of violence—more specifically, of organized violence. Eibl-Eibesfeldt referred to the !Ko-Bushmen as not bellicose: "Their cultural ideal is peaceful coexistence, and they achieve this by avoiding conflict, that is by splitting up, and by emphasizing and encouraging the numerous patterns of bonding."[1] An earlier judgment by W.J. Perry is generally accurate, if somewhat idealized: "Warfare, immorality, vice, polygyny, slavery, and the subjection of women seem to be absent among our gatherer-hunter ancestors."[2]

The current literature consistently reports that until the final stages of the Paleolithic Age—until just prior to the present 10,000-year era of domestication—there is no conclusive evidence that any tools or hunting weapons were used against humans at all.[3] "Depictions of battle scenes, skirmishes and hand-to-hand combat are rare in hunter-gatherer art and when they do occur most often result from contact with agriculturalists or industrialized invaders," concludes Taçon and Chippindale's study of Australian rock art.[4] When conflict began to emerge, encounters rarely lasted more than

1   I Eibl-Eibesfelt, "Aggression in the !Ko-Bushmen," in Martin A. Nettleship, eds., *War, its Causes and Correlates* (The Hague: Mouton, 1975), p. 293.

2   W.J. Perry, "The Golden Age," in *The Hibbert Journal* XVI (1917), p. 44.

3   Arthur Ferrill, *The Origins of War from the Stone Age to Alexander the Great* (New York: Thames and Hudson, 1985), p. 16.

4   Paul Taçon and Christopher Chippindale, "Australia's Ancient Warriors: Changing Depictions of Fighting in the Rock Art of Arnhem Land, N.T.," *Cambridge Archaeological Journal* 4:2 (1994), p. 211.

half an hour, and if a death occurred both parties would retire at once.[5] "Full-fledged war seems hardly to exist among such [hunter-gatherer] groups," is Henri Claesen's judgment; counter-examples are extremely rare.[6] Sarunas Milisauska reports that the earliest case of fairly large intergroup conflict that "can be reasonably attributed" as such is that of Jebel Sahaba, Sudan, about 13,000 years ago.[7]

The record of Native Americans in California is similar. Kroeber reported that their fighting was "notably bloodless. They even went so far as to take poorer arrows to war than they used in economic hunting."[8] Wintu people of Northern California called off hostilities once someone was injured.[9] "Most Californians were absolutely nonmilitary; they possessed next to none of the traits requisite for the military horizon, a condition that would have taxed their all but nonexistent social organization too much. Their societies made no provision for collective political action," in the view of Turney-High.[10] Lorna Marshall described !Kung bushmen as celebrating no valiant heroes or tales of battle. One of them remarked, "Fighting is very dangerous; someone might get killed."[11] George Bird Grinnell's "Coup and

---

5   Maurice R. Davie, *The Evolution of War: A Study of Its Role in Early Societies* (New Haven: Yale University Press, 1929), p. 247.

6   Henri J.M. Claessen, "War and State Formation: What is the Connection?" in Ton Otto et al., eds., *Warfare and Society: Archaeological and Social Anthropological Perspectives* (Oakville, CT: Aarhus University Press, 2006), p. 219.

7   Sarunas Milisauskas, "The Contexts of Violence," in Sarah Ralph, ed., *The Archaeology of Violence: Interdisciplinary Approaches* (Albany: State University of New York Press, 2012), p. 20.

8   A.L. Kroeber, *Handbook of the Indians of California: Bulletin 78* (Washington, D.C.: Bureau of American Ethnology, 1923), p. 152.

9   Christopher Chase-Dunn and Kelly M. Man, *The Wintu and their Neighbors* (Tucson: University of Arizona Press, 1998), p. 101.

10   Harry Holbert Turney-High, *Primitive War: Its Practice and Concepts* (Columbia: University of South Carolina Press, 1949), p. 229.

11   Lorna Marshall, "!Kung Bushman Bands," in Ronald Cohen and John Middleton, eds., *Comparative Political Systems* (Garden City: Natural History Press, 1967), p. 17.

Scalp Among the Plains Indians"[12] argues that counting coup (striking or touching an enemy with the hand or a small stick) was the highest point of (essentially nonviolent) bravery, whereas scalping was not valued. "There is strong evidence," writes R. Brian Ferguson, "that much of the tribal structure recorded by Europeans was in fact called into being by their presence."[13]

But some commentators, taking a Hobbesian/conservative view, assert that warfare was commonplace all along. A well-known example is Lawrence Keeley's *War Before Civilization*. His effort is noteworthy for a fundamental confusion: Keeley lumps together supposedly pre-civilization people as "primitive" or "small-scale" societies. He completely ignores whether or not a society practices domestication—a primary marker of civilization. Keeley's index does not contain such subjects as agriculture, cultivation, domestication, or farming. The book's bibliography omits Bar-Yosef, Binford, Sahlins, Shepard, Woodburn, and many others who have commented on this topic; he lists Richard B. Lee but does not cite him in the text.[14] The reason for this is plain; it would undo Keeley's claim that organized violence existed to any appreciable degree prior to domestication.

Herbert D.G. Maschner and Katherine L. Reedy Maschner claim that "Warfare and violence played an important role in the history and development of complex hunter-gatherer societies on the north Pacific Rim."[15] But they are re-

---

12 George Bird Grinnell, "Coup and Scalp among the Plains Indians," *American Anthropologist* 12 (1910), pp. 296–310. John Stands in Timber and Margot Liberty make the same point in their *Cheyenne Memories* (New Haven: Yale University Press, 1967), pp. 61–69. Also, Turney-High, *op. cit.*, pp. 147, 186.

13 R. Brian Ferguson, "Tribal Warfare," in Nancy Scheper Hughes and Philippe Bourgois, *Violence in War and Peace* (Hoboken, NJ: Wiley, 2004), p. 69.

14 Lawrence H. Keeley, *War Before Civilization* (New York: Oxford University Press, 1996).

15 Herbert D.G. Maschner and Katherine L. Reedy-Maschner, "Raid, Retreat, Defend (Repeat): The Archaeology and Ethnohistory of Warfare on the North Pacific Rim," *Journal of Anthropological Archaeology* (1998), p. 19.

ferring to sedentary, village-based peoples (e.g., Northwest Coast) who practiced domestication (e.g., dogs, tobacco, root-crop species). Another case of ignorance and/or dishonesty, quite frankly.

The emergence of institutionalized warfare appears to be associated with domestication, and/or a drastic change in a society's physical situation. As Glassman puts it, this comes about "only where band peoples have been drawn into the warfare of horticulturalists or herders, or driven into an ever-diminishing territory."[16] The first reliable archaeological evidence of warfare is that of fortified, pre-Biblical Jericho, c. 7500 B.C. In the early Neolithic a relatively sudden shift happened. What dynamic forces may have led people to adopt war as a social institution? To date, this question has not been explored in any depth.

Symbolic culture appears to have emerged in the Upper Paleolithic; by the Neolithic it was firmly established in human cultures everywhere. The symbolic has a way of effacing particularity, reducing human presence in its specific, non-mediated aspects. It is easier to direct violence against a faceless enemy who represents some officially defined evil or threat. Ritual is the earliest known form of purposive symbolic activity: symbolism acting in the world. Archaeological evidence suggests that there may be a link between ritual and the emergence of organized warfare.

During the almost timeless era when humans were not interested in dominating their surroundings, certain places were special and came to be known as sacred sites. This was based on a spiritual and emotional kinship with the land, expressed in various forms of totemism or custodianship. Ritual begins to appear, but is not central to band or forager societies. Emma Blake observes, "Although the peoples of

---

16   Ronald R. Glassman, *Democracy and Despotism in Primitive Societies, Volume One* (Millwood, New York: Associated Faculty Press, 1986), p. 111.

the Paleolithic practiced rituals, the richest material residues date from the Neolithic period onward, when sedentism and the domestication of plants and animals brought changes to the outlook and cosmology of people everywhere."[17] It was in the Upper Paleolithic that certain strains and tensions caused by the development of specialization first became evident. Inequities can be measured by such evidence as differing amounts of goods at hearth sites in encampments; in response, ritual appears to have begun to play a greater social role. As many have noted, ritual in this context is a way of addressing deficiencies of cohesion or solidarity; it is a means of guaranteeing a social order that has become problematic. As Bruce Knauft saw, "ritual reinforces and puts beyond argument or question certain highly general propositions about the spiritual and human world...[and] predisposes deep-seated cognitive acceptance and behavioral compliance with these cosmological propositions."[18] Ritual thus provides the original ideological glue for societies now in need of such legitimating assistance. Face-to-face solutions become ineffective as social solutions, when communities become complex and already partly stratified. The symbolic is a non-solution; in fact, it is a type of enforcer of relationships and worldviews characterized by inequality and estrangement.

Ritual is itself a type of power, an early, pre-state form of politics. Among the Maring people of Papua New Guinea, for instance, the conventions of the ritual cycle specify duties or roles in the absence of explicitly political authorities. Sanctity is therefore a functional alternative to politics; sa-

---

17 Emma Blake, "The Material Expression of Cult, Ritual, and Feasting," in Emma Blake and A. Bernard Knapp, eds., *The Archaeology of Mediterranean Prehistory* (New York: Blackwell, 2005), p. 109.

18 Bruce M. Knauft, "Culture and Cooperation in Human Evolution," in Leslie Sponsel and Thomas Gregor, eds., *The Anthropology of Peace and Nonviolence* (Boulder: L. Rienner, 1994), p. 45.

cred conventions, in effect, govern society.[19] Ritualization is clearly an early strategic arena for the incorporation of power relations. Further, warfare can be a sacred undertaking, with militarism promoted ritually, blessing emergent social hierarchy.

René Girard proposes that rituals of sacrifice are a necessary counter to endemic aggression and violence in society.[20] Something nearer to the reverse is more the case: ritual legitimates and enacts violence. As Lienhardt said of the Dinka herders of Africa, to "make a feast or sacrifice often implies war."[21] Ritual does not substitute for war, according to Arkush and Stanish: "warfare in all times and places has ritual elements."[22] They see the dichotomy between "ritual battle" and "real war" to be false, summarizing that "archaeologists can expect destructive warfare and ritual to go hand in hand."[23]

It is not only that among Apache groups, for example, that the most ritualized were the most agricultural,[24] but that so often ritual has mainly to do with agriculture and warfare, which are often very closely linked.[25] It is not uncommon to find warfare itself seen as a means of enhancing the fertility of cultivated ground. Ritual regulation of production and belligerence means that domestication has become the

19 Roy A. Rappaport, *Pigs for the Ancestors: Ritual in the Ecology of a New Guinea People* (New Haven: Yale University Press, 1967), pp. 236–237.

20 René Girard, *Violence and the Sacred*, translated by Patrick Gregory (Baltimore: Johns Hopkins University Press, 1977). Like Ardrey and Lorenz, Girard starts from the absurd view that all social life is steeped in violence.

21 G. Lienhardt, *Divinity and Experience: The Religion of the Dinka* (Oxford: Oxford University Press, 1961), p. 281.

22 Elizabeth Arkush and Charles Stanish, "Interpreting Conflict in the Ancient Andes: Implications for the Archaeology of Warfare," *Current Anthropology* 46:1 (February 2005), p. 16.

23 *Ibid.*, p. 14.

24 James L. Haley, *Apaches: A History and Culture Portrait* (Garden City, NY: Doubleday, 1981), pp. 95–96.

25 Rappaport, *op. cit*, p. 234, for example.

decisive factor. "The emergence of systematic warfare, forti-fications, and weapons of destruction," says Hassan, "follows the path of agriculture."[26]

Ritual evolves into religious systems, the gods come forth, sacrifice is demanded. "There is no doubt that all the inhab-itants of the unseen world are greatly interested in human agriculture," notes anthropologist Verrier Elwin.[27] Sacrifice is an excess of domestication, involving domesticated animals and occurring only in agricultural societies. Ritual killing, including human sacrifice, is unknown in non-domesticated cultures.[28]

Corn in the Americas tells a parallel story. An abrupt in-crease in corn agriculture brought with it the rapid elabo-ration of hierarchy and militarization in large parts of both continents.[29] One instance among many is the northward intrusion of the Hohokams against the indigenous Ootams[30] of southern Arizona, introducing agriculture and organized warfare. By about 1000 A.D. the farming of maize had be-come dominant throughout the Southwest, complete with year-round ritual observances, priesthoods, social conformi-ty, human sacrifice, and cannibalism.[31] It is hardly an under-

---

26   Quoted by Robert Kuhlken, "Warfare and Intensive Agriculture in Fiji," in Chris Gosden and Jon Hather, eds., *The Prehistory of Food: Appetites for Change* (New York: Routledge, 1999), p. 271. Works such as Lawrence H. Keeley, *War Before Civilization* (New York: Oxford University Press, 1996) and Pierre Clastres, *Archaeology of Violence* (New York: Semiotext(e), 1994), and Jean Guilaine and Jean Zammit, *The Origins of War: Violence in Prehistory* (Malden, MA: Blackwell, 2005) somehow manage to overlook this point.

27   Verrier Elwin, *The Religion of an Indian Tribe* (London: Oxford University Press, 1955, p. 300.

28   Jonathan Z. Smith, "The Domestication of Sacrifice," in Robert G. Hamerton-Kelly, ed., *Violent Origins* (Stanford: Stanford University Press, 1987), pp. 197, 202.

29   Christine A. Hastorf and Sissel Johannessen, "Becoming Corn-Eaters in Prehistoric America," in Johannessen and Hastorf, eds., *Corn and Culture in the Prehistoric New World* (Boulder: Westview Press, 1994), especially pp. 428–433.

30   Charles Di Peso, *The Upper Pima of San Cayetano de Tumacacori* (Dragoon, AZ: Amerind Foundation, 1956), pp. 19, 104, 252, 260.

31   Christy G. Turner II and Jacqueline A. Turner, *Man Corn: Cannibalism and Violence in the Prehistoric American Southwest* (Salt Lake City: University of Utah Press, 1999), pp. 3, 460, 484.

statement to say, with Kroeber, that with maize agriculture, "all cultural values shifted."[32]

Horses are another instance of the close connection between domestication and war. First domesticated in the Ukraine around 3000 B.C., their objectification fed militarism directly. Almost from the very beginning they served as machines; most importantly, as war machines.[33]

The relatively harmless kinds of intergroup fighting described above gave way to systematic killing as domestication led to increasing competition for land.[34] The drive for fresh land to be exploited is widely accepted as the leading specific cause of war throughout the course of civilization. Once-dominant feelings of gratitude toward a freely giving nature and knowledge of the crucial interdependence of all life are replaced by the ethos of domestication: humans versus the natural world. This enduring power struggle is the template for the wars it constantly engenders. There was awareness of the price exacted by the paradigm of control, as seen in the widespread practice of symbolic regulation or amelioration of domestication of animals in the early Neolithic. But such gestures do not alter the fundamental dynamic at work, any more than they preserve millions of years' worth of gatherer-hunters' practices that balanced population and subsistence.

Agricultural intensification meant more warfare. Submission to this pattern requires that all aspects of society form an integrated whole from which there is little or no escape. With domestication, division of labor now produces full-time specialists in coercion: for example, definitive evidence shows a soldier class established in the Near East by 4500 B.C. The

---

32   A.L. Kroeber, *Cultural and Natural Areas of Native North America* (Berkeley: University of California Press, 1963), p. 224.

33   Harold B. Barclay, *The Role of the Horse in Man's Culture* (London: J.A. Allen, 1980), e.g., p. 23.

34   Richard W. Howell, "War Without Conflict," in Nettleship, *op. cit.*, pp. 683–684.

Jivaro of Amazonia, for millennia a harmonious component of the biotic community, adopted domestication, and "have elaborated blood revenge and warfare to a point where these activities set the tone for the whole society."[35] Organized violence becomes pervasive, mandatory, and normative.

Expressions of power are the essence of civilization, with its core principle of patriarchal rule. It may be that systematic male dominance is a by-product of war. The ritual subordination and devaluation of women is certainly advanced by warrior ideology, which increasingly emphasized "male" activities and downplayed women's roles.

The initiation of boys is a ritual designed to produce a certain type of man, an outcome that is not at all guaranteed by mere biological growth. When group cohesion can no longer be taken for granted, symbolic institutions are required—especially to further compliance with pursuits such as warfare. Lemmonier's judgment is that "male initiations… are connected by their very essence with war."[36]

Polygyny, the practice of one man taking multiple wives, is rare in gatherer-hunter bands, but is the norm for war-making village societies.[37] Once again, domestication is the decisive factor. It is no coincidence that circumcision rituals by the Merida people of Madagascar culminated in aggressive military parades.[38] There have been instances where women not only hunt but also go into combat (e.g., the Amazons of Dahomey; certain groups in Borneo), but it is clear that gender construction has tended toward a masculinist,

---

35 Betty J. Meggers, *Amazonia: Man and Culture in Counterfeit Paradise* (Chicago: Aldine Atherton, 1971), pp. 108, 158.

36 Pierre Lemmonier, "Pigs as Ordinary Wealth," in Pierre Lemonnier, ed., *Technological Choices: Transformation in Material Cultures since the Neolithic* (London: Routledge, 1993), p. 132.

37 Knauft, *op. cit.*, p. 50. Marvin Harris, *Cannibals and Kings* (New York: Random House, 1977), p. 39.

38 Maurice Bloch, *Prey into Hunter: The Politics of Religious Experience* (Cambridge: Cambridge University Press, 1992), p. 88.

militarist direction. With state formation, warriorship was a common requirement of citizenship, excluding women from political life.

War is not only ritualistic, usually with many ceremonial features; it is also a very formalized practice. Like ritual itself, war is performed via strictly prescribed movements, gestures, dress, and forms of speech. Soldiers are identical and structured in a standardized display. The formations of organized violence, with their columns and lines, are like agriculture and its rows: files on a grid.[39] Control and discipline are thus served, returning to the theme of ritualized behavior, which is always an increased elaboration of authority.

Exchange between bands in the Paleolithic functioned less as trade (in the economic sense) than as exchange of information. Periodic intergroup gatherings offered marriage opportunities, and insured against resource shortfalls. There was no clear differentiation of social and economic spheres. Similarly, to apply our word "work" is misleading in the absence of production or commodities. While territoriality was part of forager-hunter activity, there is no evidence that it led to war.[40]

Domestication erects the rigid boundaries of surplus and private property, with concomitant possessiveness, enmity, and struggle for ownership. Even conscious mechanisms aimed at mitigating the new realities cannot remove their ever-present, dynamic force. In *The Gift*, Mauss portrayed exchange as peacefully resolved war, and war as the result of unsuccessful transactions; he saw the potlatch as a sort of sublimated warfare.[41]

---

39 The "rank-and-file" of organized labor is another product of these originals.

40 Robert L. Carneiro, "War and Peace," in S.P. Reyna and R.E. Downs, eds., *Studying War: Anthropological Perspectives* (Langhorn, PA: Gordon and Breach, 1994), p. 12.

41 Cited and discussed in Marshall Sahlins, *Stone Age Economics* (Chicago: Aldine, 1972, pp. 174, 182).

Before domestication, boundaries were fluid. The freedom to leave one band for another was an integral part of forager life. The more or less forced integration demanded by complex societies provided a staging ground conducive to organized violence. In some places, chiefdoms arose from the suppression of smaller communities' independence. Proto-political centralization was at times pushed forward in the Americas by tribes desperately trying to confederate to fight European invaders.

Ancient civilizations spread as a result of war, and it can be said that warfare is both a cause of statehood, and its result.

Not much has changed since war was first instituted, rooted in ritual and given full-growth potential by domestication. Marshall Sahlins first pointed out that increased work follows developments in symbolic culture. It's also the case that culture begets war, despite claims to the contrary. After all, the impersonal character of civilization grows with the ascendance of the symbolic. Symbols (e.g., national flags) allow our species to dehumanize our fellow humans, thus enabling systematic intra-species carnage.

THE BRONZE AGE:
ORIGINS OF THE ONE PERCENT

WITH THE NEOLITHIC Age we entered the force field of domestication, leaving—not without a struggle— the free, face-to-face world of band society/community. Ever-larger settlements, more work, the emergence of warfare and the objectification of women were among the hallmarks of the new order, starting about 10,000 years ago.

But the new era was unstable, domination far from perfected. Sedentary, agriculture-based life posed unforeseen challenges in social, economic, ideological/political, and spiritual spheres. The move from personalized Paleolithic reciprocity to large-scale Neolithic resource acquisition, production and distribution was far from smooth. New modes

were needed for domestication to become civilization.

The transition from foraging to farming is widely recognized as the most profound revolution in human history. It is the revolution *into* history, and must have commanded a completely new set of responses to a newly inhabited reality. For one thing, direct, consensual decision-making no longer worked among the burgeoning populations of early complex society. A new level of control and management had to be established. Politics began. Appropriate mental frameworks had to be forged for an increasingly stratified social existence to function. And domestication brought, for the first time, devastating epidemics that resulted from crowded, stationary settlements, along with greatly reduced health and robustness overall. Out of this wrenching defeat, according to Jacques Cauvin, came "all the existential malaises" usually thought of as much later developments.[1]

We know that given a choice, humans prefer to remain hunters and gatherers; we do not settle permanently into the toil of farming until it is forced upon us. The triumph of the Neolithic was that forcing. But domination is not inexorably or invariably linear and unidirectional, and by about 6000 B.C. the Neolithic order was beginning to fray.

Upon its ruins the Bronze Age slowly emerged, with a marked acceleration in social complexity: larger communities tending toward structured social stratification. The challenge was to engineer a new consolidation of authority to counter the social fragmentation that had occurred. The overall Neolithic ideology and its ritual structures needed replacing.[2] For example, a sense of individual property had not yet replaced the community sense of property (e.g., the persistence of village herds). A second Agricultural Revolution—the Bronze Age—was required to draw (or re-draw) and more thoroughly enforce divisions and boundaries: to anchor domestication.[3]

The first civilizations are based on the solutions to such challenges, on success at channeling energies into an altogether new scale of organization (e.g., cities), of rulership, aggression, militarism, and empire building. Fertility, a staple of domestication, was expanded into great symbolic importance in all early civilizations.

---

1 Jacques Cauvin, *The Birth of the Gods and the Origins of Agriculture*, translated by Trevor Watkins (New York: Cambridge University Press, 2000), p. 205.

2 Ian Kuit, "People and Space in Early Agricultural Villages: Exploring Daily Lives, Community, Size and Archaeology in the Late Pre-Pottery Neolithic," in *Journal of Anthropological Archaeology* 19 (March 2000), pp. 96–99.

3 John Baines, "Public Ceremonial Performance in Ancient Egypt," in Takeshi Inomata and Lawrence S. Cohen, eds., *Archaeology of Performance* (Lanham, MD: AltaMira Press, 2006), p. 263.

As daily life grew harder, religion presented distant horizons of happiness. Belief in an enhanced life after death appears to have been stronger in territorial states than in city-state systems.[4] Stronger, that is, as political power extended itself. Theocratic classes served as new organizing authorities, while the deities themselves reflected the always-advancing principle of specialization. Each had his or her allotted sphere and role. The gods needed the service of monarchs and priestly bailiffs to execute religious requirements. But despite the divine sanction or legitimation accorded to political figures, they were not immune from assassination, and the threat of violence was needed to collect taxes in early civilizations.

Art and architecture partook of the growing social complexity, reflecting the developing class hierarchy and performing ideological, social-regulatory functions. Spectacle was a new cultural component, making its appearance early on in the service of social integration. Public performance, like ritual, was often highly regimented or structured, and thus paralleled the authoritarian relations closing in among people. As John Baines observes, "It is difficult to imagine any but the smallest-scale and least differentiated society that would exist without some sort of spectacle."[5]

Another ideological support for domestication was the emerging time-consciousness that seems to have accompanied ever-increasing division of labor. In its cruder, public form, the evidence shows that all regimes of early civilizations bureaucratically commandeered time, from Stonehenge-type time computers at the beginning of the Bronze Age to the calendars that regulated official cycles and events.

---

4   Bruce G. Trigger, *Understanding Early Civilizations: A Comparative Study* (New York: Cambridge University Press, 2003), p. 673.

5   John Baines, "Public Ceremonial Performance in Ancient Egypt," in Takeshi Inomata and Lawrence S. Cohen, eds., *Archaeology of Performance* (Lanham, MD: AltaMira Press, 2006), p. 263.

Literacy is exactly congruent with state formation; the one develops in parallel with the other. As written signs take precedence over memory, a ruling version of reality can be made. Writing provided a great instrument to power and is not only, in Stanley Diamond's words, "one of the original mysteries of civilization," but also its "compulsive rite."[6]

For the past thousand years in the Western world, history has been divided into modern and pre-modern. As distant in time from the Greek and Roman eras as we are today, the Bronze Age is certainly buried in the pre-modern. But as we think our present-day, modern thoughts, how different are they, really, from those thoughts in the first Bronze Age civilizations? How many deep habits of mind, institutions, routines, go back to the Bronze Age and its brand-new spirit and ethos? Was that not the origin of the notion, so basically corrosive to autonomy and freedom, that inequality and hierarchy are normal conditions and that misfortune is not a social evil but an individual's just desserts? A notion so obviously still with us. The Bronze Age devised a mechanical order several millennia before sophisticated power-driven machinery, a stratified order that is "the basic exploitation system which has lasted until the present day."[7]

Early on, what Marx called "domestic" or household industry was already market-oriented, and the consensus is that overall, the Bronze Age was a market economy.[8] Long-distance trade, occupational/full-time specialization, supply/demand-determined prices, capital investment, credit, and other "modern" features are observable by the fourth millennium B.P. Such capitalist aspects have existed in all

---

6   Stanley Diamond, *In Search of the Primitive: A Critique of Civilization* (New Brunswick, NJ: Transaction Books, 1974), pp. 4, 3.

7   Graeme Baker, "The Conditions of Cultural and Economic Growth in the Bronze Age of Central Italy," in *Proceedings of the Prehistoric Society* (1972), p. 204.

8   Oystein S. La Bianca, Introduction, in Oystein La Bianca and Sandra Arnold Scham, eds., *Connectivity in Antiquity* (London: Equinox, 2006), p. 7.

the civilized countries of the world for as far back as economic evidence can take us. Sam Lilley saw pottery as "the first mechanized production industry, the first step on the way to the mass production factory of today."[9]

Extraction and smelting of metal ores was a principal motor of Bronze Age society, with metallurgy stimulating all other productive activities.[10] Childe found that "modern science and industry...go back to the period when bronze was the dominant industrial metal."[11] By this time, production was taking place well outside the house, and moving from luxury goods for temple and palace elites toward mass consumption.

Theodore Wertime has suggested that the principal cause of deforestation was the demands of ancient metallurgy.[12] Of course, land was also cleared for agriculture, especially after the appearance of new inventions such as the plow. Vast forests (of date palms and many other trees) were eradicated across the Near East. Overspecialization in agricultural production (monoculture) and ruling-class control of surplus met a shift toward drought, to cause the collapse of Bronze Age society in the Southern Levant in about 2200 B.P.E.[13]

From an earlier self-sufficiency to a growing dependence on experts, technological complexity brought a division of the self into narrowing roles. One's skills were no longer relatively interchangeable, as they had been in a more egalitarian society. Social class derives from this most basic division; despite Marxist claims, class society did not origi-

---

9   Sam Lilley, Men, Machines and History (London: Cobbett Press, 1948), p. 8.

10   Herbert J. Muller, Freedom in the Ancient World (New York: Harper & Brothers, 1961), p. 25.

11   V. Gordon Childe, The Bronze Age (New York: Cambridge University Press, 1930), p. 3.

12   Theodore A. Wertime, "The Furnace versus the Goat? Pyrotechnic Industries and Mediterranean Deforestation," Journal of Field Archaeology 10 (1983), pp. 445–452.

13   Arlene Miller Rosen, "The Social Response to Environmental Change in Early Bronze Age Canaan," Journal of Anthropological Archaeology 14 (1995).

nate with modern industrial society. It was there very early on and was institutionalized by civilization. The individual was enfeebled, fractionalized, without the understanding or control he/she had in smaller, less complex communities. Society moved away from its constituents, became opaque, something beyond the life of the individual: the path to urban civilization, emerging after 4000 B.C.

Slavery, nonetheless, was "less extensive and oppressive than in many later preindustrial societies," in Bruce Trigger's judgment.[14] Marxists are wrong to assert that early civilizations were slave-based, as they are in error regarding a more recent formation of social classes than was the case.

People had to "tame" themselves to live in cities, that core component of civilization, and cities couldn't exist without "intensive plant and animal domestication."[15] The taming goes on, of course (e.g., genetic engineering, nanotechnology); control, its working logic, is what maintains and reproduces civilization. In terms of daily life, notes Monica Smith, "there are considerable similarities between modern and ancient cities."[16] It is obvious that we are still faced with the social, ethical, and political problems that urban civilization introduced.

The city was "a completely new kind of settlement."[17] No early civilization, according to Trigger, had an egalitarian village base.[18] The emergent urban identities rested upon an imagined and enforced community, as if communal egali-

---

14 Trigger, *op. cit.*, p. 48.

15 Elman Service, *Origins of the State and Civilization* (New York: Norton, 1975), p. 223.

16 Monica L. Smith, *The Social Construction of Ancient Cities* (Washington, DC: Smithsonian Books, 2003), p. 28.

17 Vicente Lull and Rafael Nico, translated by Peter Smith, *Archaeology of the Origin of the State* (New York: Oxford University Press, 2011), p. 184.

18 Trigger, *op. cit.*, p. 52. There is some controversy as to whether a few large Neolithic settlements, such as Jericho and, especially, Catul Huyuk (in present-day Turkey) constituted cities.

tarian foundations survived, albeit in new forms. New, but grounded upon a highly organized system of production a long time in the making. A whole chain of specialized activities laid the groundwork for and maintained the integration process represented by full-blown cities.

While it is difficult to make inferences about ideology from archaeological evidence, it seems valid to see routine activities as the most basic component of a minimum of social cohesion and stability. Technology, especially in its organizational sense, is never outside culture. Division of labor is itself a "technology" of social domination. Robert McC. Adams thus found cultural/political complexity to be "essentially technological,"[19] and is this different today?

To the discipline based on routine must be added other civilizational forces. Referring to the early Bronze Age in Syria, Lebanon and Palestine, James Mellaart found a very characteristic feature of urbanization in a "gradual uniformity of culture."[20] Heidegger saw here a threat of "destructive error"[21] that cities bring to thought.

When a city, dependent on its surroundings as every city is, has imposed its control over a region, it is thereby a "state." A city must guarantee the inputs required for its survival, must police its trade arteries, and this is the near-universal process in state formation (and war). Civilizations commonly evolve from city-states to territorial states, and finally, to empires.

From the egalitarian world of band society in the Paleolithic there is an evident shift to ranked tribal societies in the

19 Cited in A. Mederos and C.C. Lamberg-Karlovsky, "Weight Systems and Trade Networks," in Jeremy A. Subloff and C.C. Lamberg-Karlovsky, eds., *Ancient Civilization and Trade* (Albuquerque: University of New Mexico Press, 1975), p. 207.

20 James Mellaarts, *The Chalcolithic and Early Bronze Ages in the Near East and Anatolia* (Beirut: Khayats, 1966), p. 59.

21 Quoted from Martin Heidegger, "Why Do I Stay in the Provinces?" in Thomas Sheehan, ed., *Heidegger: the Man and the Thinker* (Chicago: Precedent Publishing, 1981), p. 29.

Neolithic. The latter often included face-to-face relationships among those of lesser and greater power, within small-scale networks. But "all the qualitative components of the state were already present to some degree among advanced chiefdoms," in Marvin Harris' words.[22] Developed chiefdoms were not unlike simple states.

The state uses force, or it cannot be considered a state. A sense of human inadequacy grew apace as expansion and growing differentiation passed well beyond human scale. Gift obligations, for example, were replaced by tribute and the tax collector. And yet, as Trigger concludes, "In all early civilizations, families, wards, and small communities were permitted and even encouraged to manage their own affairs, to a much greater degree than is characteristic of developed industrial societies."[23]

The state and the new authority relations were phenomena unknown to humans for most of our 2.5-million-year history. During the Bronze Age, civilization was imposed as an abnormal condition, locking the door of a social cage that had only been closed, not secured, during the Neolithic.

All civilizations are the institutionalized appropriation by a small ruling elite of most of what is produced by the submerged classes. Their political/legal structures frequently claim to serve their subjects, but of course, then as now, they exist to protect the privileged position of a few. Punishments enacted by early states, though often cruel by modern standards, do not reflect the strength of law enforcement. They are better understood as testimony to the weakness of coercive authority, its need for drastic measures.

It was once thought that palaces and temples defined Bronze Age life, but this was due to the preponderance of evidence from such sources. More recently, artifacts from other

---

22   Marvin Harris, *Cultural Materialism* (New York: Random House, 1979), p. 100.

23   Trigger, *op. cit.*, p. 196.

institutions and groups have shed light on other important participants and factors. For instance, urban centers led to accelerated consumption by individuals, in dense networks of interaction. Later, in the Iron Age, Rome became known as the ultimate "consumer city," but the movement in that direction was underway well before. The grid plan of urban design is also associated with Rome, but many of the oldest known cities were built on those lines.[24]

As Michael Mann noted, "All civilizations of recorded history have engaged routinely in highly organized and bloody warfare."[25] Civilizations began in violence and were extended via imperialism. Warrior society was a defining Bronze Age feature, serving to deflect internal contradictions and conflicts outward into territorial expansion. The military offered some upward mobility for those at the bottom, for instance.

According to Homer, this was an age of heroes and their long-distance quests. Most famously, the *Odyssey* recounts years of travel by Odysseus, a classical myth of the Trojan War (fourteenth century B.C.). A warrior elite fostered an ideology of heroic war leaders, complete with the Middle Bronze Age invention of the chariot. Militarism expanded the range of political control, and represented the most obvious phenomenon of all civilizations: patriarchy. Originating in the goal of conquering nature (domestication), society was increasingly "a man's world."[26] Virility now became a cardinal virtue.[27]

Especially very recently there is much public discussion about globalization, about our supposedly rather new glob-

---

24 Richard Sennett, *Flesh and Stone: the Body and the City in Western Civilization* (New York: W.W. Norton, 1994), p. 106.

25 Michael Mann, *The Sources of Social Power, Volume I: A History of Power from the Beginning to A.D. 1760* (New York: Cambridge University Press, 1986), p. 48.

26 Muller, *op. cit.*, p. 27.

27 Kristian Kristiansen, *Europe before History* (New York: Cambridge University Press, 1998), pp 133, 411.

al interconnectedness and interdependence. But it is actually "strikingly old,"[28] not much newer than the rise of the earliest cities. A key text is Frank and Gills' *The World System*, which argues that "the contemporary world system has a history of at least 5,000 years."[29] It resulted from the confluence of the hegemonies of Mesopotamia and Egypt, and casts "a strong continuity"[30] with the world of today. William McNeill referred to "the emergence of the original ecumenical world system within which we live today."[31]

Concurrent with the rise of civilization there appears history's first international system, an economically and technologically integrated entity. Andrew and Susan Sherratt maintained that it included such components as "the gold, the skills, the scale, the exotic materials, the sophisticated lifestyle, and the investment capacity."[32] There are varying assessments as to when this globalization was achieved, whether it was earlier or later during the Bronze Age. But the common Marxist perspective, that a world system did not exist before the sixteenth century A.D., clearly misses the mark.

There were many and varied early civilizations on various continents; for example those of north China, Indus Valley India, Mesoamerica, and the Yoruba civilization of west Africa. To focus on civilization and mass society for this brief overview, however, I'll look at the earliest and most studied cases: Mesopotamia and Egypt.

Mesopotamia (roughly contiguous with Iraq) was home to some of the very oldest agricultural settlements. Begun

---

28 Justin Jennings, *Globalizations and the Ancient World* (New York: Cambridge University Press, 2011), p. 17.

29 Andre Gunder Frank and Barry K. Gills, *The World System: Five Hundred Years or Five Thousand?* (New York: Routledge, 1993), p. 1.

30 Kasja Ekholm Friedman and Jonathan Friedman, *Historical Transformations: the Anthropology of Global Systems* (Lanham, MD: AltaMira Press, 2008), p. 163.

31 Quoted in Frank and Gills, *op. cit.*, p. 13.

32 Andrew and Susan Sherratt, cited in Frank and Gills, *op. cit.*, p. 21.

somewhat before 8000 B.C., the domestication process had included most staple crops and herd animals by about 6000 B.C. The Tigris-Euphrates valley, often called the Fertile Crescent, also exhibited social ranking and stratification at least as early as the sixth millennium B.C. More differentials developed among the population, along with manufacturing specialization and administrative bureaucracy, and in the 3000s B.C., the world's earliest known urbanized state societies appeared.

A fundamental premise of Mesopotamian civilization was the "unconditional acceptance of the city as the one and only communal organization."[33] Urbanism was based on the breakdown of simpler, more egalitarian forms of social organization, and the primitive commune was already an anachronism by the Middle Bronze Age.[34] A single-minded city-building policy was a royal aim throughout this entire period, to enact and ensure the pacification of the country. Orlin concluded that the greatest single spur to cities in the Near East was the "forced urbanization of rebellious tribes."[35]

But there were also primary social institutions at work, more basic than that of policy. Justin Jennings observed that "most of the networks that brought goods, people, and ideas to and from the city were outside the control of city administrators."[36] The key, as always, is the prime mover known as division of labor. "Central to all accounts of urbanization or state formation is the concept of specialization," as J.N. Postgate succinctly expresses it.[37]

---

33 A. Leo Oppenheim, *Ancient Mesopotamia: Portrait of a Dead Civilization* (Chicago: University of Chicago Press, 1977), p. 111.

34 Burt Alpert, *Inversions* (San Francisco: privately published, 1973), p. 294.

35 Louis L. Orlin, *Life and Thought in the Ancient Near East* (Ann Arbor: University of Michigan Press, 2007), p. 162.

36 Jennings, *op. cit.*, p. 76.

37 J.N. Postgate, *Early Mesopotamia: Society and Economy at the Dawn of History* (New York: Routledge, 1992), p. 225.

The urban revolution of the Uruk period, fourth-millennium B.C., was a basic reordering of human social life. The first literate urban civilization had fully arrived during the 3000s B.C., borne on a wave of what Robert McC. Adams termed "hyper-developed urbanism."[38] At least half of the Sumerian (south Mesopotamian) population now resided in cities.[39] By around 2500 B.C. even most farmers lived in cities. Another datum that evokes the modern world: smaller families were the rule in cities, larger ones in the villages.[40]

It is the sense of the city, the ideological potency of the urban condition, that is of main importance. In an indirect reference to the uncivilized, seminomadic Amorite tribe, the *Gilgamesh* epic of the early second millennium B.C. introduces Enkidu. He runs wild with the animals until enticed into Uruk in Sumeria, where he becomes domesticated. This key myth, among others, expresses the founding of a civic consciousness that is pervasive in the dominant Mesopotamian literature.[41] The poem *Enuma* similarly traces the defeat of precivilized chaos by the god Marduk—a task not completed until he establishes the city of Babylon as his abode.[42] In fact, the establishment of a pan-Mesopotamian sensibility is primarily the achievement of triumphant urbanism.

It was the city itself, not forgetting temple and palace as primary power centers, that became the essential aspect of Mesopotamian civilization. A.L. Oppenheim accurately

38   Robert McC. Adams, "Patterns of Urbanism in Early Southern Mesopotamia," in Peter J. Ucko, Ruth Tringham, and G.W. Dimberly, eds., *Man, Settlement and Urbanism* (London: Duckworth, 1972), p. 745.

39   Jonathan Haas, ed., *From Leaders to Rulers* (New York: Kluwer Academic/ Plenum Publishers, 2001), p. 218. And Oppenheim, *op. cit.*, p. 72.

40   Robin Winks and Susan P. Mattern-Parkes, *The Ancient Mediterranean World* (New York: Oxford University Press, 2004), p. 24.

41   Orlin, *op. cit.*, pp. 172–173.

42   Peter Machinist, "On Self-Consciousness in Mesopotamia," in S.N. Eisenstadt, *The Origins and Diversity of Axial Age Civilizations* (Albany: State University of New York Press, 1986), p. 187.

refers to the Mesopotamian city as "the assembly of free citizens."[43] A thousand years before Athens one finds such an institution, with its modern overtones of citizenship and democracy. Arguably, however, it may serve as a reminder that democratic forms have always cloaked the rule of elites. The fact of urbanism in itself seemed to give rise to a concept of citizenship; Thorkild Jacobsen makes a case for "primitive democracy."[44] The persistence of religion, however, reminds us that the context is as far from purely secular-political as it is from pure "democracy."

The official outlook was that humans were servants of the gods, no one more so than the king, who provided justice, ultimately, on behalf of the gods. But in the course of the third millennium B.C., the state ever more transparently assumed the role of the gods and their authority.[45] Religious metaphors continued as the coin of the realm nonetheless. In this sense religion was politics. Even taxation, for example, was couched in religious terms. The distinction among terms such as "religious," "political," and "social" had far less meaning in ancient Mesopotamia than for us today.[46] Functionaries who may have been identifiably "religious" can be found to have played administrative roles in political and economic spheres. At the same time, David and Joan Oates discerned a "basically democratic orientation of society."[47]

This latter city-state ideology or ideal "endured into the first millennium B.C. despite the development of larger

---

43 Oppenheim, *op. cit.*, p. 109.

44 Cited in Karen Rhea Nemet-Nejat, *Daily Life in Ancient Mesopotamia* (Peabody, MA: Hendrickson Publishers, 2002), p. 107.

45 Oppenheim, *op. cit.*, p. 191.

46 David and Joan Oates, *The Rise of Civilization* (New York: Elsevier Phaidon, 1976), p. 134.

47 *Ibid.*, p. 135.

states and empires."[48] And despite problematic terminology, Mesopotamian society was becoming more secular; the influence of the temple waned between 2500 and 1500 B.C.[49] Hammurabi, who unified Mesopotamia (ca. 1770s B.C.), promulgated a legendary legal code that espoused a defense of the weak against the strong; it eschewed war and proclaimed tolerance and friendship among peoples. The reality was one of increasing exploitation and expansion,[50] prefiguring modern political rhetoric and the evils it tries to hide or somehow legitimate.

How "archaic" is fealty to authority? Americans sing the national anthem and recite the Pledge of Allegiance. A common custom in Mesopotamia was for the ruler to mold and/or place the first brick for a building project. How like political figures of our time, cutting a ribbon to open a bridge, or digging the first shovelful to begin construction. Political integration, including some of the forms we're used to, began in the Bronze Age.

The Oates refer to apparent "evidence for strictly observed property rights already in the sixth millennium B.C."[51] By the fourth millennium, division of labor and social stratification are linked to more demand for foreign goods, production of goods for exchange, and capitalization of long-distance trade, according to Norman Yoffee.[52] More specifically, in C.K. Maisel's words, city-states' economies were "structured around 'mass production' (sustained surpluses generated by capital-intensive means), bulk transfers and sophisticated

---

48 Trigger, *op. cit.*, p. 219.

49 Nemet-Nejat, *op. cit.*, p. 302. Postgate, *op. cit.*, p. 300.

50 Lewis Mumford, *The City in History* (New York: Harcourt, Brace & World, 1961), p. 53.

51 Oates and Oates, *op. cit.*, p. 67.

52 Norman Yoffee, "Mesopotamian Interaction Spheres," in Norman Yoffee and Jeffery J. Clark, *Early Stages in the Evolution of Mesopotamian Civilization* (Tucson: University of Arizona Press, 1993), p. 267.

manufacturing—all controlled by rigorous book-keeping that tracked inputs and outputs, profits and losses and overall efficiencies."[53]

Rulers exercised some degree of control over the economic system throughout much of the Bronze Age, but there was a fluctuating relationship between central authority and the private sector. Some craft specialists, for instance, were clients of the centralized institutions, and others were independent. The distinction is not always clear; think of defense contractors in the U.S. today, private corporations entirely dependent on government contracts.

The vocabulary of daily life in Mesopotamia is surprisingly recognizable. Terms for "street" also connote "marketplace," and by about 2000 B.C. the city of Ur, for one, had merchandise-displaying showrooms.[54] "The sophistication of the credit system" at about this time, "including the circulation of debts and titles to real assets as media of exchange is impressive," noted Morris Silver.[55]

It was significantly earlier that complexity and bureaucratization of the political economy rendered sophisticated accounting systems necessary. Piotr Steinkeller found that the taxation system alone "called for an extraordinarily high level of data-recording."[56] At base it was the scale of production that called forth standardization, efficiency principles, bookkeeping procedures, and other innovations that we wrongly tend to think of as recent developments. Modern "firm-like" approaches are indeed thousands of years old.

The production of bronze required long-distance trade,

53 Charles Keith Maisels, *Early Civilizations of the Old World* (New York: Routledge, 1999), p. 346.

54 Morris Silver, *Economic Structures of Antiquity* (Westport, CT: Greenwood Press, 1995), pp. 154, 156.

55 *Ibid.*, p. 114.

56 Quoted in Introduction, Michael Hudson and Cornelia Wunsch, eds., *Creating Economic Order* (Bethesda, MD: CDL Press, 2004), p. 9.

and commonly involved copper shipments of many tons each. Excavations at Yarim Tepe revealed copper and lead smelting from about 6000 B.C., a surprisingly early date and a "hitherto unsuspected level of industrial specialization."[57] Ceramic production changed with the emergence of urbanism; pottery was increasingly wheel-made and uniform. As Childe put it, "with the adoption of the wheel, pottery tends to become a factory product and to lose much of its individuality."[58] The manufacture of glass vessels spread across the Near East upon its invention in the second millennium B.C. Textile enterprises had already reached enormous proportions. Around 2200 B.C., a weaving factory in Guabba employed over 6,000 workers, mostly women and children.[59]

Industrialism is a control apparatus by its nature, integrative in a primary sense. Mesopotamian writing, the world's earliest, is another example of a technology that arose to meet organizational requirements of the manufacturing economy. Writing made effective management of mass enterprises possible for the first time.

Thousands of years before twentieth-century Taylorists or Stakhovanite managers applied stopwatches to workers' motions in the U.S. and USSR, such practices were common in Mesopotamia. Soon after the hour was first divided into sixty minutes there, time became a weapon of mass production labor-discipline. "Ur III [late third millennium] timekeepers were extraordinarily punctilious in reckoning precisely how long it took to make ceramic vessels of varying size."[60] In other areas beside pottery fabrication, authorities

57 Oates and Oates, *op. cit.*, p. 101.

58 Childe, *op. cit.*, p. 51. Also P.R.S. Moorey, *Ancient Mesopotamian Materials and Industries* (Oxford: Clarendon Press, 1994), p. 157.

59 Postgate, *op. cit.*, p. 235.

60 D.T. Potts, *Mesopotamian Civilization: the Material Foundations* (Ithaca, NY: Cornell University Press, 1997), p. 156.

"made constant efforts to standardize and rationalize."[61]

At this time a uniform model of beveled-rim bowls became ubiquitous. It now seems that they mainly served to provide standard wage rations (e.g., barley, oil), a very widespread usage.[62] It was a common practice for workers to borrow against wages in advance of payday, and "despite the growing emphasis on labor-saving products, techniques and organization, many people's workloads probably continued to increase," concluded Oppenheim.[63] So much of this has the ring of contemporaneity to it.

Trade union activity was widespread in the Middle Bronze Age, with unionization at far higher levels than in the U.S. today.[64] The risk of social unrest prompted "make-work" projects, such as elaborate public construction efforts[65]— more practices and sensibilities that seem distinctly modern.

Some of the people who weren't interested in civilization, or its regimen of work and cities, now were compelled to work as slaves. Debt slavery came later, but slave status was a generally fluid condition, marginal to society as a whole.[66]

Deforestation, grazing, and the extensive irrigation system created increasingly grave environmental impacts in Mesopotamia by the late third millennium. It was the last factor, unnatural amounts of water applied to the land, that may have been the most harmful. Irrigation brought up salt water through capillary action, creating wastelands and causing the abandonment of cities in the southern region.[67] The salinization effects were also felt in the Harappan civilization of India at this time (circa 2200 B.C.), and indeed

---

61 Postgate, *op. cit.*, p. 233.
62 Oates and Oates, *op. cit.*, p. 130.
63 Oppenheim, *op. cit.*, p. 96.
64 Alpert, *op. cit.*, pp. 296–298.
65 Oppenheim, *op. cit.*, p. 98.
66 Nemet-Nejat, *op. cit.*, pp. 117–118.
67 Postgate, *op. cit.*, p. 181.

are very problematic today, notably in Turkey, Australia, and Montana.[68]

By this same period, a wholesale-retail network of large-scale commodity exchange was in effect, providing the background to much that we would find familiar: commercial streets, taverns, broad avenues, plazas, alleys, empty lots, large and small houses—built of mud brick, plaster and wood, as in Iraq today. Neighborhood bakeries (likely the first shops), a very developed cuisine with a wide array of recipes (including farmed fish), sports, popular music, the first zoos, parks—many features that "must have made Mesopotamian cities vibrant, noisy, smelly, sometimes bewildering and dangerous, but also exciting places."[69] And in private life, all that survives today, from cosmetics and perfume to board games and tablecloths.

Urban Mesopotamia was virtually designed for epidemic disease, created by domestication and its first, Neolithic crowding of animals (human and otherwise), and perfected by city conditions. Another civilizational staple we have not left behind. Perhaps surprisingly, general longevity for adults was much the same as it is today.[70] Probably more unusual to us is the absence of racial divisions. For H.W.F. Saggs, it is "very clear" that "ethnic divisions played little part" in Mesopotamian society.[71] Upward mobility for the individual, then as now, was most common in periods of geographic or economic expansion.[72] There were women in business and the professions—far more so than in the Near East now—but

---

68 Jared Diamond, *Collapse* (New York: Viking, 2005), p. 48.

69 Susan Pollock, *Ancient Mesopotamia: The Eden that Never Was* (New York: Cambridge University Press, 1999), p. 48.

70 Nemet-Nejat, *op. cit.*, p. 146.

71 H.W.F. Saggs, *Civilization before Greece and Rome* (New Haven: Yale University Press, 1989), p. 45.

72 Trigger, *op. cit.*, p. 161.

they did not enjoy complete equality in law or custom.[73]

Mesopotamian complex society, for example the Uruk city-states, needed the resources of the Anatolian and Iranian highlands; they therefore tended toward expansion and war. Interference with trade routes, real or potentially real, could not be tolerated. The very recent wars in this same land demonstrate the same principle urging warfare, in the matter of guaranteed oil supply, of course.

Sargon (circa 2310 B.C.) was the first historical personality. He was the first ruler to establish a unified rule over all of Mesopotamia; in fact, his was the first world system polity. Sargon's triumph, amid growing degrees of warfare and imperialism, was not without challenges. Like most rulers he faced revolts, and agriculture as an institution met with persistent resistance.[74] Sargon II referred to the hill country Mannaeans as living "in confusion," whom he had to civilize or "put into order."[75] A crescendo of aggression and warfare led to the crisis of twelfth-century Mesopotamia, three centuries of decline and collapse that represented the end of the Bronze Age.

Egypt, like Mesopotamia, was a new chapter or project of domestication. It became a civilizational answer to the uncertainty that those in power had to contend with when the Neolithic era ended. "Irrigation agriculture was decisive in generating civilization, stratification, and the state in Egypt," the Nile supporting "the highest population density" in the ancient world.[76] Lacking some of the strong early urban development seen in Mesopotamia, Egypt was—and remains—a mainly agricultural country. Its civilization rested on the surplus created in the fields; Robert July estimated

---

73 Postgate, *op. cit.*, p. 105.
74 Service, *op. cit.*, p. 215.
75 Machinist/Eisenstadt, *op. cit.*, p. 189.
76 Mann, *op. cit.*, p. 108.

that the average Egyptian peasant produced three times as much food as he needed.[77]

By about 3000 B.C. Egypt's chiefdoms and proto-states had been forged into the region's first nation-state, with a "sophisticated populace."[78] Lynn Meskell advises us that "we have underestimated the complexities of ancient cultures—Egypt being one of the most important."[79] Sergio Donadoni observes that "the Egyptian world appears to be strikingly modern in many ways."[80]

Egyptian rulers, like those of Mesopotamia, claimed a genealogy going back to the gods. Nevertheless, it was the pharaoh's earthly power that was employed to subordinate "Egypt's own potentially rebellious population."[81] We know a lot less about how that population lived than we do about tombs and pyramids, largely because unlike cities and towns, non-urban artifacts were not repeatedly replaced and built over. Concerning the breadth and depth of religious feeling, for example, we can only really guess, although as today, various people might have looked forward to an afterlife that was a considerable improvement on the earthly one. The Egyptians were the first to embalm bodies, and the practice remained popular despite widespread tomb robbing in ancient times. "During certain epochs," observed Donadoni, "it is quite likely that entire populations made a living out of the business."[82] This phenomenon would seem to undermine

---

77   Robert W. July, *A History of the African People* (New York: Scribner, 1970), p. 14.

78   Lionel Casson, *Everyday Life in Ancient Egypt* (Baltimore: Johns Hopkins University Press, 2001), p. 1.

79   Lynn Meskell, *Archaeologies of Social Life: Age, Sex, Class et cetera in Ancient Egypt* (Malden, MA: Blackwell, 1999), p. 110.

80   Sergio Donadini, ed., *The Egyptians* (Chicago: The University of Chicago Press, 1997), p. x.

81   Edith Lustig, "Anthropology and Egyptology," in A. Bernard Knapp, ed., *Monographs in Mediterranean Archaeology* 8 (Sheffield, UK: Sheffield Academic Press, 1997), p. 14.

82   Sergio Donadini, "The Dead," in Donadini, *op. cit.*, p. 272.

the notion of strong Egyptian piety. "There is some doubt," adds A.G. McDowell, "whether the common man was much concerned with what went on behind the temple pylons."[83]

It does seem clear that Egyptians favored local gods, which may be related to the common attitude that all animals were sacred.[84] In the end, however, the spiritual culture descended into a "religion-haunted, superstitious, ritualistic" condition.[85]

Egypt was essentially an exchange economy. The presence of components such as "wage-labor, a market for land, production for the market, and state involvement"[86] certainly qualified it as capitalist. Although Egypt has been described as a public sector economy,[87] Lynn Meskell's study of Deir-el-Medina, the most thoroughly documented settlement site of Middle Kingdom Egypt, provides a more nuanced view. Meskell finds that "all the evidence points to a minimum interventionist model" where individuals "exercised a remarkable amount of social mobility and maneuvering, ignoring the sanctions of the state to their own personal benefit and profit."[88]

There were many, however, who worked directly for the state (e.g., bureaucrats, craftsmen), just as there are in any modern nation. Scribes became an intellectual class and staffed a functioning and growing bureaucracy. Many hoped to avoid manual labor by building an administrative career in the civil service. Over time a large number of immigrants,

83   A.G. McDowell, *Village Life in Ancient Egypt* (New York: Oxford University Press, 1990), p. 91. Also, "The tomb of Tutenkhamen was partially looted by the very priests responsible for the burial" (p. 199). And "By 1064 B.C. at the latest it was patently clear that all the major royal tombs in the Valley of the Kings had been looted" (p. 242).

84   Casson, *op. cit.*, pp. 89, 83.

85   *Ibid.*, p. 120.

86   David Warburton, *State and Economy in Ancient Egypt* (Freiburg, Switzerland: University Press, 1997), p. 173.

87   Eric Carlton, *Ideology and Social Order* (Boston: Routledge & Kegan Paul), p. 134.

88   Lynn Meskell, *Private Life in New Kingdom Egypt* (Princeton: Princeton University Press, 2002), p. 25.

chiefly Asians, engaged in building and industrial activity.[89] Some of the world's oldest underground mining activity took place in Egypt (e.g., Nazlet Khater-4). By the time of the New Kingdom in the late Bronze Age there was mass production of goods in several sectors. Marked craft specialization existed in metallurgy, lithic industry, stone vase production, and above all, pottery manufacturing.[90] Potters used an assembly-line mode "remarkably" early, in the judgment of Lionel Casson.[91] Increasing sameness was the rule, as quantity replaced distinctive quality as a value. Industrial vessels predominate over household pots in the archaeological record,[92] as befits a mass society.

Beer, bread, and wine were some of the production staples, plus an excellent form of paper that was widely exported. (The word derives from papyrus, the Egyptian reed from which paper was first made.) Late Egypt saw a number of sizeable textile factories.[93] The kingdom had arrived at "an unrivalled celebrity as a manufacturing country."[94] Pyramid building was a socio-economic enterprise, more focused on employment-based loyalty than motivated by religious ideology.[95] In any case, such monumentalism created an enormous demand for Lebanese cedar and pine, part of the major deforestation in the region.[96]

---

89   Gae Callender, "The Middle Kingdom Renaissance," in *The Oxford History of Ancient Egypt* (New York: Oxford University Press, 2003), p. 157.

90   Casson, *op. cit.*, p. 53.

91   *Ibid.*, p. 54.

92   Max Raphael, *Prehistoric Pottery and Civilization in Egypt* (New York: Pantheon Books, 1947), p. 135.

93   Naphtali Lewis, *Life in Egypt under Roman Rule* (Oxford: Clarendon Press, 1983), p. 134.

94   J. Gardner Wilkinson, *Manners and Customs of the Ancient Egyptians* (London, John Murray, 1841), p. 4.

95   Carlton, *op. cit.*, p. 139. The Aztec state was another that consolidated power through large-scale public works projects.

96   Mellaart, *op. cit.*, p. 68.

Egypt's chief contemporary archaeologist disclosed evidence in 2010 that the Great Pyramids were built by free workers, not by slaves.[97] This furthers the thesis that such projects had become economic necessities,[98] and that slavery was in general uneconomic and comparatively rare.[99] As in Mesopotamia, the institution had very different forms and meanings from our own definition. "Slave" was not a legal term; citizens and slaves were the same under the law, for example.[100]

In the world of work, one can pass from celebrated design perfection (e.g., tombs) and magnificent stone vessel craftsmanship to the dangerous drudgery in the mines (in any age or epoch), and the fact that scribes were as numerous as office workers are now.[101]

Workers were generally well paid in regular wages of grain, fish, vegetables, and the like, with bonus payments not uncommon.[102] Deir-el-Medina laborers "were receiving good wages even when they were not needed."[103] Eyre found "no evidence that the wage levels of the crew were ever reduced, either individually or collectively, because of absences from work."[104]

The prominence of writing is clear at Deir-el-Medina, and

---

97 Marwa Awad, "Egypt Tombs Suggest Pyramids not Built by Slaves," Thomson Reuters, January 10, 2010.

98 Kurt Mendelssohn, "A Scientist Looks at the Pyramids," in *American Scientist* 59:2 (1971), pp. 210–220. After about 2,600 B.C. some thirty-five major pyramids and many smaller ones were built, along with large monuments such as Abu Simbel. Architecture and art of this kind are ultimately about governance as well as economics. A sense of power and order is transmitted, as is the case with contemporary examples (e.g., Washington Monument).

99 Shaw, *op. cit.*, p. 421.

100 Antonio Loprieno, "Slaves," in Donadini, *op. cit.*, pp. 206–216. Also Edward Eyre, "Work in the New Kingdom," in Marvin A. Powell, ed., *Labor in the Ancient Near East* (New Haven: American Oriental Society, 1987), p. 211.

101 Casson, *op. cit.*, p. 50.

102 McDowell, *op. cit.*, pp. 7, 223. And Rosalind M. and Jac J. Janssen, *Growing Up in Ancient Egypt* (London: The Rubicon Press, 1990), p. 107.

103 *Ibid.*, p. 80.

104 Edward Eyre in Powell, *op.cit.*, p. 178.

"some workmen read Middle Egyptian classics for pleasure and not merely for training."[105] The degree of proletarian literacy and culture in ancient Egypt is a surprising fact.[106]

Workers were fairly mobile, and in the case of unsolicited transfers were commonly displeased, much as in today's world. But legal agreements (and lawsuits) were far from rare, and neither were agreements that were explicitly labor contracts, it seems.[107] Skilled craftsmen and foremen often came up from the ranks,[108] and Marfoe noted an "emphasis on 'self-made' men and personal initiative [which is] a striking parallelism with the ethical changes and transformations of a later capitalistic age."[109]

Despite whatever upwardly mobile consciousness there may have been, class struggle was definitely present, especially toward the end of the Bronze Age. Strikes broke out during the reigns of Ramses III and IV in the twelfth and eleventh centuries B.C., often over late wages. The strikes of 1160–1153 B.C. are thought to be the first in history.[110] At times even the pharaoh couldn't get them back to work![111] Other heightened conflicts involved actions such as torch-lit night demonstrations and other forms of militant political activity "of a type more familiar from our own time."[112]

Ancient Egypt was somewhat less city-oriented than Mesopotamia, but did have towns and cities of considerable den-

---

105 McDowell, *op. cit.*, p. 137.

106 Janssen and Janssen, *op. cit.*, p. 86.

107 Jill Kamil, *The Ancient Egyptians: Life in the Old Kingdom* (Cairo: The American University in Cairo Press, 1996), p. 169.

108 Dominique Valbelle, "Craftsmen," in Donadini, *op. cit.*, p. 48.

109 Leon Marfoe, "Early Near Eastern Societies," in Michael J. Rowlands, Mogen Larsen, Kristian Kristiansen, eds., *Centre and Periphery in the Ancient World* (Cambridge: Cambridge University Press, 1986), pp. 27–28.

110 Shaw, *op. cit.*, p. 298. And Casson, *op. cit.*, p. 80.

111 John Romer, *People of the Nile* (New York: Crown Publishers, 1982), p. 195.

112 Robyn Gillam, *Performance and Drama in Ancient Egypt* (London: Duckworth, 2005), p. 92.

sity.[113] Among their courtyards and byways, bars and suburbs, both opportunity and crime were present.[114] At least some municipalities had elaborate sewer systems for waste disposal and state-provided laundry services.[115] Meskell referred to evidence concerning urban masses "suggesting a richer material life than previously thought."[116] Casson tells us that despite the tombs, mummies, and grave art, Egyptians reveled in the refinement of living and "were a worldly, materialistic people."[117] There was also a relative simplicity; not a lot of property that needed guarding, and structures that were easily replaced in case of storms, flooding, or fire.[118] A lesson for us, especially in our age of worsening, volatile weather.

Much activity and social life took place at the roof level, as today in Egypt. Senet (Egyptian checkers) was played on a board of thirty squares. An Old Kingdom relief displays nineteen kinds of bread. The domestic cat makes its appearance at about 2100 B.C. Many people wore almost nothing during the hot summers, using straws to sip drinks bought at booths, cooled with ice from the mountains. The siesta was observed, and of course survives in some countries. It may be telling that a key issue in a strike of Thebes necropolis workers around 1170 B.C. was that their ration of ointment oil had not been provided.

A literature of romantic love, just as nuanced and complex as found in the West many, many centuries later, was part of the culture.[119] Along with the growth of literacy,

113 T.G.H. James, *Pharaoh's People: Scenes from Life in Imperial Egypt* (Chicago: The University of Chicago Press, 1984), p. 215.

114 Meskell 2002, *op. cit.*, p. 34.

115 Saggs, *op. cit.*, p. 122. McDowell, *op. cit.*, p. 59.

116 Meskell 2002, *op. cit.*, p. 36.

117 Casson, *op. cit.*, p. 145. Barbara Mertz, *Red Land, Black Land: The World of the Ancient Egyptians* (New York: Coward-McCann, 1966), p. 298.

118 Gaston C.C. Maspero, *Life in Ancient Egypt and Assyria* (New York: Frederick Ungar, 1971 [1892]), pp. 2–5.

119 Meskell 2002, *op. cit.*, p. 127.

"school education is perhaps the best known aspect of growing up in Ancient Egypt," paralleling the high regard for white-collar scribal professions.[120] "One surprising fact about life…is the amount of letter-writing,"[121] the extent to which persons of "fairly ordinary status" corresponded.[122]

Intellectuals gravitated toward the larger cities,[123] a tendency familiar to us. Tourism within Egypt was a popular pursuit.[124] By the late Bronze Age, festivals, celebrations, and entertainments were increasingly staged, and sports figures became glorified.[125] Justice was sought from the legal system and occasionally found, at least on the local level where juries were made up of average citizens.[126] Internalization of bureaucratic values was fairly widespread, as seen in career manuals that counseled a conformist, "quiet man" approach to success.[127]

Women could own property, run businesses, become doctors, but did not have the same rights as men.[128] Various roles were open to them, but their status was unequal, their position much more dependent on the standing of their spouses.[129] Divorce was fairly common, and same-sex relations—between men, at least—were accorded "a significant place in Middle Kingdom literature."[130] Love relationships, including marriage, could be fluid and complicated, causing the Janssens to observe that "perhaps in this respect Phara-

---

120 Janssen and Janssen, *op. cit.*, p. 89.

121 Mertz, *op. cit.*, p. 142.

122 James, *op. cit.*, p. 165.

123 Carlton, *op. cit.*, p. 105.

124 Mertz, *op. cit.*, p. 129.

125 John A. Wilson, *The Culture of Ancient Egypt* (Chicago: The University of Chicago Press, 1968), p. 195.

126 James, *op. cit.*, p. 88.

127 Trigger, *op. cit.*, pp. 627, 635.

128 Erika Feucht, "Women," in Donadini, *op. cit.*, p. 344.

129 Meskell 2002, *op. cit.*, p. 56.

130 *Ibid.*, p. 145.

onic Egypt most resembles our own days."[131]

At the end of the era the Greek Herodotus made note of the freedoms of Egyptian women: "in their manners and customs the Egyptians seem to have reversed the ordinary practices of mankind. For instance, women go to market and engage in trade, while men stay home and do the weaving."[132] A little later still, Philon was even more shocked: "As things are now, some women have reached such a degree of shamelessness that they not only, though they are women, give vent to intemperate language and abuse among a crowd of men, but even strike men and insult them...."[133] These comments may say more about their authors than about the position of women in Egypt, but Erika Feucht is on solid ground in concluding that their standing was "stronger than that of their modern sisters."[134]

From the Bronze Age as a whole, we have most of our present-day craft or hand tools, including hammers, chisels, drills, etc. Also pails, wire, safety pins, tweezers, razors, and many other common implements. The pervasive consumer culture practice of branding was begun in the fourth millennium, to boost sales.[135] There was a surprising amount of metalwork left on the ground, and thus wasted, in Bronze Age locales,[136] which could remind us that our throwaway practices are nothing new. Notions of Utopia first arose in this epoch,[137] likely evidence of movement away from what

---

131 Janssen and Janssen, *op. cit.*, p. 113.

132 Herodotus, *History* II.35, Quoted in Sennett, *op. cit.*, p. 381.

133 Quoted in Jack Lindsay, *Leisure and Pleasure in Roman Egypt* (New York: Barnes & Noble, 1966), p. 346.

134 Feucht/Donadini, *op. cit.*, p. 346.

135 David Wengrow, "Prehistories of Commodity Branding," *Current Anthropology* 49:1 (2008), pp. 7–34.

136 A.F. Harding, *European Societies in the Bronze Age* (New York: Cambridge University Press, 2000), p. 352.

137 Jack Goody, *Food and Love: A Cultural History of East and West* (New York: Verso, 1998), p. 242.

might be desired in society.

Egypt, after a long, relatively inward-looking orientation, created one of the world's earliest empires. By dominating Syro-Palestine and Nubia it temporarily achieved economic advances and overcame challenges to social order. But militarism only postponed the breakdown of political authority, exacerbated by major environmental destruction. The land surrounding the Nile, for example, had been turned into barren desert by overgrazing and deforestation.[138]

There had been a very significant crisis earlier (from circa 2150 B.C.), a so-called Dark Age that resulted in political fragmentation. Every form of looting, riot and revolution had broken forth, shattering the façade of royal security.[139] But the final breakdown, delayed by imperial adventure, came in about 1200 B.C. and brought an end to all Near East Bronze Age civilizations. A rather sudden and definitive collapse. The late Bronze Age, with its industrial progress, was a time of social turmoil and chronic war,[140] now the universal mark of civilization. The project of control and integration failed, as nomadic groups grew in prominence and palaces fell.

A "dramatic reorganization"[141] was urgently needed, and the new Iron Age arose to establish more efficient systems of power and dependence. World ("Axial") religions responded to those disoriented by the hollowness of civilization's achievements.[142] Monotheism, religion's next phase, was part of the turning-point rescue mission at a time of disinte-

---

138 Donald J. Ortner, *How Humans Adapt: A Biocultural Odyssey* (Washington, DC: Smithsonian Institution Press, 1983), p. 202.

139 Carlton, *op. cit.*, p. 67.

140 Childe, *op. cit.*, pp. 192–193.

141 A. Sestiari, A. Cazzella, and A. Schlapp, "The Mediterranean," in Barry Cunliffe, Wendy Davis, and Colin Renfrew, eds., *Archaeology: The Widening Debate* (Oxford: Oxford University press, 2002), p. 427.

142 Mumford, *op. cit.*, p. 77. See John Zerzan, "The Iron Grip of Civilization: The Axial Age," in my *Twilight of the Machines* (Port Townsend, WA: Feral House, 2008), pp. 27–37.

gration. Freud blamed Akhenaton for monotheism, but the Egyptian had failed to establish it in his own culture.

"Should we be surprised to learn that the first truly large societies had to be assembled by force, and eventually broke apart?" asks Kent Flannery.[143] Early civilizations, Mesopotamia and Egypt included, were "characterized by resistance to state power and therefore by instability and periodic breakdown."[144]

We are still in the Iron Age, civilization's current pacification effort, in the techno-industrial era of that age. Collapse has to be understood as an aspect or consequence of development itself, especially when the movement of civilization has meant more work, greater discipline, more elaborate social hierarchies, and greater economic inequality, not to mention grave psychic dislocation and impoverishment, and the destruction of nature.

Early civilizations exhibit many features that we encounter today, and one could see mass society already present in Bronze Age societies. The project of control and integration is unremitting, and as we have seen, it is not always successful. Worlds that are complex and unsatisfactory require constant legitimation and re-legitimation, evolving approaches and institutions.

As Mumford put it, "The sudden evaporation of meaning and value in a civilization, often at the moment when it seems at its height, has long been one of the enigmas of history."[145] Civilization today—a single, universal reality, its fearful toll terribly evident —is far from its "height." An opportunity to end it lies before us.

---

143 Kent V. Flannery, "Process and Agency in Early State Formation," *Cambridge Archaeological Journal* 9:1 (April 1999), p. 18.

144 Trigger, *op. cit.*, p. 27.

145 Mumford, *op. cit.*, p. 69.

گفتار نیک

CIVILIZATION TIGHTENS ITS GRIP:
THE AXIAL AGE

CIVILIZATION IS control and very largely a process of the extension of control. This dynamic exists on multiple levels and has produced a few key transition points of fundamental importance.

The Neolithic Revolution, which established civilization, involved a reorientation of the human mentality. Jacques Cauvin called this level of the initiation of social control "a sort of revolution of symbolism."[1] But this victory of domination proved to be incomplete, its foundations in need of some further shoring up and restructuring. The first

---

1 Jacques Cauvin, *The Birth of the Gods and the Origins of Agriculture* (Cambridge: Cambridge University Press, 2000), p. 2.

major civilizations and empires, in Egypt, China, and Mesopotamia, remained grounded in the consciousness of tribal
cultures. Domestication had certainly prevailed—without it,
no civilization exists—but the newly dominant perspectives
were still intimately related to natural and cosmological
cycles. Their total symbolic expressiveness was not yet fully
commensurate with the demands of the Iron Age, in the first
millennium B.C.

Karl Jaspers identified a turning point for human resym-
bolization, the "Axial Age,"[2] as having occurred between

---

2   Karl Jaspers, *The Origin and Goal of History* (New Haven: Yale University Press,
1953), especially the first 25 pages.

800 and 200 B.C. in the three major realms of civilization: the Near East (including Greece), India, and China. Citing profound cultural transformations, Jaspers singled out such sixth-century prophets and spiritual figures as Zoroaster in Persia, Deutero-Isaiah among the Hebrews, Heraclitus and Pythagoras in Greece, the Buddha in India, and Confucius in China. These individuals simultaneously—but independently—made indelible contributions to post-Neolithic consciousness and to the birth of the world religions.[3] In astonishingly parallel developments, a decisive change was wrought by which civilization established a deeper hold on the human spirit, worldwide. Jaspers called it "the most crucial turning point in history; it was then that man as he is today was born."[4]

Internal developments within each of these respective societies broke the relative quiescence of earlier Bronze Age cultures. Wrenching change and new demands on the original patterns were in evidence in many regions. The world's urban population, for example, nearly doubled in the years 600 to 450 B.C.[5] A universal transformation was needed—and effected—providing the "spiritual foundations of humanity" that are still with us today.[6] The individual was fast becoming dwarfed by civilization's quickening Iron Age pace, and warfare of a more violent nature accompanied iron production itself. The accelerating work of domestication demanded a recalibration of consciousness, as human scale and wholeness were left behind. Whereas in the earlier Mesopotamian civilizations, for example, deities were

---

3 Christianity and Islam may be properly considered later spin-offs of this Axial period, their own natures already established some centuries earlier.

4 Karl Jaspers, "The Axial Age of Human History," *Commentary* 6 (1948), p. 430.

5 Andrew Bosworth, "World Cities and World Economic Cycles," in *Civilizations and World Systems*, ed. Stephan K. Sanderson (Walnut Creek, CA: AltaMira Press, 1995), p. 214.

6 Karl Jaspers, *Way to Wisdom* (New Haven: Yale University Press, 2003 [1951]), pp. 98–99.

more closely identified with various forces of nature, now society at large grew more differentiated and the separation deepened between the natural and the supernatural. Natural processes were still present, of course, but increasing social and economic tensions strained their integrity as wellsprings of meaning. In various places, environmental crises were another destabilizing force, adding to socio-economic strains. David Kamienski et al. provide a study of the eastern Mediterranean aptly titled "Environmental Roots of the Late Bronze Age Crisis."[7]

The Neolithic era—and even the Bronze Age—had not seen the complete overturning of a nature-culture equilibrium. Before the Axial Age, objects were described linguistically in terms of their activities. Beginning with the Axial Age, the stress is on the static qualities of objects, omitting references to organic processes. In other words, a reification took place, in which outlooks (e.g., ethics) turned away from situation-related discourse to a more abstract, out-of-context orientation. In Henry Bamford Parkes' phrase, the new faiths affirmed "a human rather than a tribalistic view of life."[8]

The whole heritage of sacred places, tribal polytheism, and reverence for the earth-centered was broken, its rituals and sacrifices suddenly out of date. Synonymous with the rise of "higher" civilizations and world religions, a sense of system appeared, and the need for codification became predominant.[9] In the words of Spengler: "the whole world a dynamic system, exact, mathematically disposed, capable down to its first causes of being experimentally probed and numerically

---

7   David Kamienski et al., "Environmental Roots of the Late Bronze Age Crisis, PLOS, August 14, 2013.

8   Henry Bamford Parkes, *Gods and Men: The Origins of Western Culture* (New York: Vintage Books, 1965), p. 77.

9   John Plott, *Global History of Philosophy*, vol. I (Delhi: Motilal Manarsidass, 1963), p. 8.

fixed so that man can dominate it....."[10] A common aspect of the new reformulation was the ascendance of the single universal deity, who required moral perfection rather than the earlier ceremonies. Increased control of nature and society was bound to evolve toward increased inner control.

Pre-Axial, "animistic" humanity was sustained not only by a less totalizing repression, but also by a surviving sense of union with natural reality. The new religions tended to sever bonds with the manifold, profane world, placing closure on it over and against the supernatural and unnatural.

This involved (and still involves) what Mircea Eliade called "cosmicizing," the passage from a situational, conditional plane to an "unconditioned mode of being."[11] A Buddhist image represents "breaking through the roof"; that is, transcending the mundane realm and entering a trans-human reality.[12] The new, typically monotheistic religions clearly viewed this transcendence as a unity, beyond any particularity of existence. Superpersonal authority or agency, "the most culturally recurrent, cognitively relevant, and evolutionarily compelling concept in religion,"[13] was needed to cope with the growing inability of political and religious authority to adequately contain Iron Age disaffection.

A direct, personal relationship with ultimate spiritual reality was a phenomenon that testified to the breakdown of community. The development of individual religious identity, as distinct from one's place in the tribe and in the natural

---

10   Oswald Spengler, *The Decline of the West*, vol. II (New York: Alfred A. Knopf, 1928), p. 309.

11   Mircea Eliade, "Structures and Changes in the History of Religions," in *City Invincible*, eds. Carl H. Kraeling and Robert M. Adams (Chicago: University of Chicago Press, 1958), p. 365.

12   *Ibid.*, pp. 365–366. Karl Barth's leap into "the upper story of faith" has a similar sense; quoted in Seyyed Hossein Nasr, *Knowledge and the Sacred* (Albany: State University of New York, 1989), p. 48.

13   Scott Atran, *In Gods We Trust: The Evolutionary Landscape of Religion* (New York: Oxford University Press, 2002), p. 57.

world, was characteristic of Axial consciousness. The personalizing of a spiritual journey and a distancing from the earth shaped human societies in turn. These innovations denied and suppressed indigenous traditions, while fostering the implicit illusion of escaping civilization. Inner transformation and its "way up" was spirit divorced from body, nirvana separate from samsara. Yogic withdrawal, life-denying asceticism, etc. were deeply dualistic, almost without exception.

All this was taking place in the context of an unprecedented level of rationalization and control of daily life in many places, especially by about 500 B.C. S.N. Eisenstadt referred to a resultant "rebellion against the constraints of division of labor, authority, hierarchy, and...the structuring of the time dimension...."[14] The Axial religions formed during a period of social disintegration, when long-standing sources of satisfaction and security were being undermined, and the earlier relative autonomy of tribes and villages was breaking down. The overall outcomes were a great strengthening of technological systems, and an almost simultaneous rise of mighty empires in China (Tsin Shi hwang-ti), India (Maurya dynasty), and the West (the Hellenistic empires and, slightly later, the *Imperium Romanum*).

Domestication/civilization set this trajectory in motion by its very nature, giving birth to technology as domination of nature, and systems based on division of labor. There was mining before 3000 B.C. in Sinai (early Bronze Age), and a surge in the progress of metallurgical technology during the third millennium. These innovations coincided with the emergence of true states, and with the invention of writing. Naming the stages of cultural development by reference to metals is apt testimony to their central role. Metallurgy has

---

14 S.N. Eisenstadt, "The Axial Age Breakthroughs," *Daedalus* 104 (1975), p. 13. "May the gods destroy that man who first discovered hours and who first set up a sundial here." —Plautus, third century B.C. Eisenstadt's is the best essay on the overall topic that I have found.

long stimulated all other productive activities. By 800 B.C. at the latest, the Iron Age had fully arrived in the West, with mass production of standardized goods.

Massification of society tended to become the norm, based on specialization. For example, Bronze Age smiths had prospected, mined, and smelted the ores and then worked and alloyed the metals. Gradually, each of these processes became the purview of corresponding specialists, eroding autonomy and self-sufficiency. With respect to pottery, a common domestic skill was taken over by professionals.[15] Bread now came more often from bakeries than from the household. It is no accident that the Iron Age and the Axial Age commence at almost exactly the same time, c. 800 B.C. The turbulence and upheavals in the actual world find new consolations and compensations in the spiritual realm—new symbolic forms for further fractioning societies.[16]

In Homer's *Odyssey* (eighth century B.C.), the technologically backward Cyclops have surprisingly easy lives compared to people in Iron Age Greece of that time, when the beginnings of a factory system were already in place. Development of steel plows and weapons accelerated the destruction of nature (erosion, deforestation, etc.) and ruinous warfare.

In Persia, oil was already being refined, if not drilled. There the seer Zoroaster (a.k.a. Zarathustra) emerged, providing such potent concepts as immortality, the Last Judgment, and the Holy Spirit (which were quickly incorporated into Judaism). The dualism of the divine Ahura Mazda's struggle against evil was paramount theologically, in a religious system intimately tied to the needs of the state. In fact, the Persian legal system of the Achaemenian period (558–350

---

15   The fate of domestic hand-loom weavers almost three millennia later comes to mind; the independent weaver household was overwhelmed by the factory system of the Industrial Revolution.

16   It is a striking irony that Nietzsche named his archetypal "beyond good and evil" figure Zarathustra.

B.C.) was virtually synonymous with Zoraoastrianism, and the latter in fact quickly became the state religion. According to Harle, Zoroastrianism was "born to serve the demand for social order in a rapidly changing and expanding society."[17]

Zoroastrian monotheism was not only a definitive turning away from animism and the old gods, but also a marked elevation of the categories of good and evil as universals and ruling concepts. Both of these characteristics were Axial Age essentials. Spengler regarded Zarathustra as a "traveling companion of the prophets of Israel," who also steered popular belief away from the web of pantheistic, localist, nature-oriented rites and outlooks.[18]

The Hebrew-Judaic tradition was undergoing a similar change, especially during the same sixth-century heart of the Axial Age. The eastern Mediterranean, and Israel in particular, was experiencing a surge of Iron Age urbanization. The social order was under considerable strain in the context of a national need for identity and coherence, especially in the face of more powerful, empire-building neighbors. The Israelites spent two-thirds of the sixth century as captives of the Babylonians.

Yahweh rose from local fertility god to monotheist status in a manner commensurate with the requirements of a beleaguered and threatened people. His grandeur, and the universality of his field of relevance, paralleled the Hebrews' desire for strength in a hostile world.[19] In the eighth century B.C., Amos had announced this vision as a de-ritualizing, transcendentalizing spiritual direction. Jewish uniqueness thus unfolded against the backdrop of radical, unitary divinity.

The "new man" of Ezekiel (early sixth century B.C.) was

---

17 Vilho Harle, *Ideas of Social Order in the Ancient World* (Westport, CT: Greenwood Press, 1998), p. 18.

18 Spengler, *op. cit.*, pp. 168, 205.

19 V. Nikiprowetzky, "Ethical Monotheism," *Daedalus* 104 (1975), pp. 80–81.

part of a new supernatural dimension that, again, took its bearings from an unstable time. As Jacob Neusner pointed out, by the sixth century B.C.—at the very latest—the economy was no longer grounded in subsistence or self-sufficiency.[20] The role of the household had been greatly diminished by division of labor and the massifying market. An omnipotent god demanding absolute submission reflected rulers' aspirations for top-down, stabilizing authority. Yahweh, like Zeus, was originally a nature god, albeit connected to domestication. His rule came to hold sway over the moral and civic order, anchored by the rule of kings. The positive, redemptive role of suffering emerged here, unsurprisingly, along with refined political domination. Deutero-Isaiah (Second Isaiah), greatest of the Hebrew prophets of the Axial Age, created a royal ideology in the sixth century B.C.[21] He announced that the very essence of the Covenant with God was embodied in the king himself—that the king *was* the Covenant.[22] The force of this announcement derived from universal cosmic law, beyond any sense perception or earthly parallel; natural phenomena were only its expressions, wrought in an infinity unknowable by mortals.

In pre-Socratic Greece, especially by the time of Pythagoras and Heraclitus in the sixth century B.C., tribal communities were facing disintegration, while new collectivities and institutional complexes were under construction. The silver mines of Laurium were being worked by thousands of slaves. An "advanced manufacturing technology"[23] in large urban workshops often displayed a high degree of division

---

20 Jacob Neusner, *The Social Studies of Judaism: Essays and Reflections*, vol. 1 (Atlanta: Scholars Press, 1985), p. 71.

21 Paolo Sacchi, *The History of the Second Temple Period* (Sheffield: Sheffield Academic Press Ltd., 2000), p. 87.

22 *Ibid.*, pp. 99–100.

23 Frederick Klemm, *A History of Western Technology* (New York: Charles Scribners Sons, 1959), p. 28.

of labor. "Pottery in Athens was made in factories which might employ, under the master-potter, as many as seventy men."[24] Strikes and slave uprisings were not uncommon,[25] while home industries and small-scale cultivators struggled to compete against the new massification. Social frictions found expression, as always, in competing worldviews.

Hesiod (eighth century B.C.) belonged to a tradition of Golden Age proponents, who celebrated an original, uncorrupted humanity. They saw in the Iron Age a further debasing movement away from those origins. Xenophanes (sixth century), to the contrary, unequivocally proclaimed that newer was better, echoing Jewish prophets of the Axial Age who had contributed significantly to progressive thinking. He went so far as to see in the forward movement of civilization the origin of all values, glorying in urbanization and increasingly complex technological systems.[26] Xenophanes was the first to proclaim belief in progress.[27] Although the Cynics held out in favor of an earlier vitality and independence, the new creed gained ground. The Sophists upheld its standards, and after 500 B.C., widespread embrace of higher civilization swamped the earlier longing for a primordial, unalienated world.

The transcendentalizing foundation for this shift can be read in an accelerating distancing of people from the land that had been taking place on multiple levels. A land-based pluralism of small producers, with polytheistic attachments to local custom, was transformed by urban growth and stratification, and the detached perspective that suits them. Pla-

---

24 Charles Singer, E.J. Holmyard and A.R. Hall, eds., *A History of Technology*, vol. I (Oxford: Clarendon Press, 1954), p. 408.

25 C. Osborne Ward, *The Ancient Lowly*, vol. I (Chicago: Charles Kerr, 1888), Chapter V.

26 Ludwig Edelstein, *The Idea of Progress in Classical Antiquity* (Baltimore: Johns Hopkins University Press, 1967), pp. 15–16.

27 *Ibid.*, p. 3.

to's *Republic* (c. 400 B.C.) is a chilling, disembodied artifact of the rising tendency toward transformation of thought and society along standardized, isolating lines. This model of society was a contrived imposition of the new authoritarianism, utterly removed from the surviving richness that civilization had thus far continued to coexist with.

Social existence intruded to the furthest reaches of consciousness, and the two schema, Iron Age and Axial Age, also overlapped and interacted in India. The period from 1000 to 600 B.C. marked the early Iron Age transition from a socio-economic-cultural mode that was tribal/pastoral, to that of settled/agrarian. The reign of surplus and sedentism was greatly hastened and extended by full-fledged iron and steel plow-based cultivation. Mines and early factories in India also centered on iron technology, and helped push forward the homogenization of cultures in the Mauryan state of this period. New surges of domestication (e.g., horses), urbanization, large estates, and wage labor took place in the Ganges valley, as "tribal egalitarianism," in Romila Thapar's words, surrendered to the newly evolving system by 500 B.C.[28]

This was also roughly the time of Gautama Buddha. Buddhism's origins and role with respect to the spread of Iron Age society can readily be traced.[29] Canonical scriptures refer to early Buddhist teachers as consultants to the rulers of Indian states, a testimony to Buddhism's direct usefulness to the new urban order in a time of great flux. Various commentators have seen the Buddhist reformulation of the premises of Hinduism as an ideology that originated to serve

---

28   Romila Thapar, "Ethics, Religion, and Social Protest in India," *Daedalus* (104), 1975, p. 122. See also pp. 118–121.

29   For example, Vibha Tripathi, ed., *Archaeometallurgy in India* (Delhi: Sharada Publishing House, 1998), especially Vijay Kumar, "Social Implications of Technology."

the needs of a challenged, emerging structure.[30] The early supporters, it is clear, were largely members of the urban and rural elites.[31]

For the Buddha—and for the other Axial prophets in general—the personal took precedence over the social. He was the detached observer, seeking freedom from the world, who mainly accepted a very narrow sphere as locus of attention and responsibility. This amounts to a fatalism that founded Buddhism upon suffering as a prime fact, a condition of life that must be accepted. The message of *dukkha* (suffering) expresses the ultimate incapacity of the human condition to include happiness.

Yet Buddhism promised a way out of social dislocation and malaise,[32] through its focus on individual salvation. The goal is "extinguishedness" or Nirvana, the suppression of interest in the world by those disenchanted with it. Similarly, Buddha's presentation of the "cosmic process" was stripped of all earthly processes, human and non-human. While criticizing the caste system and hereditary priesthoods, he took no active role in opposing them. Buddhism was highly adaptive regarding changing social situations, and so was useful to the ruling classes.

Buddhism became another world religion, with global outreach and distinctive superhuman beings to whom prayers are directed. By around 250 B.C. Buddha had become the familiar seated god-figure and Buddhism the official religion of India, as decreed by Asoka, last of the Mauryan dynasty.

The Iron Age came to China slightly later than to India; industrial production of cast iron was widespread by the fourth century B.C. Earlier, Bronze Age polytheism resem-

---

30   See Greg Bailey and Ian Mabbet, *The Sociology of Early Buddhism* (Cambridge: Cambridge University Press, 2004), pp. 18-21. Bailey and Mabbet, it should be said, see more of the picture than just this aspect.

31   Thapar, *op. cit.*, p. 125.

32   Bailey and Mabbet, *op. cit.*, p. 3.

bled that found elsewhere, complete with a variety of spirits, nature and fertility festivals, etc., corresponding to less
specialized, smaller-scale modes of livelihood. The Zhou
dynasty had been gradually falling apart since the eighth
century; continuous wars and power struggles intensified
into the period of the Warring States (482–221 B.C.). Thus
the indigenous spiritual traditions, including shamanism
and local nature cults, were overtaken by a context of severe
technological and political change.

Taoism was a part of this age of upheaval, offering a
path of detachment and otherworldliness, while preserving
strands of animist spiritual tradition. In fact, early Taoism
was an activist religion, with some of its "legendary rebels"
engaged in resistance to the new stratifying trends, in favor
of re-establishing a class-less Golden Age.[33]

The primitivist theme is evident in the *Chuang Tzu* and
survives in the *Tao Te Ching*, key text of Taoism's most prominent voice, Lao-tse (sixth century B.C.). An emphasis on simplicity and an anti-state outlook put Taoism on a collision
course with the demands of higher civilization in China.
Once again, the 500s B.C. were a pivotal time frame, and the
opposed messages of Lao-tse and Confucius were typical of
Axis Age alternatives.

In contrast to Lao-tse, his virtual opposite, Confucius
(557–479 B.C.), embraced the state and the New World Order. Instead of a longing for the virtuous time of the "noble
savage," before class divisions and division of labor, the
Confucian doctrine combined cultural progressivism with
the abandonment of connections with nature. No ban was
placed on the gods of mountains and winds, ancestral spirits,
and the like, but they were no longer judged to be central,
or even important.

---

33 Joseph Needham, *Science and Civilization in China*, vol. 2 (Cambridge: Cambridge University Press, 1962), pp. 99–100, 119.

Confucianism was an explicit adjustment to the new realities, aligning itself with power in a more hands-on, less transcendent way than some other Axial Age spiritualisms. For Confucius, transcendence was mainly inward; he stressed an ethical stringency in service to authority. In this way, a further civilizational colonization was effected, at the level of the individual personality. Internalization of a rigid ruling edifice, minus theology but disciplined by an elaborate code of behavior, was the Confucian way that reigned in China for two thousand years.

These extremely cursory snapshots of Axial Age societies may serve to at least introduce some context to Jaspers' formulation of a global spiritual "breakthrough." The mounting conflict between culture and nature, the growing tensions in human existence, were resolved in favor of civilization, bringing it to a new level of domination. The yoke of domestication was modernized and fitted anew, more tightly than before. The spiritual realm was decisively circumscribed, with earlier, earth-based creeds rendered obsolete. Civilization's original victory over freedom and health was renewed and expanded, with so much sacrificed in the updating process.

The whole ground of spiritual practice was altered to fit the new requirements of mass civilization. The Axial Age religions offered "salvation," at the price of freedom, self-sufficiency, and much of what was left of face-to-face community. Under the old order, the authorities had to use coercion and bribery to control their subjects. Henceforth they could operate more freely within the conquered terrain of service and worship.

The gods were created, in the first place, out of the deepest longings of people who were being steadily deprived of their own authentic powers and autonomy. But even though the way out of progressive debasement was barred by the Axial

Age shift, civilization has never been wholeheartedly accepted; and most people have never wholly identified with the "spiritualized" self. How could these ideas be fully embraced, predicated as they were on a mammoth defeat? For Spengler, the Axial Age people who took up these new religions were "tired megalopolitans."[34] Today's faithful, too, may be tired megalopolitans—all too often still spellbound, after all these years, by ideologies of sacrifice, suffering, and redemption.

The renunciations have been legion. Buddhism was founded, for example, by a man who abandoned his wife and newborn child as obstacles to his spiritual progress. Jesus, a few centuries later, exhorted his followers to make similar "sacrifices."

Today's reality of unfolding disaster has a lot to do with the relationship between religion and politics—and more fundamentally, with accepting civilization's trajectory as inevitable. It was the sense of the "unavoidable" that drove people of the sixth century B.C. to the false solutions of Axial Age religiosity; today, our sense of inevitability renders people helpless in the face of ruin, on all fronts. 2,500 years is long enough for us to have learned that escape from community, and from the earth, is not a solution, but a root cause of our troubles.

Authentic spirituality is so importantly a function of our connection with the earth. To reclaim the former, we must regain the latter. That so very much stands in our way is the measure of how bereft we have become. Do we have the imagination, strength, and determination to recover the wholeness that was once our human birthright? It is worth noting that, as Bellah and Joas put it, Axial-type paradigms are more likely to arise in periods of social turmoil and disintegration.[35]

---

34 Spengler, *op. cit.*, p. 356.

35 Robert N. Bellah and Hans Joas, *Axial Age and its Consequences* (Cambridge, MA: Harvard University Press, 2012), p. 285.

THE CRISIS OF LATE ANTIQUITY: ARRIVEDERCI ROMA

EDWARD GIBBON wrote *The History of the Decline and Fall of the Roman Empire* in the 1780s, and it remains a classic. Beyond the merits and deficiencies of his Enlightenment creation stands its title, in itself an enduring proposition. That is, many have wondered whether their own time and place—especially in recent times—is not also experiencing a decline and fall. Today, for example, do we not see a parallel to "the spiritual and social exhaustion of the Roman world"[1]?

But getting back to the subject, it was more than just the Empire that declined and fell. Rome's authority melted away

---

1   Karl Kautsky, *Foundations of Christianity*, translated by Henry F. Mins (New York: S.A. Russell, 1953), p. 109.

in the fifth and sixth centuries A.D. And Greco-Roman civilization itself disintegrated and vanished—socially, culturally, politically, and militarily. It was a rupture unparalleled in the history of the West, another civilizational turning point.

There are some who deny this, seeing, rather, only a bit of transition or adjustment. Noel Lenski, for instance: "The model of decline and fall is…a modern invention, which we have finally begun to cast off in our postmodern world."[2] Just as postmodernism "casts off" change in general, or the possibility of change.

---

2   Noel Lenski, *Failure of Empire: Valens and the Roman State in the Fourth Century* A.D. (Berkeley: University of California Press, 2002), p. 369.

More intelligently, Aldo Schiavone—and to some degree, Michael Rostovtzeff and F.W. Walbank before him—asks a very probing question: why didn't Roman society, so fully developed a civilization, continue directly on to modernity rather than fail?[3] Why did it have to fall apart and require a new start?

A partly valid answer is the standard one, provided by Gibbon, among others. It was Rome's "immoderate greatness,"[4] with frontiers that ranged across all of Europe, North Africa, and the Levant. Rome could not persevere forever, faced with "barbarians" on every side. I will take up barbarians later, but note in passing a barbarian's remark recorded by Tacitus: "They [the Romans] make a desert and call it peace."[5]

The Marxist explanation is that Greco-Roman civilization was based on slavery, and the transition toward a feudal system meant the end of that whole structure.

Rome was fully formed, a civilization of vast extent but insufficient depth. There had been a basis of traditional bonds and reciprocities underlying all else. It slowly broke down, socially and economically, and "unraveled down to its smallest elements between the sixth and seventh centuries."[6] A malaise settled over every sphere of life, beginning in the second century, deepening into exhaustion, sterility, and resignation. Learning was neglected, for example, with the gardens of Epicurus and the portico of the Stoics almost deserted.[7] Knowledge no longer mattered.

Some achievements did endure. Oswald Spengler argued

---

3   Aldo Schiavone, *The End of the Past: Ancient Rome and the Modern World*, translated by Margery J. Schneider (Cambridge: Harvard University Press, 2000), e.g., p. 175.

4   Edward Gibbon, *The History of the Decline and Fall of the Roman Empire* (London: Thomas Figg, 1827), Vol. VI, p. 223.

5   Quoted by Herbert J. Muller, *Freedom in the Ancient World* (New York: Harper & Brothers, 1961), p. 283.

6   Schiavone, *op. cit.*, p. 29.

7   Gibbon, *op. cit.* (Modern Library edition, 1995), Vol. I, p. 437.

that the last phase of any civilization is a technological one. Trajan's second-century 3,000-foot Danube bridge comes to mind, along with aqueducts that are still standing, and public baths and latrines, the latter with heated marble seats![8] But as Andrew Wilson noted, a certain amount of technological regression (e.g., regarding hydraulic mining) was a factor in the fall of Roman civilization.[9]

Rome began as a small settlement on the Tiber, in the eighth century B.C. if not earlier. By 270 B.C. its power had been consolidated throughout Italy. And by this time, gold, silver, grain and slaves flowed into the Roman treasury from other conquests. When the new millennium arrived, however, "the people of the Empire were obsessed with a vague feeling of deterioration."[10] Well underway by 200 A.D. was a sharpening of class divisions and "the accumulation of wealth and status into ever fewer hands."[11]

At the same time that the wealth, including slaves, of far-flung regions began to run dry, it was clear that "everywhere the extension of Roman rule had elicited armed resistance."[12] Rome became increasingly dependent for its defense on barbarian warriors; there had been "virtually no Italians in the ranks of the legions since the time of Trajan" in the second century.[13] In fact, "by the late fourth century

---

8   Lionel Casson, *Everyday Life in Ancient Rome* (Baltimore: The Johns Hopkins University Press, 1998), p. 39.

9   Andrew Wilson, "Machines, Power and the Ancient Economy," *Journal of Roman Studies* XCII (2002).

10   F.W. Walbank, *The Awful Revolution: The Decline of the Roman Empire in the West* (Toronto: University of Toronto Press, 1969), p. 1.

11   Peter Brown, *The Making of Late Antiquity* (Cambridge: Harvard University Press, 1978), p. 31.

12   Peter Sarris, *Empires of Faith: The Fall of Rome to the Rise of Islam, 500–700* (New York: Oxford University Press, 2011), p. 6.

13   Jeremy K. Knight, *The End of Antiquity* (Stroud, Gloucestershire, UK: Tempus, 2007), p. 9.

even slaves were sometimes enlisted."[14]

Rising dissatisfaction within a stagnating economy brought a period of unparalleled crisis between 235 and 284, "during which the Roman Empire nearly came to an end."[15] According to Rostovtzeff, this crisis was largely brought about by "a revolutionary movement of the masses of the population which aimed at a general leveling."[16] Rome weathered the storm, and in the process became an absolute monarchy. The long period of challenge transformed the defensive Empire into what had not heretofore been seen in this part of the world: an absolutist state. Rome had emerged from the crisis, but was much weakened.[17]

Compared with the third century, the fourth was a time of governmental stability and economic improvement. It was also, as Ramsay MacMullen put it, "the great age of tax collectors."[18] There was a reason why the early medieval hymn *Dies Irae* conceived of the Day of Judgment in terms of the arrival of the late Roman tax collector. The state began to impose intolerable burdens upon town and country: "heavier taxes and an oppressive system of forced services and requisitions."[19] At the same time, the currency was repeatedly debased (with less gold and silver in the coinage), and rural depopulation set in.

The end neared in the fifth century as a period of "stark and rapid economic decline, perhaps unprecedented in re-

---

14 Joseph A. Tainter, *The Collapse of Complex Societies* (New York: Cambridge University Press, 1988), p. 144.

15 *Ibid.*, p. 137.

16 Michael Rostovtzeff, *The Social and Economic History of the Roman Empire* (Oxford: Clarendon Press, 1967), p. 525.

17 Tainter, *op. cit.*, p. 150.

18 Ramsay MacMullen, *Changes in the Roman Empire* (Princeton, NJ: Princeton University Press, 1990), p. 68.

19 Solomon Katz, *The Decline of Rome and the Rise of Medieval Europe* (Ithaca, NY: Cornell University Press, 1955), p. 31.

corded human history,"[20] afflicted much of the Empire. Early on, North Africa fell to the Vandals, with a crippling loss of tax revenues from Rome's wealthiest province. Also compromised thereby was much of the grain and oil subsidies to the Roman populace, half of the well-known "bread and circuses." Gladiatorial contests had been a legacy of the early-conquered Etruscans, with widespread construction of coliseums for the "circuses" to entertain the urban masses. These were something of a priority, usually built before public baths.

A climate of futility and decay could not be dispelled by government, despite military decrees, enforced by many agents, spies, and informers, to monitor Roman subjects.[21] In the countryside, tenant farmers were now tied to the land along with their heirs, a significant move toward serfdom.

Rome itself was breached and sacked several times, the final blow falling in 476 when barbarian mercenaries deposed the last Western Roman emperor. Byzantium and its capital of Constantinople survived, the Eastern remnant of Greco-Roman civilization. In the same year of 529 Justinian closed the university of Athens and Benedict founded the first monastery of the West on Monte Cassino. Not until 554 was Roman authority at last re-established in Italy.

A sense of decline had long been underway, along with a lurking fearfulness.[22] A basic part of the background for this, basic to civilization, is the erosion of community and the separation of the individual from communal bonds. The most primary driver of this process, and most primary to civilization, is division of labor. In Late Antiquity we see activities transformed into professions, e.g., legal specialists. Formal and informal dress codes developed to distinguish

---

20 Sarris, *op. cit*, p. 75.

21 Stewart Perowne, *The End of the Roman World* (New York: Thomas Y. Crowell Company, 1967), p. 14.

22 Gilbert Murray, *Five Stages of Greek Religion* (London: Watts & Co., 1935), Chapter IV, "The Failure of Nerve."

the various orders, and in portraiture there is less attention to individuality, "in order to focus on the insignia of a role, with laborious exactitude."[23]

The general poverty of intellectual life was a clear sign of decline, as it is today. Despite imperial support, higher studies of all types languished. Fewer schools existed, less was written and read, original thought was wanting. There was a dearth of handbooks, encyclopedias, maps, etc. According to Carlin Barton, there was "a positive hostility toward the life of the mind," dating from the 300s, possibly earlier.[24]

The universe became devoid of meaning and a stratum of irrationality thickened over Rome's final centuries. "The mass of the people, dispirited and depressed, found hope in magic and superstition or in ancient cults, Oriental mystery religions, and Christianity."[25]

Various forms of pervasive violence perhaps also forecast a failing system of domination. Painful obligations on the citizenry produced resistance and, in turn, extraordinarily punitive measures. Restraint on the part of the powerful was lost, even as the legal right of the individual to decent treatment was steadily degraded. Judicial punishment was "specially aggressive, harsh, and ruthless," really amounting to cruel savagery.[26]

The ruling classes, concluded Peter Brown, carried a "static electricity of violence."[27] At school future Church father Augustine encountered the violence of well-to-do students who called themselves the Wreckers.[28] By the fourth century

---

23 Carlin A. Barton, *The Sorrows of the Ancient Romans: The Gladiator and the Monster* (Princeton, NJ: Princeton University Press, 1995), p. 98.

24 MacMullen, *op. cit.*, p. 117.

25 Katz, *op. cit.*, p. 41.

26 MacMullen, *op. cit.*, pp. 148–150.

27 Brown, *The Making of Late Antiquity, op. cit.*, p. 40.

28 Michael Grant, *The Fall of the Roman Empire* (London: Weidenfeld and Nicolson, 1990), p. 176.

Augustine's fellow bishops had taken notice of "the endemic domestic violence of the upper classes."[29] Nor was this confined to the elites. Philosopher and anatomist Galen's *On the Passions and Errors of the Soul* had much to say about violent outbursts, judging that "The passions have increased in the souls of the majority of men to such a point that they are incurable diseases."[30]

Besides the symptoms of internal emptiness and anxiety in a civilization waning in meaning, there were barbarians; and in the popular account it was their repeated invasions that proved fatal. Kenneth Clark put it this way: "By the year 1000...the long dominance of the barbarian wanderers was over, and Western Europe was prepared for its first great age of civilization."[31] That's us, of course.

They were "not particularly numerous," as E.T. Salmon remarks.[32] The Vandals, who conquered the richest province of the Empire, were "a small people...indisputably weak when measured against Rome," found David Lambert.[33] Many historians have seen the barbarians as more notable for their incorporation into the fabric of the West than for their invasions.[34] More often than not, they were enrolled in the Empire's defense, as the number of Italians available for the legions steadily declined.

---

29 Peter Brown, *Power and Persuasion in Late Antiquity: Towards a Christian Empire* (Madison: The University of Wisconsin Press, 1992), p. 52.

30 Galen, *On the Passions and Errors of the Soul*, translated by Paul W. Harkins (Columbus: Ohio State University Press, 1963), p. 66.

31 Kenneth Clark, *Civilisation: A Personal View* (New York: Harper & Row, 1969), p. 31.

32 E.T. Salmon, *The Nemesis of Empire* (New York: Oxford University Press, 1974), p. 61.

33 David Lambert, "The Barbarians in Salvian's De Gubernatione Dei," in Stephen Mitchell and Geoffrey Greatrex, eds., *Ethnicity and Culture in Late Antiquity* (London: Duckworth, 2000), p. 104.

34 Walter Goffart seems to lead the way here. See his *Barbarians and Romans, A.D. 414–584: The Techniques of Accommodation* (Princeton, NJ: Princeton University Press, 1980).

Not that this was always a seamless proposition. The Goths, for example, made a substantial military contribution, but not as an integral part of Rome's armies. Their autonomy meant that their loyalty could be shaky. But even in Rome's worst of times, barbarians in general "regularly disclaimed any intention or desire of destroying it."[35] The Gothic chieftain Alaric sacked Rome in 410, disappointed in his desire to become a high Roman official.[36] He had already been a mercenary in the pay of both the Western and Byzantine parts of the Empire.

Sometimes loyal, sometimes untrustworthy, the "barbarian" as a figure served various ideological purposes. Violent barbarians were used to justify huge military expenditures by the state.[37] Portrayed as noble savages, they were a means of criticizing degenerate civilization. *On the Government of God* was Salvian's fifth-century Christian take on the virtuous simplicity of barbarians vs. debased Romans. Earlier and more famously, the historian Tacitus praised moral, democratic, hospitable, and happy denizens to the north in his *Treatise on the Situation, Manners and Inhabitants of Germany*.[38] Petrus Patricius described the Scythians, in the east, as having "jeered at those who were shut up in the cities, saying, 'They live a life not of men but of birds sitting in their nests aloft; they leave the earth which nourishes them and choose barren cities; they put their trust in lifeless things rather than in themselves.'"[39]

---

35 Salmon, *op. cit.*, p. 48.

36 David S. Potter, *The Roman Empire at Bay A.D. 180–395* (New York: Routledge, 2004), p. 528.

37 Ralph W. Mathisen, "Violent Behavior and the Constitution of Barbarian Identity in Late Antiquity," in H.A. Drake, ed., *Violence in Late Antiquity* (Burlington, VT: Ashgate, 2006), p. 32.

38 Tacitus, *The Works of Tacitus*, Vol. II, "A Treatise on the Situation, Manners, and Inhabitants of Germany" (London: George Bell and Sons, 1909), e.g., pp. 300, 308, 312, 342.

39 Rostovtzeff, *op. cit.*, p. 498.

In modern times J.B. Bury referred to Slavonic barbarians of late Rome "who could defy the justice of civilization in thick forests and inaccessible ravines—regions echoing with the wild songs and romances of outlaw life."[40] But the "barbarians" in Europe had been practicing domestication for at least four millennia, and the processes of state formation had been going on for four hundred years in the Germanic world. Nonetheless not all the earlier, freer modes were extinguished. Bury again: "The east German barbarians were still in the stage in which steady habits of work seem repulsive and dishonorable."[41]

And though various tribes had versions of "a warrior-aristocracy far removed from the tastes and ambitions of their own rank and file,"[42] not to mention kings, they structured their authority very much after the Roman model.[43] Theodoric wrote the emperor in 508 to assert that "Our royalty is an imitation of yours, modeled on your own good purpose, a copy of the only Empire."[44] King of the Germanic Ostrogoths, his aim was to restore the glory of Rome.

Going back as far as fifth-century B.C. Herodotus, one can find the warlike quality of barbarians seen as a result of contact with a succession of rapacious Mediterranean empires.[45] Far more recently, E.A. Thompson argued that slavery in the Germanic world was the exception and that it was only much developed "in the two areas where Roman influence was the

---

40 J.B. Bury, *A History of the Later Roman Empire*, Vol. II (New York: MacMillan and Co., 1889), p. 14.

41 *Ibid.*, Vol. I, p. 97.

42 Peter Brown, *The World of Late Antiquity* (London: Thames and Hudson, 1971), p. 123.

43 Peter Heather, "The Barbarian in Late Antiquity," in Richard Miles, ed., *Constructing Identities in Late Antiquity* (New York: Routledge, 1999), p. 248.

44 *Ibid.*, p. 253.

45 A.H. Merrills, *History and Geography in Late Antiquity* (New York: Cambridge University Press, 2005), p. 56.

most extreme" and civilization the most advanced.[46]

Aside from the nature of barbarian society and/or its dialectic with Rome—and the difficulty of generalizing about various groups—there were some connections with Romans that may seem surprising. Peter Sarris wrote of fourth-century Goths and their "campaign of destruction aimed at members of the Roman governing classes"—in which "the barbarians were expressly aided...by members of the Roman lower classes."[47] In *On the Government of God*, the Christian author Salvian declared, "A large part of Gaul and Spain is already Gothic, and all the Romans who live there have only one wish, not to become Romans again."[48] Joseph Tainter saw it similarly: "Contemporary records indicate that, more than once, both rich and poor wished that the barbarians would deliver them from the burdens of the Empire."[49]

The dominant idea remained that only those who dwelt in cities were civilized; Roman civilization promoted urbanization. This was not limited to the capital, but "the early years of the fourth century A.D. saw a great increase in the population of Rome."[50]

Oswald Spengler declared an endpoint to civilization to be the triumph of the inorganic world-city over the organic land. (See especially "The Soul of the City" in *The Decline of the West*, volume II.) The Marxist Kautsky, Spengler's opposite politically, also observed the loss of contact with nature and the unmooring of the individual from ancestral supports.[51] Excessive urbanization was the main cause of the

---

46 E.A. Thompson, "Slavery in Early Germany," in M.I. Finley, ed., *Slavery in Classical Antiquity* (Cambridge, UK: W. Heffer & Sons Ltd., 1960), pp. 28–29.

47 Sarris, *op. cit.*, p. 34.

48 Quoted in Kautsky, *op. cit.*, p. 58.

49 Tainter, *op. cit.*, p. 147.

50 Emanuele Papi, "A New Golden Age?" in Simon Swain and Mark Edwards, eds., *Approaching Late Antiquity* (New York: Oxford University Press, 2006), p. 3.

51 Kautsky, *op. cit.*, p. 144.

Roman collapse, in the opinion of Guglielmo Ferrero.[52]

It was "a world of dwindling towns and bloated cities"[53] in which the countryside was taxed and exploited to sustain urban living, resulting in rural depopulation. Meanwhile the urban framework was itself falling apart. The mounting stresses on Roman civilization, its empire in retreat, meant a "hard" regime tending toward what we would call privatization. Less expenditure for public buildings and public cults. "The cities, which had created and sustained the higher forms of economic life, gradually decayed, and the majority of them practically disappeared from the face of the earth," to quote Rostovzteff.[54]

"Mass unrest," often due to food shortages, was "an inevitable phenomenon in cities of the Roman world," in A.D. Lee's words.[55] Robert Knapp found that "the natural recourse was to riot."[56] There was substantial social war violence from the Middle Empire to the end of late antiquity.[57] The fourth-century soldier and historian Ammianus Marcellinus wrote of the prominence of violent unrest in Rome, blaming the ruling class for disturbances and squalor.[58] Significant riots include a 348 clash over delay of the grain subsidy and repeated incidents in 365 over the high price of wine.

Antioch saw major riots in the fifth century, and Peter Brown characterized Alexandria as "a notoriously riot-prone

---

52 Tainter, *op. cit.*, p. 58.

53 Salmon, *op. cit.*, p. 81.

54 Rostovtzeff, *op. cit.*, p. 532.

55 A.D. Lee, *From Rome to Byzantium AD 363–565* (Edinburgh: Edinburgh University Press, 2013), p. 214.

56 Robert Knapp, *Invisible Romans* (Cambridge: Harvard University Press, 2011), p. 40.

57 MacMullen, *op. cit.*, p. 267 and MacMullen, *Enemies of the Roman Order: Treason, Unrest, and Alienation in the Empire* (Cambridge: Harvard University Press, 1966), pp. 180–184. Also Brown, *Power and Persuasion in Late Antiquity, op. cit.*, p. 87.

58 Nicholas Purcell, "The Populace of Rome in Late Antiquity," in W.V. Harris, ed., *The Transformations of Urbs Roma in Late Antiquity* (Portsmouth, RI: Journal of Roman Archaeology, 1999), p. 156.

city,"[59] to cite just a couple of non-Rome locations. Solomon Katz mentioned "terrible peasant revolts" in various parts of the Empire,[60] while outlawry became an important presence.

Between the late third century and the first half of the fifth, the Bigaudae, described as both brigands and revolutionaries, embodied outlaw peasant rebellion in parts of Gaul and Spain. Their egalitarian risings against the rich were a powerful radical critique in action.[61]

What came to be referred to as paganism was a mainstay of Greco-Roman civilization. It was the official ensemble of gods and rites, emphasizing the citizen's responsibility to imperial authority, and embodying unity. In this way paganism was close to a general attitude of patriotism, respectful of civic tradition. Victor Ehrenberg declared paganism to be "a political rather than a religious matter...no question of belief or even emotional feeling."[62] Its ritualism left little room for spirit, its orientation more empirical than a matter of faith. And since its gods were tied to the reigning politics, paganism tended toward the same breakdown Rome was experiencing. Its gods belonged to an early age, and were far from omnipotent. Civilization renders citizens powerless, and its religious parallel is a monotheistic, unrivaled power over its subjects in the spiritual realm.

The word pagan originally meant one who lives in a *pagus*, or village. It didn't exist as a religious term before Christians began calling non-Christians pagans. But the usage is clear enough to us, and though it had about seven centuries of tradition behind it by the 400s, paganism was lacking in substance. Too impersonal and far from totalizing, this civic religion was unable to bear much weight. It was overdue for

---

59   Brown, *Power and Persuasion in Late Antiquity, op. cit.*, p. 81.

60   Katz, *op. cit.*, p. 34.

61   Knapp, *op. cit.*, p. 314.

62   Victor Ehrenberg, *Man, State, and Deity: Essays in Ancient History* (New York: Routledge, 2011), p. 15.

a crisis, along with the rest of the ruling order. The old gods were too limited and too formal. They fell into the shade.

Roman globalization acquainted people with other options, via travel, trade, and conquest. With increasing insecurity, a feeling of "cosmic pessimism" grew steadily stronger.[63] So-called "mystery religions" arrived, mainly from the east, as misery begot mysticism. Mithra worship became a mystery cult from a branch of Persian Mazdaism, via the Greeks. It was fairly strong in the army, but its appeal was limited by its exclusion of women. From Egypt arose sun-worship, the cult of Sol Invictus with his December 25 birthday, and also an Isis cult. Dionysus emerged, a powerful, universalizing god of salvation, prefiguring the Christian savior in several respects.[64] Native paganism in its last stages took on a neo-Platonic coloring, a decidedly monotheistic move like most of the other religious tendencies, but not decisively enough.

The emperor Constantine converted to Christianity in 312, made it Rome's official religion, and declared paganism illegal. Anti-pagan repression was often laxly pursued, however, and two centuries after Constantine the old cults lingered. Paganism persisted in part because of its lack of a center; still largely polytheistic, it was multiple and versatile.[65] But especially in its old Roman dress, paganism continued to fade in the sixth century, its sacrifices and temples abandoned.[66] By the 390s the Christian church, a unified institution, had already visibly secured its hegemony.[67]

63   E.R. Dodds, *Pagan and Christian in an Age of Anxiety* (Cambridge: Cambridge University Press, 1965), p. 80.

64   Glen W. Bowersock, *Selected Papers on Late Antiquity* (Bari: Edipuglia, 2000), pp. 118–119.

65   Ramsay MacMullen, *Christianity and Paganism in the Fourth to Eighth Centuries* (New Haven: Yale University Press, 1997), p. 33.

66   Brown, *The Making of Late Antiquity*, op. cit., p. 50.

67   Neil Christie, *From Constantine to Charlemagne* (Burlington, VT: Ashgate, 2006), p. 26.

Christianity had rather suddenly and unexpectedly succeeded, providing a personal religion in place of an impersonal civic one. "Seldom has a small minority played so successfully on the anxieties of society," as Peter Brown put it.[68] Its central and original message of love was preached to the poor, the burdened, the outcast, not excluding women and slaves. Christian populism caught on with many in Roman civilization, especially the miserable urban masses. It not only offered heavenly reward, but also a stronger sense of belonging than that of the devotees of Mithra or Isis, for example.[69]

Another central focus was of course Christian belief in a resurrected figure, Jesus as divine Savior. It is clear that the early Christians expected an impending return of Christ, which gave their efforts a special intensity. The unique status of women and Christian care for the sick during epidemics were more down-to-earth contributors to success. The original churches were homes, which in itself gave women prominence, but during the third century the status of women was beginning to decline.[70]

The Gospel of Luke, written in about 100, contains many condemnations of the rich, e.g., "It is easier for a camel to go through a needle's eye, than for a rich man to enter the kingdom of God" (18:24). These were typical radical sentiments—which became inconvenient as the Church grew to be a powerful financial institution by the end of the third century.[71] "The time was ripe for a reconciliation of state and church, each of which needed the other," in Rostovzsteff's

68 Brown, *The World of Late Antiquity, op. cit.,* p. 50.

69 Jack T. Sanders, *Charisma, Converts, Competitors* (London: SCM Press, 2000), p. 8.

70 *Ibid.,* pp. 154–155.

71 Shirley Jackson Case, *The Social Triumph of the Ancient Church* (New York: Harper & Brothers, 1933), p.78. Also L.W. Countryman, *The Rich Christian Church of the Early Empire: Contradictions and Accommodations* (New York and Toronto: The Edwin Mellen Press, 1980).

judgment.[72] Early on there were Christians who appreciated the relation between one god and one state, the helpful implications of monotheism for a universal and unified civilization.[73] Constantine, less abstractly, came to the conclusion that Christianity was the only glue that could help hold conflicting social elements together. The old ruling elites, or paideia, were no longer able to maintain control. With Christianity as the new public religion, religious and secular authority became integrated in a more binding and powerful partnership.

Preaching in fourth-century Antioch, John Chrysostom proclaimed, "Oh! how passing wonderful is the power of Christianity, that it restrains and bridles a man...."[74] Ambrose of Milan, another Church father and an aristocrat, in the same vein in 388: "The bishops are the controllers of the crowds, the keen upholders of peace...."[75] He also asserted that "priests should have nothing of the masses about them, nothing of the people, nothing in common with the pursuits and manners of the barbarous multitude."[76]

Christians had made the poor visible, and soon enough this made them more amenable to control. The Church took over much of the state's almsgiving and adopted a new style of pacification in civilization's never-ending task of securing its authority. More or less always stated in religious terms, the power of bishops, with their scores of guards, could hardly develop otherwise than along lines in tandem with the secular economy and society.

Rather like "closed shop" employment, where expulsion from the union spells loss of that employment, excommu-

---

72 Rostovtzeff, *op. cit.*, p. 509.

73 Bowersock, *op. cit.*, p. 58.

74 Brown, *Power and Persuasion in Late Antiquity, op. cit.*, p. 108.

75 *Ibid.*, p. 103.

76 MacMullen, *Changes in the Roman Empire, op. cit.*, p. 265.

nication had temporal as well as spiritual consequences. It enforced the temporal power; e.g., soldiers who refused to fight in a war that the Church deemed just faced excommunication. Bishops preached increasingly to the elites, and the papacy made more and more of Rome's glorious past. And yet Christianity never lost its power to offer a radical sense of community, even if that community was more symbolic than actual.

A monolithic and centrally organized religion and its professional hierarchy took charge of various administrative functions of the Christianized empire,[77] including roles performed by barbarian authorities. The growing Church to some extent took over what Rome had created. Of course, there existed various philosophical differences; the searching criticisms of Augustine and—as we have seen—Salvian come to mind. A united front against common enemies of Church and State certainly held sway, however. It is clear that almost every emperor urged the Church to define correct doctrine so as to enforce its official monopoly.[78] Intolerance in matters of dogma was a new arrival to the Mediterranean world. Doctrine is of supreme importance for the first time in civilization.

A striking counterpoint to the accommodationist, power-oriented direction of the Church was a primitivist monasticism that swept the Roman world in the 300s. It began in the deserts of Egypt, where the number of radically ascetic monks neared 200,000 by the beginning of the fourth century.[79] The impulse to return to a pre-Fall, Eden-like simplicity pitted the movement against the Church hierarchy, civic au-

---

77 Franz Borkenau, *End and Beginning* (New York: Columbia University Press, 1981), p. 21.

78 A.H.M. Jones, *The Decline of the Ancient World* (London: Pearson, 1975), p. 327.

79 Michael Grant, *The Climax of Rome* (New York: Plume, 1970), p. 222.

thority, urban life, and even culture itself.[80] Historians such as Rufinus described the ability of monks to mingle with wild animals. Their revolt favored egalitarian virtue over the achievements of civilization. "They had dropped out of the world, because they found society more than they could endure," concluded Michael Grant.[81] Bishops frequently allied with local elites to bar monks from their towns and to defend the ancient customs. "Emperors, too, in their edicts, declared the inmates of the monasteries to be fanatical, unruly, and rebellious."[82]

Violence was a not uncommon response to this challenge, which reached a high point with the Circumcellions in North Africa, in the second half of the fourth century. The anarchic offshoot of a non-radical sectarian heresy, Circumcellions (vagabonds, literally) sought to restore the primitive equality of humankind. These millennium-seekers attracted fugitive slaves and destitute peasants, and their base consisted of native Berber and Punic elements.[83] Hostile to urbanism and the dominant order, they preserved their independence until the Muslim conquests of the eighth century suppressed all forms of Christianity in the region.

Most historians have agreed that the end of late antiquity coincided with the end of slavery. Slaves in earlier civilizations tended to be few compared with those of Greco-Roman civilization.[84] In the latter era slavery was extended from the sphere of domestic labor to the mines, fields, and workshops, but it seems to have been fading in the late Empire. Walter Scheidel argues that the number of slaves in Italy was "sig-

---

80 David Rohrbacker, *The Historians of Late Antiquity* (New York: Routledge, 2002), pp. 198–199.

81 Grant, *The Fall of the Roman Empire, op. cit.*, p. 154.

82 *Ibid.*, p. 151.

83 Grant, *The Climax of Rome, op. cit.*, p. 242.

84 Bruce Trigger, *Understanding Early Civilizations* (New York: Cambridge University Press, 2003), p. 157.

nificantly smaller than previously thought"[85] even before an overall decline set in.

Peter Sarris contends that "there is every sign that agricultural slavery continued to be a widespread reality in late antiquity,"[86] but the new, bigger estates moved away from slave labor, according to Niall McKeown.[87] There were few or no slave rebellions; the Spartacus revolt, for instance, occurred several centuries earlier. But slaves escaped in large numbers, a continuous feed for outlawry.[88] The Romans, as McKeown put it, citing other historians, were "having serious difficulties controlling their slaves."[89] There was movement toward their replacement by the "colonate"—those tied to the land, toward the serf condition of medieval times.

Another transition involved the symbolic institution or dimension of time. For the Greeks, cyclical time still held sway. Their sense of historical or linear time remained quite tentative at best. Roman Stoics (e.g., Cicero and Seneca) introduced a progressive, non-repetitive concept later developed further by Augustine. We have been under the sign of historical temporality ever since. Restlessly striving to dominate it somehow, while unable to escape the helplessness resulting from civilized, complex society.

Rome's thousand years were, at base, just another civilization that came and went, subject once again to longings and anxious disquiet and requiring yet another new model of the same. Carlin Barton, in her often brilliant *Sorrows of the Ancient Romans*, refers to the Roman confrontation with time: "They were terrified by beginnings; this dread was one of the

---

85 Walter Scheidel, "Human Mobility in Roman Italy, II: The Slave Population," in *Journal of Roman Studies* XCV (2005), p. 64.

86 Sarris, *op. cit.*, p. 31.

87 Niall McKeown, *The Invention of Ancient Slavery?* (London: Duckworth, 2007), p. 59.

88 Knapp, *op. cit.*, p. 157.

89 McKeown, *op. cit.*, p. 59.

sicknesses of Roman culture."[90] One symbol of which was the gladiator, that figure of ultimate despair, with its thrill of what became inescapable. A fitting face of civilization.

90   Barton, *op. cit.*, p. 181.

REVOLT AND HERESY IN THE LATE MIDDLE AGES

IT WAS NEAR the end of the Middle Ages that authority met serious, sustained challenges. However, some opposition currents had made themselves felt centuries earlier.

Tenth-century European society consisted mainly of people on widely scattered homesteads. But during the eleventh
and twelfth centuries, a period of widespread castle-building,
people gathered into fortified settlements. Justified as a response to raids by Vikings, Saracens, and other marauders,
the consolidation had much more to do with social control.
The rural population was aware of this; their autonomy and
well-being were much reduced in the process. R.I. Moore
compared the earlier condition of Carolingian peasants to

that of hunter-gatherers, in terms of their independence and the variety of sources of sustenance. (Moore's book on the subject is *The First European Revolution, c. 970–1215.*) Thomas Bisson's *Crisis of the Twelfth Century* documents resistance, such as the communal uprising at Compostela, Spain in 1116; the Flemish crisis of 1127–28; and the rebellion of Henry of Lausanne in the 1140s.

As the fourteenth century proceeded, Europe entered a time of proliferating challenges to authority across the board. We tend to think of the Middle Ages as a time when most people were pious and accepting of their lot, but the many active crises of the late medieval period strongly belie this image. Most striking were the frequency and violence of uprisings, mostly by peasants. Even more potent were upheavals that combined the demands of the materially oppressed with the radically millenarian views of heretical movements.

Increasingly during this period, every disturbance was seized upon as an opportunity for wider rebellion. Because of the central authority wielded by the Church, it is not stretching matters a lot to infer that all that all subversive social and political ideas were necessarily also theological heresies. Growing intrusiveness by the State (e.g., heavy taxation and other assaults on local autonomy), plus the oppressive weight of the Church in daily life, provided a situation of unavoidable collision with radical movements. The power of both Church and State was on the line with mounting urgency.

Feudalism as a system, identical with society itself, was under attack, even as ecclesiastical strength declined. Revolts and radical heresies managed to persevere in the allegedly closed society of the late Middle Ages, because in fact it was no longer so effectively closed. There was an inner hollowness to ruling power that was exposed time and time again. Concerning the Church's actual power, Raoul Vaneigem went so far as to assert that the Middle Ages were no more Christian than the late Eastern Bloc was communist. As the chasm widened between rich and poor, civil authority resorted to very harsh punishments. Sound familiar? For late modernity as well, no part of the integrated whole is completely integrated...or pacified.

The three great peasant risings of the fourteenth century involved the "blue nails" of maritime Flanders (1323–1328), the French *jacquerie* (1358), and the massive English revolt of 1381. In 1378, day laborers raised a major urban challenge in Florence. And scores of other insurrections took place, shaking the reigning structures, often borne forward by apocalyptic desires. Either explicitly or just below the surface, grew chiliastic expectations of a return to the innocence, freedom and immediacy of society prior to exchange and private property. Many were inspired by some version of a lost anarcho-communal Golden Age.

Of course, specific grievances triggered upheavals according to time and place. Privations as a result of the Hundred Years War with England had much to do with fourteenth-century outbursts in France, for example. More generally, a deep and growing restlessness was noted, an anxiety in various countries related to a decisive shift in time consciousness.

In the early medieval period, there were only three "hours" based on the daily round of the monastery. But the modern twenty-four-hour day made its arrival: clocks were common after 1300, and standardized, homogeneous time was in general use beginning around 1330 in Germany and 1370 in England. This change had a tremendous effect. Heretofore, time took its meaning from the substance of life; precise clock time measured life as an external, abstract presence. A much more ordered, disciplined work life was a principal result, and a source of deep dissatisfaction. Like money, and private property itself, the clock helped those in authority enforce a significantly more quantified and regulated existence. It is no surprise that those who pursued perfected control were given to hymns of praise to dominant clock time—much as today's techno-world boosters laud the Machine.

We should also note that resistance could always be found making itself known against official mores and culture. In fact, an extensive sector of outsiders, present throughout the medieval period, swelled in size by the fourteenth century. They included the eleventh- and twelfth-century "forest people," and the thirteenth-century renegade Helmrecht, who rebelled against peasant life. The Goliards were anti-clerical wanderers who begged and sang their way from town to town, suspected of heresy and subversion. François Villon belonged to this tradition, and to the heritage of refractory Parisian students before and since. The famed poet was also a law-breaker and vagabond, and narrowly escaped the hangman's noose.

The Feast of Fools was a widespread, long-running ensemble of various kinds of performances, unmercifully mocking the Church and its authorities. Making its first appearance in twelfth-century France, the Feast included, characteristically, the Witches' Sabbath or Black Mass, ridiculing both clergy and liturgy in very pointed nocturnal celebrations. The texts that Carl Orff set to music in his *Carmina Burana* belong to this tradition; these Goliard lyrics are a decidedly non-Christian musical ode to drinking, sensual love, and the vagaries of fortune.

Violent antagonisms were on the rise in the 1200s, with the number of conflicts more and more manifest, especially in the second half of the century. The people of Piacenza and Florence revolted in 1250 because of the high cost of food and the activity of speculators. Disturbances took place in Parma in 1255, Bologna in 1256, Milan in 1258, Siena in 1262, and again in Florence in 1266. To the north, an agitation in favor of equal rights for the poor broke out in the region of Liège in 1250, leading to violence there in 1254. Flemish textile workers also revolted in Ypres, Bruges, and Douai in 1280. Before the century was out, the merchant-industrialists of Flanders were reduced to seeking French aid to suppress the workers. This move led to defeat for King Philip and the French army, for it precipitated a powerful alliance between textile laborers and artisans. At Coutrai in 1302, the united urban proletariat wiped out Philip's forces.

Also in Flanders, the first large-scale medieval revolt raged from 1323 to 1328; it was the most prolonged and intense of the many peasant revolts of the fourteenth century. Peasants waged what amounted to a war of extermination against landlords, capitalists and clergy; they were often joined by textile workers, who took up arms once again. The watchword of this rising was "war against the rich and the priests." Another civil war in 1348–49 ended when the French army massacred weavers in Bruges, Ghent, and Ypres; but the weavers rose again in 1359 and held out against all opposition for two years. Assassinations of magistrates and desecration of churches were among the features of such open warfare. And one could compile a very long list of eruptions in several countries, such as those of Calais in 1298 and St. Malo and Genoa in 1306, when the mutinies of sailors against ship owners spread to involve many others. The tally only multiplied as the fourteenth century progressed.

Both heresies and millennial outbursts long pre-dated the last two centuries of the Middle Ages. But earlier heresies, such as the Cathars and Bogomils, had been predominantly dualistic and neo-Manichean: Gnostic, repressive and anti-nature in character. Typical of a newer anti-Church outlook was the Free Spirit, a heretical movement that emerged in the early fourteenth century, honoring freedom, sensuality, and pantheistic belief in individual divinity as a natural state. Free Spirit adherents were influenced by mystics such as Joachim of Fiore and Meister Eckhart, and by the joy and innocence of Francis of Assisi. The Beguines and Beghards (partner organizations of women and men) were even closer to the Free Spirit, with their basis of simplicity and poverty.

The issue of poverty is noteworthy and curiously modern. Upholding poverty as a cardinal virtue sufficed for the Church to continually suspect the Beghards and Beguines of heresy, and quite often to persecute them. Then as now, the command to shop was implicit and its refusal was seen as a source of subversion.

In 1311, Pope Clement V, disturbed by the success of the movement of the Free Spirit, denounced its "abominable kind of life, which they call freedom of the spirit, which means the freedom to do anything they like." In Paris Margaret of Porète, author of *The Mirror of Simple Souls*, was burned at the stake in the same year. She was a Beguine who proposed that the world might be rehabilitated to its state before the Fall by "giving nature what it demands." It was in fact the major role of women that heightened the Church's active persecution of such voices, and the Free Spirit insistence on unlicensed sexuality is understood to have been related to a strong presence of women in similar groupings.

The anti-authoritarian and erotic millenarianism of the Free Spirit partook of an even wider wave of apocalyptic desire for the restoration of a lost Golden Age. Its sense of primal sinlessness and natural liberty bespoke its partisans' project of total emancipation in the present. They were opposed to private property, not in order to replace it with a world of communist cooperative labor, but with freedom from toil. Adherents fought for this general social myth; a bloody battle in 1307 near Milan in which some four hundred Free Spirit brethren were killed was not the first waged by such radical heretics. Visionary religious utopianism was beginning to form a backdrop for social struggles across Europe.

One of the best-known fourteenth-century revolts was the 1357–58 outburst of peasant energy in northern France known as the Jacquerie, for the common peasant name Jacques. Jacques has denoted a poor, rebellious peasant— and a Jacquerie a peasant uprising— ever since. Including rural artisans and craftsmen, and typical of the widespread willingness to rise up against oppression, the Jacquerie was inspired by heretical sects of several countries. "Let's let anything go and all be masters" was one of its rallying cries. An alliance formed between peasants and the people of Paris, which was especially alarming to those within the power structure. The threat was so grave that although England was then at war with France, help was rushed across the Channel to suppress this great explosion.

Florence in 1378 witnessed the "Tumult of the Ciompi," following other significant disturbances such as those in Siena in 1368 and 1371. The Ciompi (wool carders) failed to make common cause with the peasantry, but their revolt succeeded for a few months. These purely urban rebels liberated prisoners and armed themselves, but succumbed to internal divisions and to the illusion that governance would work to their advantage.

What happened in Florence was the opening round of a four-year tempest that raged across a large part of Europe until early 1382. In 1380, for example, Parisians known as *maillotins* (from the hammers and mallets they carried) attacked government buildings, burning records, killing tax collectors, and opening the jails. Similar risings took place in Rouen and other French cities and in Flanders, also precipitated by tax increases. From the Tuchin movement throughout southern France (Tuchins were "outlaws"—as designated by their enemies), to revolts in the German city of Lübeck and Novgorod in Russia, the decade opened with a rising tempo of serious contestations in Europe.

Perhaps the largest and best known was the Peasants' Revolt of spring and summer 1381 in large parts of England. Its heartlands were Kent and Essex, where imposed labor (the corvée) had actually been less onerous than in other counties; the revolt is associated with figures such as Wat Tyler and John Ball. City workers joined peasants to quickly capture and occupy London. Possibly 30,000 took part in the general and well-planned rising. Anti-clerical in spirit, the revolt nonetheless included members of the impoverished and radicalized lower clergy, known as Lollards. For a time it looked as though the monarchy would be swept away on a torrent of anger. But with the capital completely in their hands, the leaders foolishly trusted the king, who promised to act on their demands. This proved fatal, and the revolt was lost within months of its inception.

But during the spring and summer something marvelous had been pursued with great vigor. Lollard preacher John Ball gave voice to a typical sentiment: "Good folk, things cannot go well in England nor ever shall until all things are in common and there is neither villein nor noble, but all of us are of one condition." The equality of all and the original absence of social classes fired the insurgent consciousness, the goal of a primal state where no one is above another. Norman Cohn connected it to the "mystical anarchism of the Free Spirit." Of course it is more than mystical when put into practice.

This was not the end of peasant resistance in England. Between 1381 and 1405 there would be five regional revolts, especially in Kent, Cheshire, and Yorkshire. In France the vineyard workers of Auxerre gave the authorities disquieting memories of the Jacquerie and the Maillotins with the disturbances they led there in 1393. Rebellion in Catalonia brought the burning of harvests and landlords' dwellings in 1410; riots erupted in Paris in 1413 and 1418. A monk at St. Denis spoke to the nature and extent of the late fourteenth-century upheavals and their aftermath: "Nearly all the people of France had rebelled and were agitated with great fury and, according to general rumor, they were excited by messengers from the Flemish, who were themselves worked upon by the plague of a similar rebellion, stimulated by the example of the English."

The radical wave near the end of the Middle Ages reached its apogee with the great Taborite insurrection of Bohemia, the longest-lasting and most militant example of millenarianism in action. What began as a University of Prague reform program associated with Jan Hus succumbed to an immensely strong primal, Paradise-now undertow. Its passion spread like wildfire, similar to the contagious interplay described by the monk of St. Denis. Tabor was an actual society between 1420 and the mid-1430s, a movement that repeatedly destroyed large forces intent on destroying it. Women fought side-by-side with men—extraordinary for any age, much less the medieval epoch.

The most radical Taborite elements included the Pickhards (a version of "Beghard") and especially the Adamites, fighting for a return to the world before the Fall from grace— zealots who went naked at all times. Part of their philosophy prescribed that "in this time no king shall reign nor any lord rule on earth, there shall be no serfdom, all dues and taxes shall cease, nor shall any man force another to do anything, because all shall be equal, brothers and sisters."

Based on handicrafts, the key strongholds of Tabor were invincible for almost fifteen years. On August 14, 1431, the people's army met a vast pan-European army of knights and others at the battle of Tauss. These legions of feudal authority were decimated and routed there by the Taborites and their highly disciplined guerrilla tactics, but they finally succeeded in 1434 at Lipian, in Bohemia.

For some decades resistance flowered and overcame Church and State in open battle, repeatedly if not definitively. Equipped with some version of the visionary, we too may embody resistance to the domesticated world.

Selected Bibliography

Michael Barkun, *Disaster and the Millennium* (New Haven: Yale University Press, 1974)

Max Beer, *Social Struggles in the Middle Ages* (London: Leonard Parsons, 1924)

Thomas Bisson, *The Crisis of the Twelfth Century* (Princeton, NJ: Princeton University Press, 2009)

Norman Cohn, *The Pursuit of the Millennium* (Fairlawn, NJ: Essential Books, 1957)

Alfred W. Crosby, *The Measure of Reality: Quantification and Western Society, 1250–1600* (Cambridge: Cambridge University Press, 1997)

Guy Fourquin, *The Anatomy of Popular Rebellion in the Middle Ages* (Amsterdam: North-Holland Publishing Co., 1978)

John Jolliffe, editor and translator, *Froissart's Chronicles* [Jean Froissart, 1337–1410]   (London: Harville Press, 1967)

Michael Jones, editor, *The New Cambridge Medieval History, Volume VI c. 1300–c. 1415*   (Cambridge, Cambridge University Press, 1995)

John Howard Lawson, *The Hidden Heritage* (New York: Citadel Press, 1950)

Gordon Leff, *Heresy in the Later Middle Ages* (Manchester: Manchester University Press, 1967)

Robert E. Lerner, *The Heresy of the Free Spirit in the Later Middle Ages* (Berkeley: University of California Press, 1972)

Michel Mollat, *The Poor in the Middle Ages* (New Haven: Yale University Press, 1986)

Michel Mollat and Philippe Wolfe, *The Popular Revolutions of the Late Middle Ages* (London: George Allen & Unwin Ltd., 1973)

R.I. Moore, *The First European Revolution, c. 970–1215* (Malden, MA: Blackwell, 2000)

Herman Pleij, *Dreaming of Cockaigne: Medieval Fantasies of the Perfect Life* (New York: Columbia University Press, 2001)

Michael J. St. Clair, *Millenarian Movements in Historical Context* (New York: Garland Publishing, 1992)

Raoul Vaneigem, *The Movement of the Free Spirit* (New York: Zone Books, 1994)

Daniel Waley, *Later Medieval Europe* (London: Longmans, 1964)

Author's note: This chapter was written for a publication that did not want endnotes.

MODERNITY TAKES CHARGE:
RENAISSANCE TO ENLIGHTENMENT

WHAT WERE modernity's origins and what has been its trajectory? In this very brief critical survey, let's start with the Renaissance. Ever since Jacob Burkhardt's *The Civilization of the Renaissance in Italy*, the word immediately brings other words to mind: "individual," "self," "personality," usually thought of as modern. Western individualism, and a new age of domination, begin with the Renaissance.

Oswald Spengler used the word "Faustian" to designate a further realm of control. "Renaissance, Rinascita, meant...the new Faustian world-feeling, the new personal experience of the Ego in the Infinite." Of course, he refers here to the so-called Age of Discovery, when emerging European national

states reached out to colonize far-flung continents.

"Humanism" is another term that points to the future, with its emphasis on individualism. An individualism that must be seen as corporate, firmly embedded in collective networks of power and wealth. And the "self-confident artistic utopianism of fifteenth-century Renaissance Florence" existed in the context of a noisy, dirty, violent, typhus- and malaria-ridden city. Along with self-confidence there was much discontent—even despair. As Edgar Wind put it, "the most splendid release of artistic energies was attended by political disintegration."

Merchant bankers dominated the urban politics of the Renaissance, often wielding near-absolute power. In Florence the Medicis amassed huge wealth and authority, but lacked legitimacy. To make interest-bearing loans (usury) was a mortal sin, Dante's favorite target. And Medici wealth was fairly recently obtained, usually by fraudulent and violent means. It fell to artists to create an artificial aura of legitimacy (e.g., Rubens' Medici cycle of paintings). Patronage of art and architecture succeeded at this task on a grand scale, also in the service of an especially corrupt and violent Papacy (e.g., Alexander VI, Pius II).

The glories of Renaissance culture also papered over a surge of anti-semitism in Florence that "would not be matched in Italy until the rise of fascism." High culture was also deaf to the fact that European expansionism involved consigning entire peoples to non-human status. These atrocities were accompanied by what Alexander Lee termed "the most deadening artistic silence of all time." In fact, mastery of color, perspective, and the like often served the opposite of what we might think of as Renaissance values.

Spengler rightly concluded that "the Renaissance never touched the people." Case in point: the several years' rule over Florence by Dominican friar Girolama Savonarola in the waning years of the fifteenth century. Simplicity and repentance were the watchwords of his near-revolution. Thousands of youth ran through the streets smashing anything that appeared to be arrogant wealth. It was a virtual theocracy, ISIS-like to some degree, but plebeian in character. Savonarola's social and cultural bonfire did not endure; in 1498 he was hanged, then burned to ashes on the spot.

Half a century later, according to J.B. Singh-Uberoi, "the modern chapter of man and nature as well as of natural science [owed] as much (or more) to the Reformation as it did to the Renaissance." Protests against abusive practices of the Catholic Church by Luther, Calvin, Zwingli, and others became a revolt against Papal authority. Protestant denominations were the result: a full break with Catholicism. And the anti-authoritarian spirit of the Reformation was not limited to doctrinal matters. In Germany, home of the Reformation, anger at Church landlords ran high; appeals to the people by Luther and other reformers brought more radical results than these preachers intended. The radical Reformation was exemplified by Thomas Müntzer, who broke with Luther early on, announcing an imminent apocalypse wherein freedom and equality would reign. Müntzer preached dispossession of the nobility, echoing the Taborite millenarians and social revolutionaries of fifteenth-century Bohemia. The great peasant revolt in southern and central Germany (1525–1526) was the most important event of the Reformation period and one of the biggest mass movements in German history.

But sadly, the Peasants' War is not what was arguably modern about this era. The seeds of modernity are found instead in writings of people like Ulrich Zwingli. He preached the necessity of regular, industrious habits, and warned of "the danger of relaxing the incentive to work." The origin of this modern, now-internalized ethos is the main subject of Max Weber's classic, *The Protestant Ethic and the Spirit of Capitalism*.

The rise of Protestantism relied upon the print culture introduced by Johannes Gutenberg's invention: a printing press using movable type. Printed books were available in the early 1500s, accompanied by a striking increase in literacy. For Marshall McLuhan, print was a founding aspect of modernity: "With Gutenberg Europe enters the technological phase of progress, when change itself becomes the archetypal norm of social life."

Typography made possible the first assembly line, the first mass production. Not only did authorial ownership commence, but, according to Roberto Dainotto, "By embedding language in the manufacturing process of mass-produced books, the printing press transformed words and ideas into commodities." Walter Ong observed another key outcome: "Before writing was deeply interiorized by print, people did not feel themselves situated every moment of their lives in abstract, computed time of any sort." A changed sense of time seems related to a growing "passion for exact measurement" in the late Renaissance. The emphasis on precision shows that the domestication process is speeding up and tightening its grip.

The privatization of this medium through silent reading, an enormous change in itself, also altered the balance among our senses. Touch and hearing became much less important. In antiquity and in the Middle Ages, reading was social—reading aloud. Some saw typography as a powerful, alien force. Rabelais and Cervantes declared it "Gargantuan, Fantastic, Suprahuman." Print and literacy led to a marked increase in the social division of labor. Illiterates became subordinates, subject to the greater effective power of specialists, and witness to a steady dissolution of community. Community became less important than one's place in the division of labor hierarchy.

A cognate of *public* is *publish*. We come now to a foundation of mass society: mass media as a means of social control. Print greased the wheels for national uniformity and state centrism; yet at the same time it facilitated individual expression and opposition to the dominant order.

Humanism is the watchword of Renaissance thinking. *Humanitas* is its Latin reference, opposed to *immanis*, or savage. Humanism's proponents stressed individualism, but that covered a multitude of sins. An individualist spirit of inquiry and adventure helped fuel overseas invasions and territorial expansion. Humanists were often silent about the deeds of colonialist explorers, but occasionally there was a direct connection. Amerigo Vespucci, for instance, was an explorer and a humanist writer. He had also worked for the Medici bank in Florence.

Many humanists sanctioned the subjugation of women. Renaissance power was inherently masculine. During the Renaissance period, women lost status compared to their medieval sisters, although women of the middle and poorer classes retained more self-determination than those of higher rank. Between 1480 and 1700 (the heyday of humanism), large numbers of women were condemned and executed as witches.

Renaissance humanists were filled with zeal to rekindle the Crusades and wipe out Muslims. The early and much-cited humanist Petrarch was especially venomous against Islamic infidels.

As always, intellectuals were called upon to legitimate the dominant order, and humanists performed this service. Michel de Montaigne, a sixteenth-century magistrate and essayist, is principally noted for his project to question everything—a very modern idea. He is seen as the first fully humanist writer, the first to express a coherent version of the doctrine. He denied that commoners and women could engage in the search for self-knowledge.

The earthy François Rabelais, Montaigne's contemporary, was the rare antinomian figure of the period. His utopian Abbey of Thélème was a place of pleasure and freedom, not of sanctioned individualism.

As 1600 approached, humanism's legitimacy was challenged. "Late humanism was beset with a crisis of confidence," in Katherine Eggert's words. Something seemed to be missing. Something human was being lost. But what would take its place?

In 1582 time was brought up to date with the introduction of the Gregorian calendar, which reigned over a time of "a general malaise" and active disaffection in Europe. The late sixteenth century was marked by serious peasant revolts. France and the Netherlands experienced urban disorder, not forgetting the great 1585 rising in Naples. In 1600 Giordano Bruno was burned at the stake in Rome's Campo Fiori for defending Copernicus and espousing dangerous ideas of atomic theory and an infinite universe.

Seventeenth-century thinkers dethroned scholastic Aristotelianism and indeed, theology itself. Not only Church orthodoxy, but animism and magic that had survived into the Renaissance were rejected. The mental universe was still animate rather than mechanical, though, despite the concept of conquest of nature whose roots lay in the Renaissance.

The scientific revolution of the 1600s was a decisive break with the past, a thorough re-evaluation of what had come before. Francis Bacon (1561–1626) has come to represent the shift. Inaugurating methods of induction and experimentation, his project was to restore the dominion over creation that had been lost with the expulsion of Adam and Eve from the Garden of Eden. Bacon saluted America's first colonizers, their work in a "Newfound Land of inventions and sciences unknown."

But Bacon did not achieve a full break with Church scholasticism (of Thomas Aquinas and others). That task fell to René Descartes, and Michel Serres' words are worth noting: "Mastery and possession: these are the master words launched by Descartes at the dawn of the scientific and technological age, when our Western reason went off to conquer the universe. We dominate and appropriate it: such is the shared philosophy underlying industrial enterprise as well as so-called disinterested science, which are indistinguishable in this respect."

A self-proclaimed original, Descartes was an arch-rationalist who refused to trust his own senses. His dis-embodied approach sought to derive sensory information from mathematics instead of the other way around, and virtually equated math and natural science. Having created analytic geometry, he wanted to mathematize thought. Descartes' famous formulation of mind-body dualism is consonant with his view of reality as immutable and inflexible mechanical order. It should come as no surprise that he saw humans, among other living beings, as fundamentally machines.

The Cartesian project did much to initiate modern thought and at base, still obtains. Now we witness the Artificial Intelligence technicians striving for Artificial Consciousness, pursuing a machine model. And contemporary philosophy seems to take seriously hyper-estranged Alain Badiou's mathematics-equals-ontology concept. Descartes subverted humanism, and gravely worsened the un-health of the West.

Among Descartes' contemporaries was Gottfried Leibniz, whose new system of "pre-established harmony" offered a mechanistic explanation of Creation—a further move in the onslaught on scholasticism. John Locke, founder of the modern liberal, individualist tradition, rejected Descartes' dualism as too God-oriented. Locke attacked political absolutism for the non-productivity of the land-owning aristocracy. He argued for a more modern form of exploitation, the enclosure of communal land into privately owned property. The seventeenth-century backdrop to these published ideas was burgeoning occupation and enslavement on other continents by European profiteers. Thomas Hobbes was party to this through his involvement with the Virginia Company. He condemned life in the state of nature as "nasty, brutish, and short," and termed indigenous people "savages," providing ideological justification for conquest and slavery.

Price hikes and tax increases provoked resistance, such as the 1630 rising in Dijon and revolts in Aix-en-Provence between 1631 and 1638. Silk workers in Amiens attacked their masters' establishments in 1637. Bayeux tanners rose up briefly in 1639, and sailors' wives went on the offensive in Montpelier in 1645, to cite a few insurrectionary incidents in seventeenth-century France. During this period the Thirty Years' War (1618–1648), Europe's last mainly religious war, ravaged a third of the continent, with millions of casualties.

1648 was a year of revolts, particularly in the context of the English Civil War. Levellers, Ranters, Diggers, and others espoused radical, anti-authority, anti-enclosures orientations. But Oliver Cromwell's Protectorate prevailed over the resistance, establishing mercantile capitalism as the core of the economy.

By this time, and commencing in earnest around 1600, division of labor was transforming the ground of social existence. New production techniques ushered in proto-industrialization, especially in rural areas. "Proto-industries arose in almost every part of Europe in the two or three centuries before industrialization."

The ideas of Bacon, Descartes, Leibniz, and other mathematical and scientific thinkers interwove with and supported technological innovation during the seventeenth century. As Margaret Jacob notes, "The road from the Scientific Revolution to the Industrial Revolution...is more straightforward than we may have imagined."

What we call the Enlightenment of the 1700s owed much to the canon of seventeenth-century empirical philosophy and natural science. Denis Diderot's iconic *Encyclopédie* was based on his "tree of knowledge," derived from Bacon's seventeenth-century ideas. Although initially an English phenomenon, Enlightenment is best known for its flowering in Paris, between the death of Louis XIV in 1715 and the onset of the French Revolution in 1789. Its most important figures were Voltaire, Montesquieu, and Rousseau.

During this period, protests and riots continued to flare (e.g., Geneva experienced risings in 1717, 1738, 1768, and 1782). Newspapers and commercialized leisure became part

of everyday life. In the 1750s and 1760s the modern chrono-
logical timeline was first introduced, and modern education
forms (such as measurable results via written examinations)
became common.

Enlightenment voices decried superstition and tyranny.
Christianity came under fire, most forcefully by the pro-
grammatic disbelief of Diderot and David Hume, among
others. The Church retreated, dissolving the militant Jesuit
order (it would not be re-established until 1814). The new
outlook overturned the Renaissance belief that what came
first was best, replacing it with faith in progress and the
future. A favorite target of Enlightenment's materialist orientation was animism, the once-prevailing conception of a
living spirit in nature was denounced as superstition.

The supposed anti-tyranny credo bears a closer examination. Voltaire and other leading Enlightenment lights
were friendly with Frederick the Great, despite his despotism and support of feudalism. Frederick's proclamation of
the Enlightenment as Prussia's official ideology seems like a
strange fit.

Enlightenment reason certainly did some demythologiz
ing, but it also installed new myths along with its claims and
promises. One such myth held that history, in Couze Venn's
words, as "the universal and rational project of the becoming
of humanity as a whole"—a myth with grave implications
and consequences for indigenous people. There is an evident connection between imperialist expansion as a system
of power, and the diffusion of Enlightenment thought as a
global pattern of culture.

A forbear of dissent from the vision of universalizing
Progress was Rabelais. He declared his "enduring affinity
with the alien spirits, of whom there are always some in
every society, who at any sacrifice resist, or rather, quietly
elude, all pressure towards conformity, towards standardiza-

tion and mechanization of thought." In his utopian Abbey of Thélème, there are no clocks; a swimming pool and other non-monastic features are inspired by the abbey's all-encompassing watchword, Do What Thou Wilt. Eighteenth-century philosopher and novelist Jean-Jacques Rousseau took a dim view of civilization and proclaimed the natural goodness of humankind. He refused abstract geometry and its method, preferring the promenade as a way of visiting "idle and lazy" nature, as Michel Serres put it.

Central to Enlightenment thought and probably the most important modern philosopher, Immanuel Kant did much to shape how people understand reality even today. He also revealed something of the less than liberatory side of Enlightenment. Silke-Maria Weineck placed his thinking "on the side of certifiable calculations, of the exchange of goods, of sound economics." Similarly, Heinrich Heine referred to Kant's "petty-bourgeois values." Theodor Adorno took this further, observing that "All the concepts...[Kant's] Critique of Practical Reason proposes, in honor of freedom—...law, constraint, respect, duty—all of these are repressive." He found that "Kant's moral philosophy...will not let him visualize the concept of freedom otherwise than repression." And "reason itself is to Kant nothing but the lawmaking power.... He glories in an unmitigated urge to punish." Montesquieu is closely aligned with Kant in this: "Law, generally speaking, is human reason."

The empire of Reason also liquidates difference, in the direction of the "total, perfect political unification of human species," in Jacques Derrida's words—a cold, universalizing agenda. The German poet Novalis found a conformist spirit of disenchantment in the "harsh, chilly light of the Enlightenment."

Its supposed higher form of rationality provided cover for Europe's "civilizing mission" and for Western hegemony. Without the new imperialism, as Paulos Gregorios saw it, the

Enlightenment "could hardly have taken place." Ideas and actions deeply influence each other.

In France the Enlightenment emerged after the reign of Louis XIV, when it "began to set the tone in polite society." Enlightenment *philosophes* felt confidence, at least in part, because of their close relationships with bourgeois notables. Not only Frederick the Great, but other ministers and sovereigns looked to them for guidance and legitimation. The patronage of absolutist princes created influential positions for them; as J.B. Bury reminds us, "They never challenged the principle of a despotic government, they only contended that the despotism be enlightened." Before the Revolution that began in 1789, Enlightenment standard-bearers were "part of the new ruling elite."

It is also true that the modern understanding of citizenship is a creation of the Enlightenment. But as Voltaire said, "Better not teach peasants how to read; someone had to plow the fields." Yet Voltaire also passionately denounced slavery, as did Condorcet and Raynal. There were also protests against the oppression of colonial peoples, though not against the practice of colonization itself.

Summing up their mid-twentieth-century critique of the Enlightenment, Max Horkheimer and Theodor Adorno declared that the "fully enlightened earth radiates disaster triumphant." Modern exploitation of nature and modern, atomized mass society commence with this epoch.

Enlightenment thought was an ideological bridge between a pre-industrial, aristocratic culture and an industrialized, consumerist society. Some large-scale production facilities existed in mid-eighteenth-century Europe: examples include van Robais' textile factory at Abbeville, the Lombe brothers' silk mill at Derby, and the iron industry initiated by Peter the Great in the Ural Mountains. Some Enlightenment proponents were directly involved in these enterprises. Diderot studied the mechanical order of production; Vaucanson designed efficient silk mills. Early manufacturers breathed the air of the dominant liberal, humanistic creed of the Enlightenment. Its spirit of classification and analysis was a practical aid to industry. Enlightenment materialism fostered "mastery by technological and commercial means over the material world."

The principle of individual autonomy, even with the necessary qualifiers, gained acceptance during the Renaissance and the Protestant Reformation. But as Bruno Latour argues, "modern" only applies to societies in which artisanal, personal kinds of making are superseded by broad-scale, impersonal modes. Modernity is an Enlightenment word, and Latour's watershed distinction can be found in that era. The Enlightenment was the first take-off point of the non-conscious praxis of amoral technicism.

Major claims and promises were made. There would be an end to religious intolerance, and a Brave New World ushered in by science and technology. Given the evident failure of these promises, it is little wonder that there is now "a global backlash...against the Enlightenment itself," as John McCumber has put it. I concur with Onora O'Neill's assessment: "A world of isolated and alienated individuals who find to their horror that nihilism, terror, domination, and the destruction of the natural world are the true offspring of the Enlightenment."

We are still in the Enlightenment era, and its "light" is spreading everywhere. The fully enlightened world, the fully civilized world, is indeed disaster. The prospect of modernity without end faces each and all of us.

Author's note: This chapter was written for a publication that did not want endnotes.

WHO KILLED NED LUDD?

> *[A papier-mâché likeness of Ned Ludd is one of the]*
> *symbols of the days that have gone, a reminder of what*
> *the workers' attitude to the new ideas might be if the*
> *unions had not grown strong and efficient.*
> —Trade Union Congress magazine *Labour*,
> at the time of the Production Exhibition, 1956

IN ENGLAND, the first industrial nation, and beginning in textiles, capital's first and foremost enterprise there, arose the widespread revolutionary movement (between 1810 and 1820) known as Luddism. The challenge of the Luddite risings—and their defeat—was of very great impor-

tanre to the subsequent course of modern society. Luddism could not be tolerated if society was to industrialize. Machine-wrecking, a principal weapon, pre-dates this period to be sure; historian Frank Darvall accurately termed it "perennial" throughout the eighteenth century, in good times and bad. And it was certainly not confined to either textile workers or England. Farm workers, miners, millers, and many others joined in destroying machinery, often against what would generally be termed their own "economic interests." Similarly, as Fülöp-Miller reminds us, there were the workers of Eurpen and Aix-la-Chapelle who destroyed the important Cockerill Works, the spinners of Schmollen and Crimmitschau who razed the mills of those towns, and countless others at the dawn of the Industrial Revolution.

Nevertheless, it was the English cloth workers—knitters, weavers, spinners, croppers, shearmen, and the like—who initiated a movement, which "in sheer insurrectionary fury has rarely been more widespread in English history," as E.P. Thompson wrote, in what is probably an understatement. Though generally characterized as a blind, unorganized, reactionary, limited, and ineffective upheaval, this "instinctive" revolt against the new economic order was very successful for a time and had revolutionary aims. It was strongest in the more developed areas, the central and northern parts of the country especially. The *Times* of February 11, 1812 described it as "the appearance of open warfare" in England. Vice-Lieutenant Wood wrote to Fitzwilliam in the government on June 17, 1812 that "except for the very spots which were occupied by Soldiers, the Country was virtually in the possession of the lawless."

The Luddites indeed were irresistible at several moments in the second decade of the century and developed a very high morale and self-consciousness. As Cole and Postgate put it, "Certainly there was no stopping the Luddites. Troops ran up and down helplessly, baffled by the silence and connivance of the workers." Further, an examination of newspaper accounts, letters, and leaflets reveals insurrection as the stated intent; for example, "all Nobles and tyrants must be brought down," read part of a leaflet distributed in Leeds. Evidence of explicit general revolutionary preparations was widely available in both Yorkshire and Lancashire, for instance, as early as 1812.

An immense amount of property was destroyed, including vast numbers of textile frames that had been redesigned for the production of inferior goods. In fact, the movement took its name from young Ned Ludd, who, rather than do the prescribed shoddy work, took a sledgehammer to the frames at hand. This insistence on either the control of the productive processes or their annihilation fired the popular imagination and brought the Luddites virtually unanimous support. Hobsbawm declared that there existed an "overwhelming sympathy for machine-wreckers in all parts of the population," a condition which by 1813, according to Churchill, "had exposed the complete absence of means of preserving public order." Frame-breaking had been made a capital offense in 1812 and increasing numbers of troops had to be dispatched, to a point exceeding the total Wellington had under his command against Napoleon. The army, however, was not only spread very thin, but was often found unreliable due to its own sympathies and the presence of many conscripted Luddites in the ranks. Likewise, the local magistrates and constabulary could not be counted upon, and a massive spy system proved ineffective against the real solidarity of the populace. As might be guessed, the volunteer militia, as detailed under the Watch and Ward Act, served only to "arm the most powerfully disaffected," according to the Hammonds, and thus the modern professional police system had to be instituted, from the time of Peel.

Intervention of this nature could hardly have been basically sufficient, though, especially given the way Luddism seemed to grow more revolutionary from event to event. Cole and Postgate, described the post-1815 Luddites as more radical than those previous and from this point imputes to them that they "set themselves against the factory system as a whole." Also, Thompson observed that as late as 1819 the way was still open for a successful general insurrection.

Required against what Mathias termed "the attempt to destroy the new society" was a weapon much closer to the point of production, namely the furtherance of an acceptance of the fundamental order in the form of trade unionism. Though the promotion of trade unionism was as clear a consequence of Luddism as was the creation of the modern police, there had been a long-tolerated tradition of unionism among textile workers and others prior to the Luddite risings.

Hence, as Morton and Tate almost alone point out, the machine-wrecking of this period cannot be viewed as the despairing outburst of workers having no other outlet.

Despite the Combination Acts, an unenforced ban on unions between 1799 and 1824, Luddism did not move into a vacuum but was successful for a time in opposition to the refusal by the extensive union apparatus to compromise capital. In fact, the choice between the two was available, and the unions were thrown aside in favor of the direct organization of the workers and their radical aims.

During the period in question it is quite clear that unionism was seen as basically distinct from Luddism and promoted as such, in the hope of absorbing the Luddite autonomy. Contrary to the intent of the Combination Acts, unions were often held to be legal in the courts, for example. When unionists were prosecuted they generally received light punishment or none whatever, whereas Luddites were usually hanged.

Some members of Parliament openly blamed mill owners for the social distress, for not making full use of the trade union path of escape. This is not to say that union objectives and control were as clear or pronounced as they are today. But the indispensable role of unions vis-à-vis capital was becoming clear, illumined by the crisis at hand and industry's need for allies to help pacify the workers.

Members of Parliament in the Midlands counties urged Gravenor Henson, head of the Framework Knitters Union, to combat Luddism—as if this were needed. His method of promoting restraint was of course his tireless advocacy of the extension of union strength. The Framework Knitters Committee of the union, according to Church's study of Nottingham, "issued specific instructions to workmen not to damage frames." And the Nottingham Union, the major attempt at a general industrial union, likewise set itself against Luddism and never employed violence.

Unionism played the critical role in Luddism's defeat through the divisions, confusion, and deflection of energies the unions engineered. It "replaced" Luddism in the same way that it rescued the manufacturers from the taunts of the children in the streets, and from the direct power of the producers.

Thus the full recognition of unions in the repeal in 1824 and 1825 of the Combination Acts "had a moderating effect upon popular discontent," in Darvall's words. The repeal efforts, led by Place and Hume, easily passed an unreformed Parliament, with much pro-repeal testimony from employers as well as from unionists, and only a few reactionaries opposed. In fact, while the conservative arguments of Place and Hume included a prediction of fewer strikes post-repeal, many employers understood the cathartic, pacific role of strikes and were not much dismayed by the rash of strikes that accompanied repeal. The Repeal Acts also officially delimited unionism to its traditional marginal wages and hours concern, the forerunner of the universal presence of "management's rights" clauses in collective bargaining contracts to this day.

The mid-1830s campaign against unions by some employers only underlined in its way the central role of unions: the campaign was possible only because the unions succeeded so well as against the radicalism of the unmediated workers in the previous period. Hence Lecky was completely accurate later in the century when he judged that "there can be little doubt that the largest, wealthiest and best-organized

Trade-Unions have done much to diminish labor conflicts." The Webbs also conceded late in the nineteenth century that labor revolt was far more common before unionism became the rule.

As for the Luddites, we find very few first-person accounts and a virtually secret tradition, mainly because they projected themselves through their acts, seemingly unmediated by ideology. What was it really all about? Stearns, perhaps as close as the commentators come, wrote, "The Luddites developed a doctrine based on the presumed virtues of manual methods." He all but calls them 'backward-looking wretches' in his condescension, yet there is a grain of truth here certainly. The attack of the Luddites was not occasioned by the introduction of new machinery, however, as is commonly thought, for there is no evidence of such in 1811 and 1812 when Luddism proper began. Rather, the destruction was leveled at the new slipshod methods which were ordered into effect on the extant machinery. Not an attack against production on economic grounds, it was above all the violent response of the textile workers (soon joined by others) to their attempted degradation in the form of inferior work; shoddy goods—the hastily assembled "cut-ups," primarily—was the root issue at hand.

While Luddite offensives generally corresponded to periods of economic downturn, it was because employers often took advantage of these periods to introduce new production methods. But it was also true that not all periods of privation produced Luddism; and Luddism appeared in areas not particularly distressed. Leicestershire, for instance, was the least hit by hard times; it was an area producing the finest quality woolen goods. Yet Leicestershire was a strong center of Luddism.

To wonder what was so radical about a movement which seemed to demand "only" the cessation of fraudulent work, is to fail to perceive the inner truth of the valid assumption, made on every side at the time, of the connection between frame-breaking and sedition. As if the fight by the producer for the integrity of his work-life can be made without calling the whole of capitalism into question. The demand for the cessation of fraudulent work necessarily becomes a cataclysm, an all-or-nothing battle insofar as it is pursued; it leads directly to the heart of the capitalist relationship and its dynamic.

The communal aspect of pre-industrial culture is also worth mentioning, in its own right and as a source of solidarity in struggle. For the knitters, handloom weavers, and others it was obviously work, but there were also real bonds involved. Thomas Pennant, writing at the time, provides a glimpse of women knitters at Dent in the West Riding: "During the winter the females, through love of society, often assemble at one another's house to knit; sit round a fire, and listen to some old tale, or some ancient, or the sound of a harp; and this is called Cymnorth Gwan, or, the knitting assembly." (Quoted in Brian Bailey, *The Luddite Rebellion* [1998].)

Another element of the Luddite phenomenon generally treated with condescension, by the method of ignoring it altogether, is its organizational aspect. Luddites, as we all know, struck out wildly and blindly, while the unions provided the only organized form to the workers. But in fact, the Luddites organized themselves locally and even federally, including workers from all trades, with an amazing coordination. Eschewing an alienating structure, their organization was without a center and existed largely as an "unspoken code"; theirs was a non-manipulative, community organization which trusted itself. All this, of course, was essential to the depth of Luddism, to the appeal at its roots. In practice, "no degree of activity by the magistrates or by large reinforcements of military deterred the Luddites. Every attack revealed planning and method," stated Thompson, who also gave credit to their "superb security and communications."

An army officer in Yorkshire understood their possession of "a most extraordinary degree of concert and organization." William Cobbett wrote, concerning a report to the government in 1812: "And this is the circumstance that will most puzzle the ministry. They can find no agitators. It is a movement of the people's own."

Coming to the rescue of the authorities, however, despite Cobbett's frustrated comments, was the leadership of the Luddites. Theirs was not a completely egalitarian movement, though this element may have been closer to the mark than was their appreciation of how much was within their grasp and how narrowly it eluded them. Of course, it was from among the leaders that "political sophistication" issued most effectively in time, just as it was from them that union cadres developed in some cases.

In the "pre-political" days of the Luddites—now developing in our "post-political" days, also—the people openly hated their rulers. They cheered Pitt's death in 1806 and, more so, Perceval's assassination in 1812. These celebrations at the demise of prime ministers bespoke the weakness of mediations between rulers and ruled, the lack of integration between the two. The political enfranchisement of the workers was certainly less important than their industrial enfranchisement or integration, via unions; it proceeded more slowly for this reason. Nevertheless, it is true that a strong weapon of pacification was the strenuous effort made to interest the population in legal activities, namely the drive to widen the electoral basis of Parliament. Cobbett, described by many as the most powerful pamphleteer in English history, induced many to join Hampden Clubs in pursuit of voting reform, and was also noted, in the words of Davis, for his "outspoken condemnation of the Luddites." The pernicious effects of this divisive reform campaign can be partially measured by comparing such robust earlier demonstrations of anti-government wrath as the Gordon Riots (1780) and the mobbing of the King in London (1795) with such massacres and fiascoes as the Pentridge and Peterloo "risings," which coincided roughly with the defeat of Luddism just before 1820.

But to return, in conclusion, to more fundamental mechanisms, we again confront the problem of work and unionism. The latter, it must be agreed, was made permanent upon the effective divorce of the worker from control of the instruments of production—and of course, unionism itself contributed most critically to this divorce, as we have seen.

Some, certainly including the Marxists, see this defeat and its form, the victory of the factory system, as both an inevitable and desirable outcome, though even they must admit that in work execution resides a significant part of the direction of industrial operations even now. A century after Marx, Galbraith located the guarantee of the system of productivity over creativity in the unions' basic renunciation of any claims regarding work itself. But work, as all ideologists sense, is an area closed off to permanent falsification. Work activities are the kernel, impervious to the intrusion of ideology and its forms, such as mediation and representation. Thus ideologists ignore the unceasing universal Luddite contest over control of the productive processes, even as every form of "employee participation" is now frequently promoted. Thus class struggle is something quite different to the producer than to the ideologue.

In the early trade union movement there existed a good deal of democracy. For example, there was a widespread practice of designating delegates by rotation or by lot. But what cannot be legitimately democratized is the real defeat at the root of the unions' victory, which makes them the organization of complicity, a mockery of community. Form on this level cannot disguise unionism, the agent of acceptance and maintenance of a grotesque world.

The Marxian quantification elevates output-per-hour over creation as the highest good, as leftists likewise ignore the ending of the direct power of the producers and so manage, incredibly, to espouse unions as all that "untutored" workers can have. The opportunism and elitism of all the Internationals, indeed the history of leftism, sees its product finally in fascism, when accumulated ideological confines bring their result. When fascism can successfully appeal to workers as the removal of inhibitions, as the "Socialism of Action," etc.—as *revolutionary*—it should be made clear how much was buried with the Luddites.

The Luddite rebellion could be seen as a mere blip in the inevitable march of industrial progress. And yet it is far from forgotten. The lethal history of industrialism is unmistakable in its fullness and promises of further tolls on life at every level. Kirkpatrick Sale's *Rebels Against the Future: The Luddites and their War on the Industrial Revolution* (1995) sees past and present in terms of what's at stake, now at least as much as ever, calling for a renewal of Luddite resistance.

Selected Bibliography

Brian Bailey, *The Luddite Rebellion* (New York: New York University Press, 1998).

G.D.H. Cole and Raymond Postgate, *The Common People, 1746–1946* (London: Methuen, 1938).

Frank Darvall, *Popular Disturbances and Public Order in Regency England* (New York: Oxford University Press, 1969).

Frank Peel, *The Rising of the Luddites* (New York: Routledge, 1968).

John and Barbara Hammond, *The Skilled Labourer: 1760–1832* (London: Longmans, 1919).

Kirkpatrick Sale, *Rebels Against the Future: The Luddites and Their War on the Industrial Revolution* (New York: Basic Books, 1995).

E.P. Thompson, *The Making of the English Working Class* (New York: Vintage Books, 1966).

Sidney and Beatrice Webb, *The History of Trade Unionism* (London: published by the authors, 1919).

Author's note: This chapter was written for a publication that did not want endnotes.

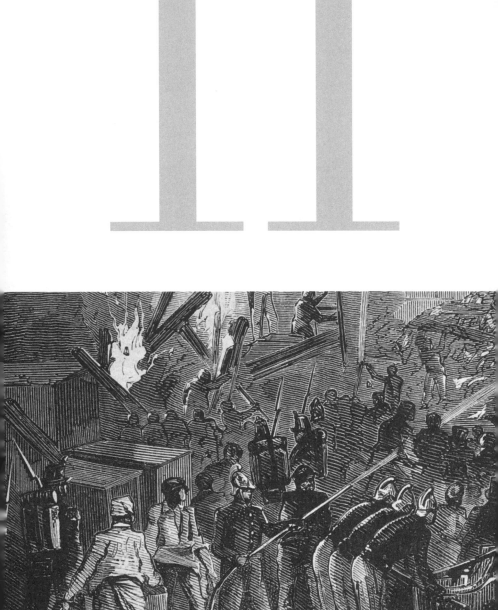

CULTURAL LUDDISM: ENDURING ANTI-INDUSTRIAL CURRENTS

JUST AS THE Luddites met their defeat, Mary Wollstonecraft Shelley gave us a classic warning about the hubris of technology's combat against nature. Her late Gothic novel, *Frankenstein, or the Modern Prometheus* (1818), depicts the revenge nature takes upon the presumption of engineering life from the dead. Victor Frankenstein and his creation perish, of course; his "Adam" is as doomed as he is. If this monster cannot be saved by his father/creator, however, today's cyborg/robot/Artificial Intelligence products *do* expect to be saved. For those at the forefront of technological innovation today, there will be no return to a previous, monster-free state.

From our hyper tech world we can look back to Mary Shelley's time and see the prototype, the arrival of modern techno-industrial reality. Between 1800 and 1820, England underwent the strains, storms and challenges of the ascendant Industrial Revolution. We are living with the outcome of that decisive battleground time.

Ugo Perone put it this way: "One day the big O with which the Ottocento [the 1800s] begins exploded, and philosophy as the great tale of totality started to be abandoned. The age of specializations began...."[1]

---

1   Ugo Perone, *The Possible Present* (Albany: State University of New York Press, 2011), p. 60.

Of course, few changes happen overnight. Industrial output had been tending sharply upward since the early 1780s.[2] And one could easily look much further back, to deforestation in Neolithic and Bronze Age times, to find out why many English moors and heathlands are now barren.[3] But it is in the early nineteenth century that power was passing from the hands of the titled landowners to those who owned the factories and foundries. Much more fundamentally, the time and space of social existence were fundamentally altered. As the equality of all citizens before the law began to emerge, so did the reality of an unprecedented subjugation or domestication.

Nothing in the canon of the (fairly recent) Enlightenment, with its claims and promises, had prepared anyone for this. The road to complete mastery of the physical and social environments was indeed opening, as the industrial system became, in Toynbee's words, "the sole dominant institution in contemporary Western life."[4] The picture thus presented was laden with far more pain and absence than promise.

With the nineteenth century begins the "winter of the West."[5] Spengler's conclusion is more apt than he knew. It was not a beginning, but the beginning of the end. Dickens' depiction of Coketown in *Hard Times* did much to capture the repercussions of industrialism: the new mass society, ruled by the regime of the factory and its pace, its polluted and despoiled landscape, its inhabitants anonymous and dehumanized. Spengler saw how "the machine works and forces the man to cooperate," rending nature beneath him as

---

2   T.S. Ashton, *An Economic History of England: The 18th Century*, vol. 3 (London: Methuen, 1955), p. 125.

3   G.W. Dimbleby, *The Development of British Heathlands and Their Soils* (Oxford: Clarendon Press, 1962), e.g., pp. 29, 44.

4   Arnold J. Toynbee, *A Study of History*, vol. I (London: Oxford University Press, 1934–1958), p. 8.

5   Oswald Spengler, *The Decline of the West*, vol. II (New York: Alfred A. Knopf, 1928), e.g., p. 78.

this "Faustian" machine passion alters the face of the earth.[6]

There was a long lead-in to the pivotal developments, a long process of mechanization and privatization. In England, more than six million acres of open field and common pasture were enclosed between 1760 and 1844.[7] The pressures of the new industrial society were increasing enormously, pushing the dispossessed relentlessly toward the despotic mills and mines. New power-driven shearing frames and fully mechanized spinning machines encroached on the relative autonomy of family-based handloom weavers, for example. By the 1820s the pace of change was dizzying.

Especially in the late eighteenth century, Enlightenment theories of rights were advanced as arguments against severe challenges to popular prerogatives. Although the dawn of 1789 had been a moment of great promise, the early idealism of the French Revolution was betrayed by authoritarian terror. In the first years of the nineteenth century, however, "the solidarity of the community [and] the extreme isolation of the authorities" were still political realities.[8]

At issue, in an unprecedented way, is a new state of being, untouched by political claims and reform efforts: a world becoming decisively independent of the individual. The quantum leap in division of labor which is industrialism means the generic interchangeability of parts—and people. From identity and particularity to the stage, in Joseph Gabel's term, of "morbid rationalism."[9] Michel Foucault noted that up to the end of the eighteenth century, "life does not

---

6   *Ibid.*, p. 503.

7   Harold Perkin, *The Origins of Modern English Society, 1780–1880* (London: Routledge & Kegan Paul, 1969), p. 125.

8   E.P. Thompson, *The Making of the English Working Class* (New York: Vintage Books, 1966), p. 583.

9   Joseph Gabel, *False Consciousness: An Essay on Reification* (Oxford: Basil Blackwell, 1975).

exist: only living beings."[10] The stakes were as high as they could be, the ensuing struggle a world-historical one in this first industrializing nation. It's clear that Emile Durkheim had it entirely wrong when he proclaimed "that in the industrial societies...social harmony comes essentially from the division of labor."[11]

The march of the factories was a sustained attack on irregular work routines, in favor of the time-disciplined work environment.[12] Centralized production aimed at control over recalcitrant and decentralized workers. By its nature it demanded discipline and regimentation.

Heretofore the customary and numerous holidays from work were supplemented by the celebration of Saint Monday, a day of recovery and play following a typical weekend's drinking. Enshrined in custom and long-standing local tradition, the popular culture—especially among artisans—was independent and contemptuous of authority. Hence factory servitude did not exactly beckon. F.M.L. Thompson noted that it was "extremely difficult to find satisfactory workers," and that "even higher wages were not enough in themselves."[13] For example, the reluctance of weavers (many of them women) to leave their homes has been widely documented.[14]

But at least as early as the beginning of the period under review, the beginnings of the destruction of the handicraft artisan and the yeoman farmer could be seen. "The small

---

10 Michel Foucault, *The Order of Things* (New York: Vintage Books, 1970), p. 161.

11 Robert N. Bellah, ed., *Emile Durkheim on Morality and Society* (Chicago: University of Chicago Press, 1973), p. 86.

12 Somewhat recent scholarship has challenged Ashton, Landes and others as having overgeneralized the irregularity of pre-industrial work habits; e.g., Mark Harrison, *Crowds and History* (New York: Cambridge University Press, 1988), ch. 5, especially p. 111. But the overall description seems valid.

13 F.M.L. Thompson, *The Cambridge Social History of Britain 1750–1950*, vol. 2 (New York: Cambridge University Press, 1990), pp. 129, 130.

14 Ashton, *op. cit.*, p. 117.

agricultural cloth-making household units...each so easily identifiable by its tenter of white cloth—would be gone in a few years," observed Robert Reid.[15] Manchester, the world's first industrial city, was one contested ground, among many other English locales, as everything was at stake and the earth was made to shift. By the late 1820s, Thomas Carlyle wrote this summary: "Were we required to characterise this age of ours by a single epithet, we should be tempted to call it, not an Heroical, Devotional, Philosophical, or Moral Age, but above all others, the Mechanical Age."[16]

The widespread "hatred of authority and control"[17] and "general levelling sentiment"[18] meant that resistance was powerful and certainly predated the early nineteenth century. The Northumberland minders destroyed pit-head gear with regularity during clashes with owners, leading to the passage of no less than eight statutes directed against such destruction between 1747 and 1816: quite ineffectual statutes, evidently.[19] The briefest sampling reveals the range of late eighteenth-century contestation: the anti-toll Bristol bridge riots of 1793, the great food riot year of 1795 (when groups of women waylaid shipments of corn, and attacked government press gangs seeking to kidnap men for military service), and naval mutinies at Portsmouth and the Nore in 1797, to cite only a few prominent examples.[20]

Machine-breaking and industrial arson soon became fo-

---

15   Robert Reid, *Land of Lost Content: the Luddite Revolt, 1812* (London: Heinemann, 1986), pp. 294–295.

16   Quoted in Ben Wilson, *Decency and Disorder: The Age of Cant 1789–1837* (London: Faber and Faber, 2007), p. 356.

17   *Ibid.*, p. 74.

18   E.P. Thompson, "The Crime of Anonymity," in Douglas Hay et al., eds., *Albion's Fatal Tree: Crime and Society in Eighteenth-Century England* (New York: Verso, 2011), p. 277.

19   Ian R. Christie, *Stress and Stability in Late Eighteenth-Century Britain* (Oxford: Clarendon Press, 1984), pp. 150–151.

20   Nicholas Rogers, *Crowds, Culture, and Politics in Georgian Britain* (Oxford: Clarendon Press, 1998), p. 229.

cused tactics against the ravages of industrialism, and to some often hard-to-pinpoint degree, against industrialism itself. Such forms of combat are seen among the west England "shearmen and clothing workers, in the Luddite resistance" to the introduction of mechanized devices between 1799 and 1803.[21] This was also the time (1801–1802) of the underground workers' movement known as the Black Lamp, in the West Riding of Yorkshire. Not coincidentally, the 1790s was the golden age of the Lancashire handloom weavers, whose autonomy was the backbone of radical opposition to the factory system.

Marx's idea of revolution was severely limited, confined to the question of which class would rule the world of mass production. But even on those terms he completely failed to predict which groups were most likely to constitute a revolutionary force. Instead of becoming radicalized, factory workers were domesticated to a far greater degree than those who held out against "proletarianization." The quiescence of factory workers is well known. It wasn't until the 1820s that they were first drawn into protest against the progress of the industrial revolution.[22]

"Class" as a social term became part of the language in the 1820s, a by-product of the rise of modern industry, according to Asa Briggs.[23] "It was between 1815 and 1820 that the working class was born," as Harold Perkin had it,[24] but the distinctive consciousness did not, as noted, mean a militant, much less a radical, orientation during the pivotal two decades under review. A workerist identity was "scarcely

---

21 Thompson in Hay et al., *op. cit.*, p. 275.

22 Neil J. Smelser, "Sociological History," in M.W. Flinn and T.C. Smout, eds., *Essays in Social History* (Oxford: Clarendon Press, 1874), pp. 31–32.

23 Asa Briggs, "The Language of 'Class' in Early Nineteenth-Century England," in Flinn and Smout, *op. cit.*, p. 154.

24 Perkin, *op. cit.*, p. 213.

involved" in the Luddite risings between 1800 and 1820.[25]

The most sustained Luddite destruction of newly intro-duced textile machinery occurred between 1811 and 1816 and took its name from Ned Ludd, a young frame-work knitter in Leicestershire who had an aversion to confinement and drudge work. More than just identification with Ned's famous frame-smashing episode, Luddism may be properly understood as a widely held narrative or vision.[26] At the heart of this shared outlook was a grounded understanding of the corrosive nature of technological progress. The focus is underlined in Robert Reid's wonderfully titled *Land of Lost Content*, wherein he describes a Luddite attack on the hosiery workshop of Edward Hollingsworth on the night of March 11, 1811. Having successfully breached Hollingsworth's for-tified works, frame-breaking, à la Ned, ensued. The armed workers proceeded "selectively. Only the wide machines which knitted the broader, cheaper cloth came under the destructive hammer."[27] Such targeting exhibits a combative hostility to standardization and standardized, mass-pro-duced life, hallmarks of industrial progress writ large.[28]

Byron, the most famous poet of the age, was moved to write, "Down with all kings but King Ludd!"[29] More import-ant was the very widespread support for Luddite actions. Across the area, according to E.P. Thompson, "active mor-al sanction [was] given by the community to all Luddite

25 Smelser, *op. cit.*, p. 31.

26 Katrina Navickas, "The Search for 'General Ludd': The Mythology of Lud-dism," *Social History* 30:3 (August 2005).

27 Reid, *op. cit.*, pp. 59–60.

28 The radical impulse in Ireland was diverted into Ribbonism, somewhat like Luddism, but lost in a nationalist emphasis. Simon Edwards, "Nation and State," in Zachary Leader and Ian Haywood, eds., *Romantic Period Writings 1798–1832: An Anthology* (New York: Routledge, 1998), p. 125.

29 Kirkpatrick Sale, *Rebels Against the Future: The Luddites and their War on the Industrial Revolution* (Cambridge, MA: Perseus, 1996), p. 17.

activities short of actual assassination."[30] Women did not play a key role in the machine-breaking attacks, but were very much a part of the movement. In the April 1812 assault on the Burton power-loom mill in Middleton, women were conspicuously present; five were charged with riot and breaking windows.[31]

Parallel examples of militancy were the East Anglian bread riots of 1815, and the victorious five-month seamen's strike in the same year that paralyzed coal-shipping ports and the east coast coal trade. Frame-breaking had been made a hanging offense in 1812, and repression hit its high point in 1817 with suspension of habeas corpus rights.

But upon the end of the Napoleonic wars in 1815, a long era began that was decisively centered on political reform (e.g., reform of parliamentary representation) and trade unionism. Unions, then as now, exist to broker the relationship between owners and workers. A more or less scattered, independent and often recalcitrant population becomes combined, represented, and disciplined via unionism.[32] This is much less some kind of conspiracy than an accommodation to the great pressures pushing industrial wage-slavery.

As early as Lord Holland's 1812 efforts to channel Luddite energy in a reform direction, there had been interest in somehow moving it away from its real focus. Luddism had to do with something incomparably more basic than politics and unions, but it failed in its frontal assault. A major late-inning target was John Heathcote's lace factory at Longborough in June 1816, and the Folly Hill and Pentrick risings a year later "can be regarded as the last flicker of Luddism in its

---

30 E.P. Thompson, *The Making of the English Working Class*, p. 585.

31 Rogers, *op. cit.*, p. 238.

32 For the conservative role of unions see John Zerzan, "Who Killed Ned Ludd?" in John Zerzan, *Elements of Refusal* (Columbia, MO: C.A.L. Press, 1999), pp. 205–211.

desperate, violent and political phase."[33] This last adjective refers to a key aspect of the defeat of machine destruction: its diversion into reform channels.

Oppositional energies could still be found, but from this point on they were more often in evidence in more approved contexts. In Bristol, for example, "gangs of disorderly fellows there assembled, throwing stinking fish, dead cats, dogs, rats, and other offensive missiles" during an election campaign.[34] The "Swing" riots throughout southeast England in 1830–1831 harkened back to anti-industrial militancy. Agricultural laborers resented threshing machines that were turning farms into factories; they resorted to destroying them and burning owners' property.[35] Their direct action and communal organization marked them as agricultural Luddites. Another, and pretty much final, outbreak was the Plug riots in the summer of 1842, when a thousand armed workers held Manchester for several days in a general strike. But the second and third generation came to accept as natural the confinement and deskilling of industrial labor. Only starvation could conquer a few holdouts, notably hand-loom weavers, terribly outflanked by the factories. What happened, or failed to happen, in the turning point years of 1800 to 1820 sealed people's fate. The ultimate victor was a new, much deeper level of domestication.

The Luddite challenge to the new order stood out, and continues to inspire. Another somewhat neglected aspect or current was that of religious utopianism, known as millenarianism. This movement (or movements) shed virtually all association with traditional religious belief. It was distant

---

33 Edward Royle, *Revolutionary Brittania?: Reflections on the Threat of Revolution in Britain, 1789–1848* (Manchester: Manchester University Press, 2000), p. 51.

34 M. Harrison, *op. cit.*, p. 179.

35 Roland Quinault, "The Industrial Revolution and Parliamentary Reform," in Patrick K. O'Brien and Roland Quinault, eds., *The Industrial Revolution and British Society* (New York: Cambridge University Press, 1993), p. 197.

from that agent of social control, the Church of England, and turned its back(s) on the C of E's main rival, Methodism (a.k.a. Dissenting or Non-Conformist). The millennials were anti-clerical and even at times anti-Christian.[36] They promised a vast transformation; their prophets threatened to "turn the world upside down," similar to the aims of secular revolutionaries.[37] Millenarianism was "directed to the destruction of existing society," and the reigning authorities believed in the possibility that it "might be sufficient to spark off the explosive mixture of social discontent and radical sentiment" then prevailing.[38]

The Methodist leadership recoiled in horror from the Luddite momentum and likewise from the many faces of millenarian extremism, some number of which were breakaways from Methodism. The Primitive Methodist Connexion was steadily growing, along with the "magic Methodists" of Delamere Forest, and the "Kirkgate screamers" of Leeds, among the many disaffected offshoots.[39] Some of these (and other similar groups) were explicitly referred to as Ranters, recognizing a link to the Ranters (and Diggers) of the seventeenth-century millenarianist rebellion. Already in the 1790s "cheap reprints of long-buried works of Ranter and Antinomian [literally, anti-law] complexion" were circulating.[40]

The Scottish Buchanites, followers of Elspeth Simpson Buchan, wished to hold all things in common and rejected the bonds of official marriage. The Wroeites were largely wool-combers and handloom weavers, fighting against the

---

36 J.F.C. Harrison, *The Second Coming: Popular Millenarianism 1780–1850* (New Brunswick, NJ: Rutgers University Press, 1979), p. 10.

37 Iain McCalman, *Radical Underworld* (New York: Cambridge University Press, 1988), p. 61.

38 J.F.C. Harrison, *op. cit.*, pp. 50, 77.

39 Eric J. Evans, *The Forging of the Modern State: Early Industrial Britain, 1783–1870* (New York: Longman, 1983), p. 53.

40 Iain McCalman, "New Jerusalem: Prophecy, Dissent and Radical Culture in England, 1786–1830," in Knud Haakonsen, ed., *Enlightenment and Religion: Rational Dissent in Eighteenth-Century Britain* (New York: Cambridge University Press, 1996), p. 324.

extinction of their crafts. The more numerous Muggleto-nians, led by the tailor Ludovic Muggle, offered a refuge to the oppressed and excluded. Among the myriad groups and sects a range of millennial faiths can be found. Joanna Southcott, with her thousands of Southcottians, was a feminist—but not a radical one. Some of her flock, like Peter Morison and John Ward, were on the fiery side; in 1806 Morison preached the confiscation of "all the property and land belonging to the rich."[41] Richard Brothers of the New Jerusalem proclaimed that "now is the whore of Babylon falling" and the future will see "no more war, no more want."[42] Robert Wedderburn, a black sailor, attracted the "most extreme and impoverished radicals" to his London chapel.[43]

The millenarian impulse was by no means an isolated, cranky, or unrepresentative passion. In the 1790s it emerged "on a scale unknown since the 17th century," judged E.P. Thompson.[44] "From the 1790s to at least the 1830s radical millenarianism could pose a real threat" to the dominant system, precisely because it did not accept the ruling paradigm or participate within it.[45] It was an active critique of the deep assumptions of the ruling order.

Domestic servants and small shopkeepers were among the adherents, as well as artisans and other dispossessed craftspeople who were the spearhead of the Luddite ranks. And in 1813 a New Connexion minister, George Beaumont, was charged with inspiring the Luddite attacks in the Huddersfield area.

Thomas Spence was an influential, apocalyptic figure who found inspiration in the seventeenth-century visionaries. He

---

41 J.F.C. Harrison, *op. cit.*, p. 127.

42 Quoted in E.P. Thompson, *The Making of the English Working Class, op. cit.*, p. 118.

43 I. McCalman, *op. cit.*, p. 139.

44 E.A. Thompson, *Making, op. cit.*, p. 116.

45 E. Royle, *op. cit.*, p. 45.

reprinted a Digger tract from that era by Gerald Winstanley, and likewise attacked private property as standing against God's common storehouse. Spence was convinced that "God was a very notorious Leveller" and that it was possible and necessary for humble men to turn the world upside down.[46]

Alas, the world wasn't turned upside down. The civilizing machine persevered through the storms. Religion, in its usual role, taught respect for authority and had a new weapon in its arsenal: the evangelical revival's campaign for industrial discipline.

William Blake, of "dark Satanic mills" fame, was an enigmatic, idiosyncratic figure who certainly played a part in this period. Not fully a millenarian or a Romantic either, Blake took as his central theme "the need to release the human spirit from bondage."[47] Starting from an orientation toward class struggle, Blake ultimately opposed kingship, and rulership itself.[48]

His *Songs of Experience* (1790s) point in a radical and millenarian direction, and he provided a radical critique of the limits of Swedenborgianism. But Blake can be characterized more as a Jacobin reformer than a revolutionary millennial. Consistency may be hard to find overall, though some observations, rendered in his own inimitable style, hit the mark. He found the factory and the workhouse terribly wrong and, as with the Luddites, saw the destruction of traditional workmanship as the end of working people's integrity. Mechanized time was a particularly important target: "the hours of folly are measured by the clock, but of wisdom: no clock can measure," for example.[49]

Blake's outlook on both nature and women has to be seen

---

46   I. McCalman, *op. cit.*, p. 63.

47   Shiv Kumar, "The New Jerusalem of William Blake," in Shiv Kumar, ed., *British Romantic Poets* (New York: New York University Press, 1966), p. 169.

48   Michael Ferber, *The Social Vision of William Blake* (Princeton: Princeton University Press, 1985), pp. 191–192.

49   Quoted in *Ibid.*, p. 135.

as quite flawed. His antifeminism is hard to miss, and there is a contempt for nature, as female and therefore secondary to the male. Social harmony is a major goal, but harmony or balance with nature, as championed by the Romantics or William Morris, for instance, was of no interest to Blake.[50] He desired the "Immediate by Perception or Sense at once,"[51] but it did not occur to him to ground this desire in the non-symbolic natural world.

E.P. Thompson clearly went too far in asserting, "Never, on any page of Blake, is there the least complicity with the kingdom of the Beast."[52] More accurate was his appraisal that few "delivered such shrewd and accurate blows against the ideological defenses of their society."[53]

The first two decades of the nineteenth century were the heart of the Romantic period, and the course of this literary movement reflects what took place socially and politically in those years. At the beginning, Coleridge, Wordsworth, Shelley and others gave voice to "an explosion of millenarial and apocalyptic enthusiasm for the new dawn."[54] Writing in 1804, Wordsworth recalled the exhilaration of ten years or so earlier, when the French revolution announced a new world and the factory system had not yet metastasized: "Bliss was it in that dawn to be alive,/But to be young was very Heaven!"[55] In its first bloom especially, Romanticism sought to reconcile humans and nature, consciousness and unconsciousness. As Northrup Frye put it, "the contrast between

---

50 Ibid., pp. 83, 86, 99, 105.

51 Quoted in Heather Glen, Blake's Songs and Wordsworth's Lyrical Ballads (New York: Cambridge University Press, 1983), p. 206.

52 E.P. Thompson, Witness Against the Beast: William Blake and the Moral Law (New York: Cambridge University Press, 1983), p. 229.

53 Ibid., p. 114.

54 Carl Woodring, Politics in English Romantic Poetry (Cambridge, MA: Harvard University Press, 1970), p. 47.

55 Quoted in R.W. Harris, Romanticism and the Social Order (London: Blandford Press, 1969), p. 178.

the mechanical and the organic is deeply rooted in Romantic thinking."[56] René Wellek noted that such thinking could be seen as "an upsurge of the unconscious and the primitive."[57]

Events, soon to be defined by Marx and other industrializers as Progress, undid optimism and a sense of possibilities, as we have seen. Sunny Enlightenment predictions about the perfectibility of society were already turning to ashes, as people became increasingly separated from nature and entered the state of modern, industrial slavery. A great sense of disappointment overtook the earlier aspirations, which were rapidly being destroyed by each new advance of industrial capitalism. From this point onward, disillusionment, ennui, and boredom became central to life in the West.

William Wordsworth acknowledged the existence and importance of a spirit of wild nature, which Blake resisted in him. Wordsworth was particularly moved by the decline of the domestic or pre-industrial mode of production and its negative impact on the poor and on families.[58] Privation, a sense of what has been lost, is a key theme in Wordsworth. His well-known decline as a poet after 1807 seems linked to the pessimism, even despair, that began to get the upper hand. He saw that the Enlightenment enshrining of Reason had failed, and he abandoned Nature as a source of value or hope.

Samuel Taylor Coleridge's anguish at the erosion of community brought surrender and drug addiction. His *Rime of the Ancient Mariner* testifies to the erosion of values in the absence of community. His "Michael" poems completed a series on abandonment and meaningless loss. A major poet who collapsed back into Anglican orthodoxy—as did Wordsworth—and nationalist conservatism.

---

56 Northrup Frye, "The Drunken Boat," in Northrup Frye, ed., *Romanticism Reconsidered* (New York: Columbia University Press, 1963), p. 7.

57 René Wellek, "Romanticism Reconsidered," in Frye, *op. cit.*, p. 117.

58 R.W. Harris, *op. cit.*, p. 193.

One who kept the liberatory Romantic flame burning longer was Percy Bysshe Shelley. Influenced by the anarchist William Godwin, Shelley's *Queen Mab* (1813) contains these lines:

> Power, like a desolating pestilence,
> Pollutes whate'er it touches; and obedience,
> Bane of all genius, virtue, freedom, truth,
> Makes slaves of men, and, of the human frame,
> A mechanized automaton. (III, 176)[59]

Shelley's *Mask of Anarchy* (1819) is an angry call to arms following the government assault on protestors, known as the Peterloo Massacre (e.g., "Rise like Lions after slumber/In unvanquishable number").[60] But he too flamed out, lost his way. The *Hyperion* project was dropped, and a major work, *Prometheus Unbound*, presents a confusing picture. By 1820 his passion had been quelled.

Of aristocratic lineage, George Gordon, Lord Byron was a lifelong radical. He spoke out against making frame-breaking a capital offense, and defended the impoverished. His brazen, bisexual behavior shocked a society he despised. With *Childe Harold* and *Don Juan*, transgressors escaped their "just deserts" and instead were glamorized. Byron saw nature as a value in itself; his nature poetry is correspondingly instinctive and immediate (as is that of his contemporary, John Keats).

He was the most famous of living Englishmen but said goodbye to England in 1816, first to join forces with Carbonari partisans in Italy, and later on the side of Greek rebels, among whom he died in 1824. "I have simplified my politics into an utter detestation of all existing governments," he had declared.[61]

---

59 Quoted in *Ibid.*, p. 288.
60 Quoted in *Ibid.*, p. 299.
61 Quoted in *Ibid.*, p. 361.

Dino Falluga recognized that some celebrated the death of Byron and what he represented. Victorian novelist Edward Bulwer-Lytton wrote a few decades after the fact that thanks to Byron's death the culture was finally able to grow up. It "becomes accustomed to the Mill," rather than quixotically defending the Luddites as Byron did.[62] Expectations of change did indeed die with Byron, if not before. Frustration with individual disappointments, also with a generalized, now chronic condition. Now the solitary poet becomes a true fixture, true to the reality that the poet—and not only the poet—is losing the last resource, one's own authority over oneself. Another deep loss of this era, perhaps the deepest. The age of no more autonomy, of no more hope of making things basically different.

The Gothic novel represents the dark side of Romanticism. It had been launched decades earlier, with Horace Walpole's anti-Enlightenment *The Castle of Otranto* (1764), and outlived Romanticism considerably. Its rise suggests resistance to the ideas of progress and development. The more psychoanalytically inclined see the Gothic as a return of what had been repressed: "a rebellion against a constraining neoclassical aesthetic ideal of order and unity, in order to recover a suppressed primitive and barbaric imaginative freedom."[63]

A common feature of many Gothic novels is a look backward to a simpler and more harmonious world—a connection to Rousseauian primitivism. Gothic's revolt against the new mechanistic model for society often idealizes the medieval world (hence the Gothic) as one of organic wholeness. But this rather golden past could hardly be recognized through the distorting terror of the intervening years. Gothic ruins and haunted houses in print reflected the pro-

---

62 Dino Franco Felluga, *The Perversity of Poetry: Ideology and the Popular Male Poet of Genius* (Albany: State University of New York Press, 2004), p. 133.

63 Maggie Kilgour, *The Rise of the Gothic Novel* (New York: Routledge, 1995), p. 3.

duction of real ruins, real nightmares. The trauma of fully Enlightened modernity finds its echo in inhuman literary settings where the self is hopelessly lost and ultimately destroyed. The depravity of Matthew Lewis' *The Monk*, hailed by the Marquis de Sade, comes to mind, as does Mary Shelley's *Frankenstein*, which demonizes its own creation. Soon, however, the Gothic became as mechanistic a genre as the social order it rejected. Its formulaic products are still being churned out.

The formation of malleable character, adaptable to the regimen of industrial life, was of obvious importance to the various managers in the early nineteenth century. Hence a key argument for support of schools was that they were "a form of social insurance."[64] In Eric Evans' summary, "By 1815 the argument was not whether education for the lower orders was proper but how much should be provided."[65]

The dinnerware manufacturer Thomas Wedgwood wanted a rigorous, disciplinary system of education and tried to enlist Wordsworth as its superintendent. His response, in *The Prelude*, includes these stinging lines:

> The Guides, the Wardens of our faculties,
> And Stewards of our labor, watchful men
> And skillful in the usury of time,
> Sages, who in their prescience would controul
> All accidents and to the very road
> Which they have fashion'd would confine us down,
> Like engines...[66]

Private, usually Christian schools received some govern-

64 A.P. Wadsworth, "The First Manchester Sunday Schools," in Flinn and Smout, *op. cit.*, p. 101.

65 E. Evans, *op. cit.*, p. 54.

66 E.P. Thompson, "Time, Work-Discipline, and Industrial Capitalism," *Past and Present* 38:1 (1967), p. 97.

ment funding, but a national system of education was rather slow in arriving.

Food rioters, anti-enclosure fence-breakers, not to mention Luddites, could end up on the gallows, but a modern uniformed police force was not implemented much earlier than was a standardized school system. While those in authority had great need of law enforcement, they faced the deep-rooted hostility of the majority. Prevailing sentiment held that personal morality should not be subject to scrutiny by the armed force of society and law. Police were opposed as "paid agents of the state who informed on their neighbors and interfered in private life."[67]

Uniformed police were on the streets of London with passage of the Metropolitan Police Act of 1829, but strong antipathy to the new institution persisted. At a political reform rally in Coldbath Fields, London in 1833 a struggle broke out and three officers were stabbed, one fatally. The subsequent coroner's jury brought in a verdict of justifiable homicide.

The change toward formal policing was just one aspect of an enforced social shift already underway. Increased control of mores introduced laws against "public indecency," and other punitive measures were enshrined in the Vagrant Act of 1822. This was part of the transition from "a largely communal to a primarily state-oriented, bureaucratically organized and professionally supported civic culture," in the words of M.J.D. Roberts.[68] Idleness was a mark against the overall industrial future, so the treadmill was introduced. (Idleness among the rich was quite different, needless to say.) Unauthorized fairs were subject to suppression, though they showed considerable staying power; the Vagrant Act of 1824 was aimed at a variety of popular entertainments. The

---

67 B. Wilson, *op. cit.*, p. 261.

68 M.J.D. Roberts, "Public and Private in Early Nineteenth-Century London: The Vagrant Act of 1822 and its Enforcement," *Social History* 13:3 (October 1988), p. 294.

outlawing of "blood sports" like cock-fighting and bull-baiting may be seen as a positive move; but there was no talk of banning hunting of fox, rabbit, and deer by the upper crust.

Driven by the enclosure movement at base, privatization struck on all levels. Domesticity tended to crowd out the social, and happiness became "a fireside thing."[69] Enclosure meant an absolutization of private property; enjoyment was increasingly private and confined. The home itself becomes more specifically divided, isolating family members within the household.[70] Movement is toward segregation of the sexes and identification of women with domesticity. The family and its division of labor become integrated with the trajectory of industry.

Consumer demand for cheap manufactured goods was an underlying, emergent key to the Industrial Revolution. This "demand" was not exactly spontaneous; new wants were now very widely advertised and promoted, filling the vacuum of what had been taken away. The decline in traditional self-sufficiency was everywhere apparent; beer and bread were now more often bought than brewed and baked at home, for example. Standardized goods—and a standardized national language—were in full flow.[71]

A stronger emphasis on the need for regular, predictable labor is shown by the prevalence of factory clocks, schedules, and timetables; also domestic clocks and personal watches, once luxury items and now consumer necessities. By the 1820s, nostalgic images were being reproduced using the kinds of technology that erased the lost, commemorated

---

69   Robert W. Malcomson, *Popular Recreations in English Society, 1700–1850* (Cambridge: Cambridge University Press, 1973), p. 156.

70   Jurgen Habermas, *The Structural Transformation of the Public Sphere* (Cambridge, MA: MIT Press, 1989), p. 45.

71   Fiona Stafford, *Local Attachments: the Province of Poetry* (New York: Oxford University Press, 2010), pp. 84–85.

world.[72] As a relatively self-sustaining arrangement of life, rural society was ending, fast becoming a commercial item to be wistfully contemplated.

Bulwer-Lytton wrote in 1833 of the ascendant standards of decorum and conformity: "The English of the present day are not the English of twenty years ago."[73] Diversions that many had enjoyed throughout their lives—public drinking, many holidays from work, boisterous street fairs, etc.—were seen as disgraceful and disgusting under the new order.

As the average person was being subdued and tamed, a few were lionized. Industrial modernity ushered in what is so prominent today, celebrity culture. The flamboyant actor Thomas Kean was an early star, but none surpassed the fame of Byron. He was one of the first ever to receive what we would call fan mail, that is, unsolicited letters on a mass scale.[74] Massified life also initiated widespread psychic immiseration. The best-seller of 1806 was *The Miseries of Human Life*, testifying to the large-scale anxiety and depression that had already set in, inevitable fruit of modern subjugation.

The door that was forced open decisively between 1800 and 1820, roughly speaking, inaugurated both global warming and an ever-mounting rise in global population. Globalizing industrialization is the motive force behind both developments. A deepening technological dimension becomes more and more immersive and defining, driving the loss of meaning, passion, and connection. This trajectory continually reaches new levels, at an ever-accelerating rate. As early as the 1950s, new technology was hailed by many as a "Second Industrial Revolution."[75] In 1960 Clark Kerr and

---

72 David Bindman, "Prints," in I. McCalman, *op. cit.*, p. 209.

73 Quoted in B. Wilson, *op. cit.*, p. 316.

74 Tom Mole, *Romanticism and Celebrity* (New York: Cambridge University Press, 2009), p. 228.

75 For example, Norbert Weiner, *The Human Use of Human Beings* (London: Eyre and Spottiswoode, 1954).

others announced that "the world is entering a new age—the age of total industrialization."[76]

As the nineteenth century waned, William Morris, who disliked all machinery, concluded that "Apart from the desire to produce beautiful things, the leading passion of my life has been and is hatred of modern civilization."[77] His *News from Nowhere* expresses a wonderful reversal of perspective, in which Ellen speaks from a time that has set aside the techno-desolation: "And even now, when all is won and has been for a long time, my heart is sickened with thinking of all the waste of life that has gone on for so many years." "So many centuries, she said, so many ages."[78]

76 Clark Kerr et al., *Industrialism and Industrial Man* (Cambridge, MA: Harvard University Press, 1960), p. 1.

77 Quote in E.P. Thompson, *William Morris: Romantic to Revolutionary* (New York, Pantheon Books, 1977), p. 125.

78 William Morris, *News from Nowhere* (New York: Routledge, 1970), p. 176.

12

INDUSTRIALISM AND RESISTANCE:
THE CASE OF THE U.S.

THE 1820s constituted a watershed in U.S. life. By the
end of that decade, about ten years after the last of the English Luddite risings had been suppressed, industrialism secured its decisive American victory; by the end of the 1830s
all of its cardinal features were definitively present.

The many overt threats to the coherence of emerging
industrial capitalism, the ensemble of forms of resistance to
its hegemony, were blunted at this time and forced into the
current of that participation so vital to modern domination.
In terms of technology, work, politics, sexuality, culture, and
the whole fabric of ordinary life, the struggles of an earlier
relative autonomy—that threatened both old and new forms

of authority fell short. A dialectic of domestication, so familiar to us today, broke through.

American "industrial consciousness," which Samuel Reznek judged to have triumphed by 1830, was in large measure and from the outset a project of the State. Lawrence Peskin saw a "recognizable working class" emerging as of 1827, when it had become clear that industrialization was a very significant reality. In 1787, generals and government officials sponsored the first promotional effort, the Pennsylvania Society for the Encouragement of Manufactures and the Useful Arts. With Benjamin Franklin as the Society's official patron, capital was raised and a factory equipped, but arson put an end to this venture early in 1790.

Another benchmark of the period was Alexander Hamilton's *Report on the Subject of Manufactures*, drafted by his tirelessly pro-factory technology Assistant Secretary of the Treasury, Tench Coxe. It is noteworthy that Coxe received government appointments from both the Federalist Hamilton and his archrival Jefferson, "Democratic-Republican" and career celebrator of the yeoman free-holder as the basis of independent values. While Hamilton pushed industrialization, arguing, for example, that children were better off in mills than at home or in school, Jefferson is remembered as a constant foe of that evil, alien import—manufacturing.

To correct the record is to glimpse the primacy of technology over ideological rhetoric, as well as to remember that no Enlightenment figure was not also an enthusiast of science and technology. In fact, it is fitting that Jefferson, the American most closely associated with the Enlightenment, introduced and promoted the idea of interchangeability of parts, key to the modern factory, from France as early as 1785.

Also to the point is Charles V. Hagnar's remark that in the 1790s "Thomas Jefferson...a personal friend of my father... indoctrinated him with the manufacturing fever," and induced him to start a cotton mill. As early as 1805, Jefferson, at least in private, complained that his earlier insistence on independent products as the bedrock of national virtue was misunderstood; his condemnation of industrialism, he explained, was only meant to apply to the cities of Europe.

Political spin aside, it was becoming clear that mechanization was in no way impeded by government. The role of the State is tellingly reflected by the fact that the term "armory system" now rivaled the older "American system of manufactures" as a more accurate description of new production methods. Along these lines, Cochran referred to the need for federal authorities to "keep up the pressure," around 1820, to soften local resistance to factories and their methods.

In the 1820s, a fully developed industrial lobby in Congress, and the extensive use of technology fairs and exhibits, along with nationalist pro-development appeals (e.g., to anti-British sentiment after the War of 1812) contributed to the assured ascendancy of industrialization by 1830.

Ranged against the efforts to achieve that ascendancy was an unmistakable antipathy, described by historians in classic works on the era. Norman Ware found that the Industrial Revolution "was repugnant to an astonishingly large section of the earlier American community," and Victor S. Clark noted the strong popular prejudice that existed "against factory industries as detrimental to the welfare of the working people."

This aversion persisted, though declining, as a pivotal force. The July 4, 1830 of pro-manufacture Whig Edward Everett contained a necessary reference to the "suffering, depravity, and brutalism" of industrialism in Europe, for the purpose of deflecting hostility from its American counterpart. Later in the 1830s, the visiting English liberal Harriet Martineau, in her efforts to defend manufacturing, indicated that her difficulties were precisely her audiences' antagonism to the subject.

Yet despite the "slow and painful" nature of the changeover and especially the widespread evidence of deep-seated resistance (of which the foregoing citations are a minute sample), there lingers the notion of an enthusiastic embrace of mechanization in America by craftsmen and capitalists alike. Fortunately, late twentieth-century scholarship contributed to a better grasp of the struggles of the early to mid-nineteenth century. Merritt Roe Smith's excellent *Harpers Ferry Armory and the New Technology* is a prime example. "The Harpers Ferry story diverges sharply from oft-repeated generalizations that 'most Americans accepted and welcomed technological change with uncritical enthusiasm,' Smith declared in his introduction.

No valid separation exists between anti-technology feelings and the more commonly recognized elements of class conflict; in practice the two were (and are) intertwined. References to the "massive and irrefutable" class opposition to early industrialism, or to Taft and Ross' dictum that "the United States has had the bloodiest and most violent labor history of any industrial nation," find their full meaning when we appraise both levels of anti-authoritarianism, especially in the watershed period of the 1820s.

In early 1819 English visitor William Faux declared that "Labour is quite as costly as in England, whether done by slaves, or by hired whites, and it is also much more troublesome." Later that year his travel journal further testified to the "very villainous" character of American workers, who "feel too free to work in earnest, or at all, above two or three days in a week." Indeed, travelers seemed invariably to remark on "the independent manners of the laboring classes," in slightly softer language.

Dissent by skilled workers, as has often been noted, was the sharpest and most persistent. Given the "astonishing versatility of the average native laborer," however, it is also true that a generalized climate of resistance confronted the impending debasement of work by the factory.

Those most clearly identified as artisans give us the clearest look at resistance, owing to the self-reliant culture that was a function of autonomous handicraft production. Bruce Laurie, commenting on some Philadelphia textile craftsmen, illustrates the vibrant pre-industrial life in question, with its blasé attitude toward work: "On a muggy summer day in August 1828 Kensington's hand loom weavers announced a holiday from their daily toil. News of the affair circulated throughout the district and by mid-afternoon the hard-living frame tenders and their comrades turned the neighborhood avenues into a playground. Knots of lounging workers joked and exchanged gossip.... The more athletic challenged one another to foot races and games... [and] quenched their thirst with frequent drams. The spree was a classic celebration of St. Monday."

It was no accident that mass production—primarily textile factories—first appeared in New England, with its relative lack of strong craft traditions, rather than in Philadelphia, the center of American artisan skills. Traditions of independent creativity obviously posed an obstacle to manufacturing innovation, causing Carl Russell Fish to assay that "craftsmen were the only actively dissatisfied class in the country."

The orthodox explanation of industrialism's triumph stresses the much higher U.S. wage levels, compared to Europe, and an alleged shortage of skilled workers. These are, as a rule, considered the primary factors that produced "an environment affording every suggestion and inducement to substitute machinery for men," and that nurtured that "inventiveness and mechanical intuition which are sometimes regarded as a national trait," in the descriptive phrases of Clark.

But as the preceding discussion indicates, it was the presence of work skills that challenged the new technology, not their absence. Research shows no dearth of skilled workers, and there is abundant evidence that "the trend toward mechanization came more from cultural and managerial bias than from carefully calculated marginal costs."

Habakkuk's comparison of American and British antebellum technology and labor economics cites the "scarcity and belligerency of the available skilled labour," and we must accentuate the latter quality, while realizing that scarcity can also mean the ability to make oneself scarce—namely, the oft-remarked high turnover rates.

It was industrial discipline that was missing, especially among craftsmen. The manufacture of guns was the widely known example of American mass production; at mid-century Samuel Colt confided to a British engineering group that "uneducated laborers" made the best workers in his new mass-production arms factory because they had so little to unlearn." Skills, and the recalcitrance that accompanied them, were hardly at a premium.

Strikes and unionization (though not always linked) became common from 1823 forward, and the modern labor movement showed particular vitality during the militant "great uprising" period of 1833–1837. However, especially by the 1830s, these workers and their struggles (for shorter hours and secondarily, for higher pay) were situated within the world of a standardizing, regimenting technology. In the main, it was the "unorganized" workers who mounted the most extreme forms of opposition, Luddite in many instances, contrary to the time-honored wisdom that Luddism and America were strangers.

Gary Kulik's groundbreaking scholarship on industrial Rhode Island determined that in Pawtucket alone more than five arson attempts were made against cotton mill properties, and that the deliberate burning of textile mills was far from uncommon throughout early nineteenth-century New England, declining by the 1830s. Jonathon Prude reached a similar conclusion: "Rumors abounded in antebellum New England that fires suffered by textile factories were often of 'incendiary origin.'" The same reaction was reported slightly later in Philadelphia: "Several closely spaced mill burnings triggered cries of 'incendiarism' in the 1830s, a decade of intense industrial conflict."

The hand sawyers who burned Oliver Evans' new steam mill at New Orleans in 1813 also practiced machine-wrecking by arson, like their Northeastern cousins. Soon after,

Massachusetts rope makers attacked machine-made yarn, boasting that their handspun product was stronger.

Sailors in New York often inflicted damage on vessels during strikes, according to Dulles, who noted that "the seamen were not organized and were an especially obstreperous lot." In the eighteenth century sailors had often proved unruly, "deserting at the first opportunity," according to Marcus Rediker.

Luddite-type violence continued, though its impact declined after the 1820s. The unpopular superintendent of the Harpers Ferry Armory, Thomas B. Dunn, was shot dead in his office in 1830 by an angry craftsman, Ebenezer Cox. Though Cox was hung for his act, he became a folk hero among the Harpers Ferry workers, who hated Dunn's emphasis on supervision and factory-type discipline, and "never tired of citing Dunn's fate as a blunt reminder to superintendents of what could be expected if they became overzealous in executing their duties and impinged on the traditional freedoms of employees."

Construction laborers, especially in railroad work, frequently destroyed property; Gutman provides an example from 1831 in which about three hundred workers punished a dishonest contractor by tearing up the track they had built. The destructive fury of Irish strikers on the Baltimore and Ohio Canal in 1834 occasioned the inaugural use of federal troops in a labor dispute, on orders of Andrew Jackson. And in the mid-1830s anti-railroad teamsters (wagon drivers) still ambushed trains and shot at their crews.

In the Philadelphia hand loom weavers' strike of 1842, striking artisans used machine breaking, intimidation, destruction of unwoven wool and finished cloth, house wrecking, and threats of even worse violence. During this riotous struggle, weavers marched on a water powered, mass-production mill to burn it; the attack was driven off, with two constables wounded. Around the same time in New England, as Prude describes the situation there after 1840, "Managers were rarely directly challenged by their hands; and although mills continued to burn down, contemporaries did not as quickly assume that workers were setting the fires."

There were social-political reasons for the culture of industrialism. Official efforts to domesticate the ruled, via the salutary effects of poor relief, led Boston officials to put widows and orphans to work beginning in 1735. The intent was to inculcate habits of industry and routine. But even threats of denial of subsistence aid failed to establish industrial discipline over irregular work habits and independent attitudes.

Artisanal and agricultural work was far more casual than its regimented counterpart in modern productionist models. Unlike factory work, workshop and farm work could almost always be interrupted in favor of an encounter, an adventure, or simply a distraction. This easy entry to gaming, drinking, personal projects, hunting, extended and often raucous revelry on a great variety of occasions, among other interruptions, was a preserve of independence from authority in general.

On the other hand, the regulation and monotony that adhere to the work differentiation of industrial technology combat such casual, undomesticated tendencies. Division of labor embodies, as an implicit purpose, the control and domination of the work process and those tied to it. Adam Smith saw this, and so did Tocqueville, in the 1830s: "As the principle of the division of labor is ever more completely applied, the workman becomes weaker, more limited, and more dependent.... Thus, at the same time that industrial science constantly lowers the standing of the working class, it raises that of the masters."

This subordination, including its obvious benefit, social control, was widely appreciated (especially, but not exclusively) by the early industrialists. Manufacturers, with un-ruliness very visible to them, came quickly to identify tech-nological progress with a more subdued populace. In 1816 Walton Felch, for instance, claimed that the "restless dis-positions and insatiate prodigality" of working people were altered, by "manufacturing attendance," into patterns of regularity and calmness. Another New England mill owner, Smith Wilkinson, judged in 1835 that factory labor imposed a "restraining influence" on people who "are often very ig-norant, and too often vicious." Harriet Martineau was of like mind in the early 1840s: "The factories are found to afford a safe and useful employment for much energy that would otherwise be wasted and misdirected." She determined that unlike the situation that had prevailed "before the introduc-tion of manufactures...now the same society is eminently orderly...disorders have almost entirely disappeared."

Eli Whitney provides another case in point of the social design inhering in mechanization. His Mill Rock armory moved from craft shop to factory status during the peri-od of the late 1790s until Whitney's death in 1825. Long associated with the birth of the "American system" of in-terchangeable parts production, Whitney was thoroughly unpopular with his employees because of the regimentation he developed by increased division of labor. His penchant for order and discipline was embodied in his view of Mill Rock as a "moral gymnasium" where "correct habits" of diligence and industry were inculcated through systematic control of all facets of the workday.

Andrew Ure, the English ideologue of early industrial capitalism, summed up the control intentionality behind the new technology by typifying the factory as "a creation designed to restore order," while proclaiming that "when capital enlists science into her service, the refractory hand of labor will always be taught docility."

As skill levels were forcibly reduced, the art of living was also purposefully degraded by the sheer number of hours involved in industrial work. Emerson, usually thought of as an advocate for human possibilities, applauded the suppression of potential enacted by the work hours of 1830s railroad building. He observed that long, hard construction shifts were "safe vents for peccant humors; and this grim day's work of fifteen or sixteen hours, though deplored by all humanity of the neighborhood, is a better police than the sheriff and his deputies." A hundred years later Simone Weil supplied a crucial part of the whole equation of industrialization: "No one would accept two daily hours of slavery. To be accepted, slavery must be of such a daily duration as to break something in a man." Similar is Cochran's more recent (and more conservative) reference to the twelve-hour day, that it was "maintained in part to keep workers under control."

Pioneer industrialist Samuel Slater wondered in the 1830s whether national institutions could survive "amongst a people whose energies are not kept constantly in play by the pursuit of some incessant productive employment." Indeed, technological "progress" and the modern wage-slavery that accompanied it offered a new stability to representative government, because of its magnified powers for suppressing the individual. Slater's biographer recognized that "to maintain good order and sound government, [modern industry] is more efficient than the sword or bayonet."

A relentless assault on the worker's historic rights to free time, self-education, craftsmanship, and play was at the heart of the rise of the factory system; "increasingly, a feeling of degradation spread among factory hands," according to Rex Burns. By the mid-1830s a common refrain in the working-class press was that the laborer had been debased "into a necessary piece of machinery."

Assisted by sermons, a growing public school system, a

new didactic popular literature, and other social institutions that sang the praises of industrial discipline, the factory had won its survival by 1830. From this point on, and with increasing visibility by the end of the 1830s, conditions worsened and pay decreased. No longer was there a pressing need to lure first-time operatives into industrialized life and curry their favor with high wages and relatively light duties. After 1840, the pace of work in textile mills was greatly speeded up. This coincided with the first major influx of immigration, by impoverished Irish and French Canadians.

Henry Clay asked, "Who has not been delighted with the clockwork movements of a large cotton factory?" A concomitant of such regimentation was the spread of a new conception of time. Things did not always go "like clockwork" for the industrialists; "punctuality and absenteeism remained intractable problems for management" throughout the first half of the nineteenth century, for example. But a new industrial time made gradual headway, against great resistance.

In the task-oriented labors of artisans and farmers, work and play were freely mixed. A constant pace of unceasing labor was the ideal not of the mechanic but of the machine— more specifically, of the clock. Largely spontaneous games, fairs, festivals, and excursions gave way, along with working at one's own pace, to enslavement to the uniform, unremitting technological time of the factory whistle, centralized power, and unvarying routine.

At the Harpers Ferry armory early in the century, workshops opened at sunrise and closed at sunset, but workers were free to come and go as they pleased. They had long been accustomed to controlling the scheduling and duration of their tasks, and "the idea of a clocked day seemed not only repugnant but an outrageous insult to their self-respect and freedom." Hence the bitter and protracted opposition to 1827 regulations that installed a clock and announced a ten-hour day.

For those already under the regimen of factory production, struggles against the alien time were necessarily of a lingering, rear-guard character by the end of the 1820s. An interesting illustration is that of Pawtucket, Rhode Island, a mill village whose citizens built a town clock by public subscription in 1828. In their efforts to counter the mill owner's monopoly of recording time, one can see that the level of contestation had degenerated. The issue was no longer industrial time itself, but merely the democratization of its measurement.

The clock, favorite machine of the Enlightenment, is a master device in the depiction of the American economy by Thoreau and others. Its function is decisive because it links the industrial apparatus with consciousness. It is fitting that clockmaking, along with gun manufacture, was a model of the new technology. The U.S. led the world in production of inexpensive timepieces by the 1820s, testimony to the encroaching industrial value system and the marked anxiety about the passage of time that it provoked.

Though even in the first decades of the Republic there was a permanent operative class in at least three urban centers of the Mid-Atlantic seaboard, industrialization began in earnest with New England cloth production twenty years after the Constitution was adopted. For example, forty-one new woolen mills were built in the U.S., chiefly along New England streams, between 1807 and 1813. The textile industry selected the most economically deprived areas, and with cheery propaganda and, initially, relatively good working conditions, enticed women and children (who had no other options) into the mills. That they "came from families who could no longer support them at home" means that theirs was essentially forced labor. In 1797 Obadiah Brown, in a letter to a partner regarding the selection of a mill site, determined that "the inhabitants appear to be poor, their homes very much on the decline. I apprehend it might be a very good place for a Cotton Manufactory, Children appearing very plenty." "In collecting our help," a Connecticut mill owner said thirty years later, "we are obliged to employ poor families and generally those having the greatest number of children."

New England factory cloth output increased from about 2.4 million yards in 1815 to approximately 13.9 million yards in 1820, and the shift of weaving from home to factory was almost complete by 1824. Although arson, absenteeism, stealing, and sabotage persisted with particular emphasis into the 1830s, the march of industrialism proceeded in textiles, as elsewhere. If a prime element of modernity is the amount of time spent in factories, as Inkeles and Smith (among others) have contended, the 1820s was indeed a watershed decade.

"Certainly by 1825 the first stage of industrialization of the United States was over," in Cochran's estimation. In 1820, factories were capitalized to $50 million, by 1840, to $250 million; and the number of people working in them had more than doubled. Also, by the 1820s the whole direction of specialized bureaucratic control, realized a generation later in large corporations such as the railroads, had already become clear.

As the standardizing, quasi-military machine replaced the individual's tools, it provided those in authority with an invaluable, "objective" ally against "disorder." Not coincidentally did modern mass politics take root in the 1820s; political hegemony, as a necessary part of social power, had failed to dominate during the struggles of the early republic. Conflict of all kinds was rampant, and a "terrible precariousness," in Page Smith's phrase, characterized the cohesion of national power. By the 1820s, the legitimacy of traditional rule by informal elites was breaking down, and a serious restructuring of American politics was required.

Part of the restructuring dealt with law, paralleling the social meaning of technology: "neutral" universal principles came to the fore to justify increased coercion. Modern bourgeois society was forced to rely on an increasingly objectified legal system, which reflected, at base, the progress of division of labor. It must, in David Grimsted's words, "elevate law because of what it is creating and what it has to destroy." By the time of Jackson's ascendancy in the late 1820s, America had become largely a government of laws, not men (though juries mitigated legality). The unpopularity of this development can be measured by the widespread disdain for lawyers.

Along with the need to mobilize the lower orders into industrial work, it was important to greatly increase political participation, in the interests of legitimizing the whole system. Although by the mid-1820s almost every state had extended the franchise to include all white males, numbers of voters remained very low during the decade. By this time, newspapers had proliferated and were playing a key role in working toward critical integration into the dominant order, achieved with Jackson and the new, mass political machinery.

In 1826, a workingman was chosen for the first time as a mayoral candidate in Baltimore, explicitly to attract workingmen's participation. This is an early example of the felt necessity of moving away from narrow-based, old-style rule. However, John Quincy Adams, who had become president in 1825, "failed to comprehend that voters needed at least the appearance of consultation and participation in making decisions." A conservative and a nationalist, Adams was at least occasionally candid; as he told Tocqueville, there is "a great equality before the law...[which] ceases absolutely in the habits of life. There are upper classes and working classes."

Following Adams, the election of Andrew Jackson in 1828 symbolized and accelerated a shift in American life. At the moment when mechanization was securing its domination of life and culture, the Jacksonian era signaled the arrival of professional politics, and a crucial diversion of what potentially dangerous energies remained. Embodying this domestication in his successful appeal to the "common man," the old general was in reality a plantation owner, land speculator, and lawyer, whose first case in 1788 defended the interests of Tennessee creditors against their debtors.

Jackson reversed the decline in executive power that had plagued his three predecessors. For the first time in U.S. history, a president renewed the authority of the state by a direct appeal to the working classes. The mob at the 1829 White House inaugural, celebrated in history textbooks with its smashing of china and trampling of furniture, did in fact "symbolize a new power," in Curti's phrase—a power tamed, and delivering itself to government.

Jackson's "public statements address a society divided into classes, invidiously distinguished and profoundly antagonistic." Employing Jefferson's rhetoric, he identified the class enemy in misleading terms as the money power, the moneyed aristocracy, etc. By the presidential contest of 1832 the gentleman-leader had been rendered anachronistic, in large part through the use of class-oriented rhetoric. After Jackson was overwhelmingly re-elected on the strength of his attacks on the Bank of the United States, he vetoed the rechartering of the bank—the most popular act of his administration.

Although many conservatives feared that Jackson's policies and conduct would result in a "disastrous, perhaps a fatal" revolution, that the Jacksonians "had raised up forces greater than they could control," the bank proved a safe target for the Jacksonian project of deflecting popular anger. As Fish noted, "hostility was merely keenest against banks; it existed against all corporations."

Thus the "Monster" Bank, which reaped outrageous profits and openly purchased members of Congress, was inveighed against as the incarnation of aristocracy, privilege, and the spirit of luxury. Missing the essential point, Daniel Webster and others warned against such inflaming of the poor against the rich. Needless to say, the growth of an enslaving technology was never attacked; rather, as Bray Hammond maintained, Jackson represented "a blow at an older set of capitalists by a newer, more numerous set." And meanwhile, along with the phrasemaking of this "frontier democrat," class distinctions widened, and tensions increased, without the means to successfully overcome them.

In the mid-1830s various workers' parties also sprang up. Many were far from totally proletarian in composition, and few went much further than Jacksonian democracy, in their denunciations of "monopolists" and such demands as free public schools and equality of "opportunity." This political workerism only advanced the absorption of working people into the new political system and displayed, for the first time, the now familiar interchangeability of labor leader and politician.

But integration was not accomplished smoothly or automatically. Political insurrection was a legacy from the eighteenth century: from Bacon's Rebellion in Virginia (1675), by 1760 there had been eighteen uprisings aimed at overthrowing colonial governments. Soon after the Revolution followed Shay's Rebellion in Massachusetts (1786–1787), the Whiskey Rebellion in western Pennsylvania (1794), and Fries' Rebellion in eastern Pennsylvania (1798–1799).

Twenty-five years after the Constitution was signed, extensive anti-Federalist rioting in Baltimore seemed to connect with this legacy, rather than to less authentic political alternatives to the old informal means of social control. Significantly, over the course of those upheavals in the summer of 1812, the composition of the mob shifted toward an exclusively proletarian, propertyless group.

Moving into the focus period of the 1820s, the extent of general contestation is shown by a most unlikely revolt, a "vicious cadet mutiny" at West Point in 1826. On Christmas morning, "drunken and raging cadets endeavored to kill at least one of their superior officers and converted their barracks into a bastion which they proposed to defend, armed, against assault by relieving Regular Army troops on the Academy reservation." Despite its fury, this amazing turn of events, though detailed in much Board of Inquiry and courts-martial testimony, remains a little-known episode in U.S. history. It can be seen to have introduced a whole chapter of wholesale tumult, nonetheless.

By the late 1820s, group violence had reached great prominence in American life, such that "many Americans had a strong sense of social disintegration." In November 1830, New York's annual parade of artisans was another incident that told a great deal about the mounting unruliness. Printers, coopers, furniture makers, and a great many other tradesmen assembled at the culmination of the procession to hear speeches expressing the usual republican virtues. But on this day, politicians mouthing the same old ritual phrases about political freedom and the dignity of labor were suddenly confronted by curses, scuffling, and a defiant temper. "As the militia tried to quiet the militants, the dissatisfied crowd knocked out the supports of the scaffolding, causing the entire stage to crash to the ground," and bringing the ceremonies to an undignified end.

The public violence of the 1830s was more a prolonged aftershock, however, than a moment of revolutionary possibility. As shown above, industrial technology had triumphed by the end of the 1820s. The ensuing aftermath, though major, could not be decisive.

But it was the case that, by Hammett's reckoning, "A climate of disorder prevailed...which seemed to be moving the nation to the edge of disaster." As Page Smith described life in the early 1830s, "What is hard to comprehend today is the constant ferment of social unrest and bitterness that manifested itself almost monthly in violent riots and civic disorders." For example, Gilje's research revealed "nearly 200 instances of riot between 1793 and 1829 in New York City alone," and Weinbaum counted 116 such incidents in that city between 1821 and 1837. Philadelphia, Baltimore, and Boston witnessed outbreaks on a similar scale, often directed at banker Gilje s and "monopolists."

Michael Chevalier wrote a chapter entitled "Symptoms of Revolution" against the backdrop of four days of rioting in Baltimore over exploitive practices of the Bank of Maryland, in the summer of 1835. In the same year, disorders that caused Jackson to resort increasingly to the use of federal troops, occasioned William Ellery Channing's report from Boston: "The cry is, 'Property is insecure, law a rope of sand, and the mob sovereign.'" Likewise, the *Boston Evening Journal* pondered the "disorganizing, anarchical spirit" of the times in an August 7, 1835 editorial.

February 1836 saw hundreds of debtor farmers attack and burn offices of the Holland Land Company in western New York. In 1836 and 1837 crowds in New York City several times broke into warehouses, furious over the high price of food, fuel, and rental housing. The Workingmen's Party in New York, also known as the Locofoco Party, has been linked with these "flour riots," but interestingly, at the February 1837 outburst most closely tied to Locofoco speechmaking, of fifty-three rioters arrested none was a party member.

Despite the narrow chances for the ultimate success of the 1830s uprisings, it is clear that deep and bitter class feelings were involved. Poor men could see that the promise of equality contained in the Declaration of Independence was mocked by reality. Serious disturbances continued: the 1838 "Buckshot War," in which Harrisburg was seized by an irate, armed crowd in a Pennsylvania senatorial election dispute; the "anti-rent" riots by New York tenants of the Van Rensselaer family in 1839; the "Dorr War" of 1842 (echoing the independent "Indian Stream Republic" of 1832–1835 in New Hampshire) in which thousands of Rhode Islanders approached civil war in a fight over rival state constitutions; and the sporadic anti-railroad riots in the Kensington section of Philadelphia from 1840 to 1842, were among the major hostilities.

But ethnic, racial, and religious disputes began fairly early in the 1840s to supersede class-conscious struggles, though often disparate elements fought on the same side. This decline in consciousness showed itself in riots against Irish, abolitionists, and Catholics, and must be placed in the context of the earlier defeat of working people by the factory system in the 1820s. Cut off from the only terrain where challenge could gain basic victories, could change life, the upheaval of the 1830s was destined to sour. The end of that decade saw both the professionalization of urban police forces and organized gang violence—both in place as permanent fixtures.

If by 1830 most aspects of American life had undergone major alteration, the startling changes in drinking habits shed particular light on the industrialism behind this transformation. The "great alcoholic binge of the early nineteenth century," and its precipitous decline in the early 1830s, have much to say about how the culture of the new technology took shape.

Drinking, on the one hand, was part of the pre-industrial blurring of the distinction between work and leisure. Through the early decades of the nineteenth century, small amounts of alcohol were commonly consumed through the day, at work and at home (sometimes the same place). There were frequent spontaneous holidays, and three-day "Blue Monday" weekends, "which run pretty well into the week," according to one complaining New York employer. Drinking was the universal accompaniment to these days off, as it was to the normal workday.

The tavern or grog-shop, with its "unstructured, leisurely, and wholly unproductive, even anti-productive, character," was a social center well suited to a non-mechanized age. It became more than ever the workingman's club, as modernization cut him off from other emotional outlets.

But drunkenness—especially binge-drinking and solitary drinking—was increasing by 1820; significantly, alcoholic delirium tremens (the D.T.s) first appeared in the U.S. during the 1820s. Alcoholism is an obvious register of strains and alienation, of people's inability to cope with the burden of daily life. Clearly, there is little healthy or resistant about such drinking practices.

Temperance reform was part of the larger syndrome of social discipline expressed in industrialization. Irregular drinking habits were an obstacle to a well-managed population. Not surprisingly, factory owners were in the forefront of such efforts; they had to contend with troublesome wage-earners who had little taste for such dictums as "the steady arm of industry withers from drink." Tyrell's examination of Worcester, Massachusetts found that "the leading temperance reformers were those with a hand in the work of inventions and of innovations in factory or machine production."

While at one point workers considered a daily liquor issue a non-negotiable right and an emblem of their independence, increasing reliance on alcohol signified the debility that went along with their domination by machine culture. The Secretary of War estimated in 1829 that "three-quarters of the nation's laborers drank daily at least four ounces of distilled spirits," and in 1830 the average annual consumption of liquor exceeded five gallons, nearly triple the amount 150 years later.

The anti-alcohol crusade began in earnest in 1826 with the formation of the American Temperance Society, and local groups such as the Society for the Promotion of Industry, Frugality and Temperance in Lynn, Massachusetts. In the same year Henry Ward Beecher published his *Six Sermons on Intemperance*, the leading statement of anti-drinking of the period; he pronounced tippling to be politically dangerous. In Gusfield's summation, Beecher's writings "displayed the classic fear the creditor has of the debtor, the propertied of the propertyless, and the dominant of the subordinate—the fear of disobedience, renunciation, and rebellion."

Temperance exertions in the 1820s revealed in their propaganda what a tenuous influence the respectable held over the laboring classes, at the height of the battle to establish industrial values and a reliable workforce. As this battle was won by the end of the 1820s, drinking suddenly leveled off, and began to plummet toward an unprecedented low in the early 1830s. As working people became domesticated, the temperance movement shifted toward the goal of complete abstinence. In the 1840s a "dry" campaign swept the nation.

A second major reform movement, the demand for a public school system, arose in the mid-1820s. Like the temperance campaign, it was explicitly undertaken to "make the dangerous classes trustworthy." The concept of mass schooling had arrived by the early Jacksonian period, when innovative forms of coercion were necessitated by deteriorating restraints on social behavior, and auxiliary institutions came to the aid of the factory.

The "willingness of early nineteenth-century school promoters to intervene directly and without invitation in the lives of the working class" was a consequence of the notion that education was something the ruling orders did to make the populace orderly and tractable. Thus "the first compulsory schools were alien institutions set in hostile territory," as Katz put it, owing largely to the spirit of autonomy and egalitarianism that parents had instilled in their children. Faux noted in 1819 the "prominent want of respect for rule and rulers," which he connected with a common refusal of "strict discipline" in schools; Marryat's diary reported that students "learn precisely what they please and no more."

Drunkenness and rioting occurred in schools as well as in the rest of society, and educators interpreted the overall situation as announcing general subversion. In an 1833 address on education, John Armstrong declared, "When Revolution threatens the overthrow of our institutions, everything depends on the character of our people." Industrial morality—obedience, self-sacrifice, restraint, and order—constituted the most important goal of public education; character was far more important than intellectual development. The school system came into being to shape behavior and attitudes and thus reinforce the emerging industrialized world. The belief that attendance should be universal and compulsory followed logically from these assumptions.

Moral instruction was also amplified by the churches during the 1820s and 1830s, an antidote to that tendency to "rejoice in casting off restraints and unsettling the foundations of social order," woefully recorded by the Reverend Charles Hall. Sunday School and societies for diffusion of religious tracts were new ecclesiastical contributions to social control in this period.

The Jacksonian period is also synonymous with the "Age of the Asylum," a further development in the quest for civic docility. The regularity and efficiency of the factory was the model for the penitentiaries, insane asylums, orphanages, and reformatories that now appeared. Embodying uniformity and regularity, the factory had become the model for the whole of society.

Religious revivalism and millenarianism grew in strength after the mid-1820s, and one of the new denominations to appear was the Millerites (forerunners of today's Seventh-Day Adventists). On October 22, 1844 the group gathered to await what they predicted would be the end of the world. Their expectation was but the most literal manifestation of a feeling that began to pervade the country after 1830; without unduly elevating the pre-industrial past, one can recognize a lament for a world that was indeed ended.

The early stages of industrial capitalism introduced a sharpened division between the worlds of work and home, male and female, and private and public life, with large extended families devolving toward small, isolated nuclear families. Along with this process of increasing separation and isolation came a focused repression of personal feelings, stemming from new requirements for rationalized, predictable behavior. As planning and organization moved ahead via the progress of the machine model of the individual, the range of human sentiments became suspect, a target for suppression. For example, whereas in 1800 it was not considered "unmanly" for a man to weep openly, by the 1830s a proscription against any extreme emotional display, especially crying, was gaining strength. This tendency became pronounced in child training; in the widely distributed *Advice to Christian Parents* (1839), the Reverend John Hersey emphasized that "in every stage of domestic education, children should be disciplined to restrain their appetites and desires."

The seventeenth-century Puritans were hardly "puritanical" about sexual matters, and eighteenth-century American society—especially in the latter part of the century—was characterized by very open sexuality. During the seventeenth and eighteenth centuries, moreover, much emphasis was placed on the arousal, pleasure, and satisfaction of women. *Aristotle's Master Piece*, for example, was a very popular work of erotica and anatomy in the eighteenth and early nineteenth centuries, predicated on the sexual interest of women. There were at least one hundred editions of the book prior to 1830, and no known complaints about it in any newspapers or periodicals.

In 1831, the year when the last edition of *Aristotle's Master Piece* was published, J.N. Bolles' *Solitary Vice Considered* appeared, an anti-masturbation booklet of a type that would proliferate from the early 1830s on. While the advice books on sex of the early part of the century could be quite explicit concerning women's sexual satisfaction, the trend now was that "medical, biological, instructional, and popular literature contained countless defenses of extreme moderation and self-control." The turning point, again, was the 1820s. By the 1840s the very idea of women's sexuality was fading. By mid-century Dr. William Acton's *Functions and Disorders of the Reproductive Organs*, a popular standby; summed up the official view: "The majority of women (happily for them) are not very much troubled with sexual feelings of any kind. What men are habitually, women are only exceptionally."

Among working and non-white women (not exclusive categories, obviously), this ideology had less impact than among those of higher station, for whom the relentless quelling of the recognition of "animal passions" caused vast physical and psychological damage. The cult of female purity, or cult of the lady, or "true womanhood," emerged among the latter in the 1830s, stressing piety and domesticity. This American woman was now exclusively a consumer of her husband's income, at a period when advertising developed on a scale and sophistication unique in the world.

Not surprisingly, national expansionist policy came into

its own now, too. The hemispheric imperialism proclaimed in late 1823—the Monroe Doctrine—coincided with the beginnings of intensifying Indian genocide, both occurring against a backdrop of a gathering industrial cancer. The Seminoles and Creeks were crushed at this time, an answer to the "especially menacing" specter of a combined Indian and runaway slave coalition. The First Seminole War was in large part undertaken "to secure Indian lands and therewith deny sanctuary to runaway slaves."

From 1814 to 1824, Jackson had been "the moving force behind southern Indian removal," a policy inherited from Jefferson and one which he completed upon becoming president in 1828. Indian destruction, surely one of the major horror tales of the modern age, was more than an ugly stain on American politics and culture; Rogin's argument that its scope "defines for America the stage of primitive capitalist accumulation" is at least partly true. At the very least it presaged the further acquisitiveness that blossomed in the Manifest Destiny conquest of the 1840s. But the more monstrous perhaps is its moral dimension, committed under Jackson's description of "extending the area of freedom."

The Red Man, as Noble Savage, had to disappear; he was "savage," after all. The Dead Indian is a more apt symbol for the trajectory of industrial capitalism, though the romantic use of the Indian reached its height at the moment of capital's victory, when, by the 1830s Nature truly became an evil to be subdued, while the machine was the fountainhead of all values that counted. The word "machino-culture" had come into use, an apt enough term for what had come to pass.

Nevertheless, voices and symbols of opposition survived, and Jonathan Gluckstein concluded that "only toward the end of the nineteenth century" was the condition of wage labor itself accepted as permanent. Johnny Appleseed (Jonathan Chapman), for instance, who was respected by Indians during the first forty years of the century, represented riches of a wholly non-productionist, non-commodity type. There were such doubters of the period as Thoreau, Hawthorne, Poe, and Melville. Lee Clark Mitchell, among other contemporary scholars, has found in letters, diaries, and essays the record of a popular sense of deep foreboding about the conquest of the wild by technological progress.

Author's note: This chapter was written for a publication that did not want endnotes.

13

DECADENCE AND THE MACHINE

FIN-DE-SIÈCLE EUROPE from 1880 to 1900, and especially the 1890s, is known as a period of cultural and social Decadence. This term is somewhat elusive, though there are at least a few parallels to our own time. The philosopher C.E.M. Joad went so far as to conclude, "There is not, I think, any word whose meaning is vaguer, and more difficult to define."[1]

In the arts as in bohemia in general, one thinks of Baudelarian dandyism, irreverent wit, a cultivated languor. Oscar Wilde comes to mind. As R.K.R. Thornton put it,

1   C.E.M. Joad, *Decadence: A Philosophical Inquiry* (London: Faber and Faber Ltd., 1948), p. 55.

"some young men in various countries...call themselves Decadents, with all the thrill of unsatisfied virtue masquerading as uncomprehended vice."[2] There is little doubt that Decadence made twentieth-century modernism possible by breaking long-standing strictures and conventions.

More basically, Decadence was a darkening disillusionment that pervaded thought, imagination, and material life, and which was inseparable from the triumph of industrialism. The characteristic sense of general decay flowed from being lost in the darkness of a completely ascendant Indus-

2   Ian Fletcher, ed., *Decadence and the 1890s* (Teaneck, NJ: Holmes and Meier, 1978), R.K.R. Thornton, "'Decadence' in Later Nineteenth-Century England," p. 17.

trial Revolution. In the words of Nietzsche, "Many chains have been laid upon man.... He suffers from having worn his chains for so long."[3]

An unsettled time of doubt, but more than that—an epoch when defeat was deeply felt. "This sense of unrest, of disease, penetrates down even into the deepest regions of man's being," according to Edward Carpenter.[4] When the world presents itself as a mechanism of impersonal forces beyond human control, a done deal, with the full connivance of both Left and Right, Decadence is unavoidable. Ennui reigns; only technology is dynamic. Everything healthy is in decline and "the decadent mentality resigns itself to awaiting it passively, with anguished fatality and inert anxiety."[5] Sound familiar? The ethos of failure was palpable. The chief power of the era was that of industrialism, hands down.

In the first half of the century E.T.A. Hoffmann, Mary Shelley, and Edgar Allen Poe shuddered at automatons and other mechanical figures as if they saw in them the future reality of industrializing humanity. There was of course a persistent Romantic critique of mechanistic Progress. From about 1830 when the impact of the factory was really registering, various oppositional voices were heard, including Zola, Balzac, and Flaubert in France; Heine, Hesse, and Thomas Mann in Germany; Carlyle, Dickens, Ruskin, Morris, and Carpenter in England; and Tolstoy in Russia, to name a few.

But Decadence was not an extension of Romanticism but a reaction to it. In the absence of significant anti-industrial movements and in a world where simplicity, balance, harmony were being systematically erased by the Machine, cul-

---

3   Friedrich Nietzsche, *Human, All Too Human* (New York: Cambridge University Press, 1986), p. 393.

4   Edward Carpenter, *Civilization—Its Cause and Cure* (London: S. Sonnschein, 1897), p. 3.

5   Renato Poggioli, *The Theory of the Avant-Garde* (Cambridge, MA: Belknap Press, 1968), p. 75.

tural expression followed suit. Deformed by a colossal defeat, a revolt against the primitive and natural sets in. Industrial discipline—the latest and deepest form of domestication—infects all of society. Toynbee noted that "mechanization spelled regimentation…[which] had taken the spirit out of a Western industrial working class and a Western middle class in succession."[6] Early on Stendhal saw that "one of the consequences of the modern dedication to productivity was sure to be the exhaustion of the natural human gift for the enjoyment of life."[7] Weariness of mind; potentially subversive energies suppressed.

The dominant minds—Comte, Darwin, Marx, etc.—agreed: the ascending order of civilization required always more complexity, homogeneity, work. In the 1880s Havelock Ellis recounted his "feeling that the universe was represented as a sort of factory filled with an inextricable web of wheels and looms and flying shuttles, in a deafening din."[8] The philosopher Arthur Schopenhauer did not at all join in the official optimism. His idea of pessimism, however—in view of the overall failure of desire and will—posited that will itself was the underlying problem. A classic case of deformed thinking.

Decadent literati in the West gave voice to a sense of nothingness at the heart of things.[9] In 1890 Max Nordau's very popular *Degeneration* depicted the fin-de-siècle mood as that of the impotent despair of a sick individual, dying by inches. The book is uneven, to say the least, but Nordau pointed accurately, in particular, to the nervous hysteria

6   Arnold J. Toynbee, *A Study of History*, Volume IX (New York: Oxford University Press, 1954), p. 577.

7   Cesar Grana, *Fact and Symbol: Essays in the Sociology of Art and Literature* (New Brunswick, NJ: Transaction Publishers, 1994), pp. 169–170.

8   Karl Beckson, *London in the 1890s: A Cultural History* (New York: W.W. Norton, 1992), p. 318.

9   John A. Lester, Jr., *Journey Through Despair 1880–1914* (Princeton, NJ: Princeton University Press, 1968), p. 32.

brought on by industrialization and the growth of cities. He wrote of an enormous increase in hysteria, and countless others concurred. Already in 1881, the French journalist Jules Claretie had declared, "The illness of our time is hysteria. One encounters it everywhere."[10] This was the paradigmatic psychological malady of late nineteenth-century Europe. Suicide rates rose to unprecedented levels, occasioning a considerable literature on the subject.[11] Suicide also became a common feature in fiction; Thomas Hardy's *Jude the Obscure* (1896) contains perhaps the most sensational fictional suicide of the era.

A proliferation of occult movements was another aspect of Decadent malaise, as was the rise in opium use. The strong popularity of Wagner's music, with its mythic religiosity, often assumed cultish proportions. The redemptive eroticism of operas like *Tristan and Isolde* provided a pseudo-utopian refuge from reality. The late-century rise of anti-semitism, especially in Austria and France, was the disgrace of the century. Strange, even pathological phenomena, in an ugly industrial world that is not being challenged.

Decadence is self-consciously artificial.[12] It bears an unmistakably anti-natural quality that is a sad reflection of the technological dominion that literally destroys nature. "My own experience," remarked Oscar Wilde in *The Artist as Critic*, "is that the more we study Art, the less we care for Nature."[13] The retreat into artifice, closing the door on the outside reality. As William Butler Yeats put it, referring to poetry: it is "an end in itself; it has nothing to do with

---

10   Mark S. Micale, ed., *The Mind of Modernism* (Stanford, CA: Stanford University Press, 2004), Micale, "Decades of Hysteria in Fin-de-Siècle France," p. 84.

11   John Stokes, *In the Nineties* (Hemel Hemstead, UK: Harvester Wheatsheaf, 1989), pp. 121–122.

12   R.K.R. Thornton, *The Decadent Dilemma* (London, Edward Arnold, 1983), p. 32.

13   Elaine Showalter, *Sexual Anarchy: Gender and Culture at the Fin-de-Siècle* (New York: Viking, 1990), p. 170.

thought, nothing to do with philosophy, nothing to do with life, nothing to do with anything...."[14]

Decadents saw a world in which survival meant keeping one's distance. With Symbolism, as the name proclaims, came a fuller retreat, into the strictly symbolic. Language as an independent quality takes over from meaning. This literary style is the effort of the Word to somehow express everything while confronting nothing. Meanwhile the International Date Line was established in 1884, a milestone of global, integrated industrialism. The gatling gun lifted power imperialism to new heights, while skyscrapers and the Eiffel Tower (1889) showcased new vistas for the new order.

Outside of what we might call mainstream Decadence, however, there were some oppositional voices and actors. *News from Nowhere*, an 1890 novel by William Morris, depicts a harmonious, face-to-face world, devoid of factories. This utopian world of great beauty and humanness was a powerful response to Edward Bellamy's Marxist-oriented *Looking Backward* (1889). Morris rejected Bellamy's hymn to factories and regimented industrialism: "a machine life is the best which Bellamy can imagine for us on all sides; it is not to be wondered at then, that his only idea of making labor tolerable is to decrease the amount of it by means of fresh and ever fresh developments in machinery."[15] How prescient Morris was. Well over a century later, it is easier still to see that work not only increases, but is steadily more alienated.

In France, Alfred Jarry, in his Ubu plays, also expressed antipathy to "machine life"—indeed to any routinized approach. In *Ubu Agog*, for example, "free men" in an anti-disciplinary army scrupulously disobey every order.[16] Jarry

---

14   Beckson, *op. cit.*, p. 87.

15   William Morris, "Looking Backward," *Commonweal*, 22 June 1989.

16   Roger Shattuck, *The Banquet Years: The Arts in France, 1885–1914* (New York. Harcourt Brace and Company, 1958), p. 227.

must have been quite aware of those who did not confine their anti-authoritarianism to the stage—the anarchists. In fact the anarchist upsurge of the early 1890s was a major public preoccupation in France, featuring as it did a series of bombings.

The French working class had been decimated by the bloody repression of the Paris Commune in 1871, but by the mid-1880s intolerable conditions provoked more and more wildcat strikes and made anarchism appealing. Belgium, too, experienced similar developments, including the 1886 wave of vandalism and strikes in Liège, and bands of unemployed people roaming towns and countryside in the Meuse and Hainaut regions. Eleven anarchist bombs exploded in Paris between 1892 and 1894; French President Sadi Carnot was assassinated in 1894.

This decidedly non-Decadent aspect of fin-de-siècle Europe not only appealed to various workers, especially to artisans threatened by the ascendant industrializing order, but also to some of the intelligentsia. "Propaganda by the deed" reached its peak coincident with the mature phase of Symbolism, and some writers were won over to the cause. Several well-known painters also stood with the anarchists, including Georges Seurat, Paul Signac, Maximilien Luce, Camille and Lucien Pissarro, and others. Renato Poggioli even referred to the "alliance of political and artistic radicalism."[17]

Of course anarchists, no matter how militant, were not all opposed to the Machine, any more than were writers and artists as a group. Kropotkin, for instance, believed in the potential of modern technology and wholeheartedly accepted industrialization, the foundation of all modern technology. Henri Zisly spoke out for Nature and decried the industrial blight, but was definitely in the minority within anarchism. He was part of the naturist movement

---

17 Poggioli, *op. cit.*, p. 11.

that emerged in the 1890s, but did not flourish.[18]

France underwent fairly sudden, profound changes with the industrializing process, including a collision with its long-running craft tradition. The overall breakdown in craftsmanship reverberated in the cultural sphere and led, in desperation, to methodical, scientistic styles that resembled those of technology.[19] It was a time of endings, of the loss of long-established foundations. "Never before have so many artists and writers been so obsessed with various processes and manifestations of decay," according to David Weir.[20] The founding in 1886 of a literary and cultural journal called *Le Décadent* announced the arrival of a cult of highly self-conscious sensual and aesthetic decadence. The ethos is one of decreasing vitality and hopelessness,[21] of standing "in the presence of the dissolution of a civilization."[22]

Again, one could find contrary sentiments. Reviewing Jarry's *Ubu Roi*, Arthur Symons noted the "insolence with which a young writer mocks at civilization itself."[23] A mural by Paul Signac entitled "In the Time of Harmony: The Golden Age is Not in the Past, It is in the Future" (1893–1895) recalled Morris' *News from Nowhere* with its bucolic, anti-industrial pleasures. The primitivist paintings of Henri Rousseau and Paul Gauguin also come to mind.

Gustave Flaubert's *Madame Bovary* (1856) was an early, deadly satire of French Romanticism; Emma Bovary's suicide was a bitter commentary on the fruits of emerging consum-

---

18 Anonymously edited, *Disruptive Elements: The Extremes of French Anarchism* (Berkeley, CA: Ardent Press, 2014), pp. 228–231.

19 Wylie Sypher, *Literature and Technology* (New York: Random House, 1968), p. 73.

20 David Weir, *Decadence and the Making of Modernism* (Amherst, MA: University of Massachusetts Press, 1995), p. xii.

21 William Barry, *Heralds of Revolt: Studies in Modern Literature and Dogma* (London: Hodder and Stoughton, 1904), p. 215.

22 Arnold Hauser, *The Social History of Art*, Volume Four (New York: Vintage Books, 1958), p. 185.

23 Beckson, *op. cit.*, p. 336.

erism. Naturalism's gritty realism was a tableau of subjugation; Emile Zola's *Germinal* (1885), for example, a tale of misery and hopelessness.

Joris-Karl Huysmans provided in 1884 what has been widely called the bible of Decadence with his novel *À Rebours*, usually translated as *Against the Grain* or *Against Nature*. Here nature has truly been left behind by an over-civilized seeker of rare sensations, the protagonist the Duc des Esseintes. His escape into artifice ends in ridiculous exhaustion as he finally seeks a consoling faith. The full range of Decadent sensibilities are displayed or predicted.

One can notice that in Claude Monet's paintings after 1883, the human figure shows up less and less and finally disappears. Something similar is happening with the new Symbolist poetry, championed by Paul Verlaine, Stéphane Mallarmé and others. In fact, Symbolism and Decadence became more or less synonymous in the 1890s.

The essence of Mallarmé's impersonal syntactical mannerisms is revealed by his description of a dancer. He said she is not a woman who dances, nor even a woman, but a metaphor; that is, it requires a poet to make the dancer real.[24] Mallarmé realized that there can be no stable art, no classical forms, in an unstable society. From this he derived the axiom that all great poetry must be incomprehensible. Arthur Rimbaud's 1870s work pioneered what came to be called Symbolism, but R.C. Kuhn's assessment seems valid: "Rimbaud's poetry is a rejoicing in presence; Mallarmé's is a celebration of absence."[25] Borne along by a current of language and very little else.

Many of these writers ended up becoming everything they once abhorred. Rimbaud was a gun-runner in Africa, Jarry and Verlaine died of alcohol, Huysmans died a Catholic—a litany

---

24   Richard Candida Smith, *Mallarmé's Children* (Berkeley, CA: University of California Press, 1999), p. 71.

25   Reinhard Clifford Kuhn, *The Demon of Noontide: Ennui in Western Literature* (Princeton, NJ: Princeton University Press, 1976), p. 317.

of failed and foreshortened lives. The ugly anti-semitism of the Dreyfus Affair from 1898 onward marked the end of the period of Decadence in France. Before long a healthier, combative era in culture began. We may say this change was already in the air when a student riot erupted without warning in Paris in June 1893. An art ball crowd of painters, poets and the like became an unstoppable force, occupying the Latin Quarter and requiring no fewer than 30,000 troops to disperse.[26]

English Decadence, though generally a bit less hard-core, drew a lot from French models and precepts. Less absolute than the French but with the same lack of interest in life and action, the same sense of the futility of it all. John Ruskin, who like William Morris after him championed craftsmanship, saw in the 1860s that "progress and decline" were "strangely mixed in the modern mind."[27] In 1893 Arthur Symons described Decadence as a "beautiful and interesting disease."[28] Gossip and its enactment, scandal, were symptomatic. Decadents seemed titillated, even seduced, by the idea of corruption. The word "morbid" became something of a cliché by the end of the century.

The earlier cultural synthesis of Victorianism was unraveling in an ethos of exhaustion and pointlessness. In Wilde's *The Picture of Dorian Gray* is the following all-too-resonant exchange:

> "Fin de siècle," murmured Lord Henry.
> "Fin du globe," answered his hostess.
> "I wish it were fin du globe," said Dorian with a
> sigh. "Life is such a great disappointment."[29]

---

26 Cesar Grana, *On Bohemia* (New Brunswick, NJ: Transaction Publishers, 1980), pp. 374–375.

27 J. Edward Chamberlin and Sander L. Gilman, eds., *Degeneration: The Dark Side of Progress* (New York: Columbia University Press, 1985), Sandra Siegel, "Literature and Degeneration: The Representation of Decadence," p. 199.

28 Beckson, *op. cit.*, p. xii.

29 Oscar Wilde, *The Complete Works of Oscar Wilde*, Vol. 3 (New York: Oxford University Press, 2005), *The Picture of Dorian Gray*, p. 318.

The disintegration of a high Victorian ideal of English civilization bore the usual marks of increasing mechanization,
notably greater nervous exhaustion from a more intense
pace of life.[30] A boom in interest in the occult, more drug
use, the usual Decadent-era escape routes. And in response,
new efforts at social integration, like more compulsory education and a bigger emphasis on organized sports.

Meanwhile, Decadents pursued their perverse and es-
capist paths. They saw ugly industrial urbanization—and
embraced the city as the supreme work of artifice. They
embraced what they saw as inescapable rather than try to
oppose it. It is ironic, in an age of irony, that world-weary
and ennui-filled Decadents were often obsessively drawn to
the vitality of working-class pubs and music halls.[31] But the
typical Decadent poet, Ernest Dowson, does not appear to
have made even vicarious use of such vitality. Bored to death
by the nothingness of everything, his lines seem to almost
always end on a note of disillusionment. The Pre-Raphaelite
art of Gabriel Rosetti and others in the 1850s, in its Ruskin-
like distaste for industrialism, was something of an influence
much closer to the end of the century. But its subjects appear
flat and doll-like, depthless—qualities that generally fit the
Decadent profile.

Elaine Showalter has explored what she called the sexual
anarchy of fin-de-siècle England, in particular the threat of
feminism to a very sexist culture. Robert Louis Stevenson's
The Strange Case of Dr. Jekyll and Mr. Hyde (1886) as a myth
of warning to women of the dangers outside the home, also
a case study of male hysteria and homophobic panic; Bram

---

30   Peter N. Stearns, *The Industrial Revolution in World History* (Boulder, CO: Westview Press, 2007), p. 172.

31   Mikulas Teich and Ray Porter, eds., *Fin-de-Siècle and its Legacy* (New York:
Cambridge University Press, 1993), Alison Hennegan, "Aspects of Literature and
Life in England," p. 197.

Stoker's *Dracula* (1897) as a fantasy of reproduction through transfusion, that is, without the need of women.[32] The Sherlock Holmes figure is also of interest; he turns to cocaine out of his ennui and boredom. The Arts and Crafts movement of the 1880s, itself an outgrowth of Pre-Raphaelite sensibilities, failed to gain traction. Its key figure, William Morris, was reduced to designing wallpaper and furniture for the rich, which he privately called "rubbish."[33] A rare sign of life was *Jude the Obscure*, Thomas Hardy's last novel. Influenced by the French utopian Charles Fourier, it contains very explicit social criticism and an early ecological awareness.

Weak, low-energy Decadence had little with which to sustain itself. Despite its showy and sometimes shocking bohemianism, several prominent Decadents retreated into the Catholic church: the artist Aubrey Beardsley, Oscar Wilde, and the poets Ernest Dowson, Lionel Johnson, and John Gray. Beardsley died of TB in 1898 (at age 25), as did Dowson in 1900. Critic Arthur Symons suffered a mental breakdown in 1908, and poet John Davidson commited suicide in 1909. Oscar Wilde, who did sense the underlying rot of civilization, died in 1900, which was already just past the sell-by date of Decadence in England.

"Vienna in the fin de siècle [experienced] acutely felt tremors of social and political disintegration."[34] Receptive to ideas of Decadence elsewhere, the Hapsburg Empire capital exhibited ever stronger symptoms of decline. Writing of 1890s Austria, Robert Musil recalled a sense that "time was moving faster than a cavalry camel.... But in those days, no one knew what it was moving towards."[35] Even more than in France, the pace of industrialization was intense and

---

32 Showalter, *op. cit.*, pp. 127, 107, 179.

33 E.P. Thompson, *William Morris* (New York: Pantheon Books, 1977), p. 109.

34 Carl E. Schorske, *Fin-de-Siècle Vienna: Politics and Culture* (New York: Alfred A. Knopf, 1980), p. xvii.

35 *Ibid.*, p. 116.

disruptive, the "new conditions of modern life emerging suddenly and uncontrollably."[36] Czech critic Frantisek Salda characterized 1890s Vienna as a culture in which "young men imitated old with their tiredness, wornness, blague and cynicism."[37] Progress as a positive thing seemed at an end.

This deflation or defeat, again, had a deeper basis. Life on a human scale was being erased in society at large. Frederick Morton referred bitterly to the "industrial flowering" and its effects on the worker, who before "served the needs of specific men. Now he was a nameless lackey to faceless machines."[38] Along with Europe's highest suicide rate came well-trodden Decadent dodges: avoidance of socio-political reality; an occult revival; the elevation of subjectivism; Wagner worship with its ersatz pietism, pseudo-redemption, and virulent anti-semitism; embrace of Schopenhauerian pessimism/ nihilism; aversion to nature.

In terms of subjectivism or inwardness, the emergence of Sigmund Freud fits the overall predicament. 1890s Vienna saw his metaphysic mature. At base, Freud's analysis rules out the relevance of any politics in favor of the primacy of very early sexual development and the primal conflict between father and son. Certainly no decadent, Freud was nonetheless part of the retreat from outside reality.

Another precursor of modernism was Robert Musil, whose *The Man Without Qualities*, while not published until 1930, was set in Decadent Austria. The characters in the novel search for order and meaning in a culture which has broken down into a state of spiritual crisis. The sense of a loss of reality is paramount, and although Musil is not explicitly

---

36 Micale, *op. cit.*, p. 88.

37 Robert B. Pynsent, ed., *Decadence and Innovation: Austro-Hungarian Life and Art at the Turn of the Century* (London: Weidenfeld and Nicolson, 1989), Magda Czigany, "Imitation or Inspiration," p. 119.

38 Frederick Morton, *A Nervous Splendor: Vienna 1888/1889* (Boston: Little, Brown, 1979), p. 314.

interested in social specifics, he invokes the slide-rule as a reigning symbol, not unlike the computer today. Mainly we see the turn toward language, away from the moral standstill at large, soon to be so greatly stressed by Wittgenstein and others. Musil's hero Ulrich is indeed "without qualities." His character dissolves into a multiplicity of divergent, even opposing selves. The non-coherence of the modern mind is another feature, along with Musil's stress on the merely linguistic, previewing postmodernism a century later.

What could be termed gigantism in serious Viennese music echoed enormous factory growth at this time. Gustav Mahler, key composer and conductor, orchestrated long symphonies for one hundred or more players, often accompanied by huge choruses.

Gustav Klimt led the art nouveau Secession movement, but this artist-heretic "quickly acquitted strong social and financial backing."[39] Modern art, somewhat ironically, came into official favor just when parliamentary government was virtually falling apart, largely because of the poisonous rise of anti-semitism early in the 1890s.

In Germany, too, pessimism led to the cultivation of aestheticism as avoidance. The novels of the 1890s are devoid of realist content, and the major poets (e.g., Stefan George, Rainer Maria Rilke, Hans von Hofmannsthal) likewise refrained from dealing with the world, in favor of giving voice to fleeting impressions, moods, and perceptions. A spate of plays and novels, however, depicted how German secondary education produced adolescent misery, including suicides.[40] As in most countries, industrialization increased inequalities of wealth and income, while tuberculosis was a scourge in Berlin and other cities.

---

39 Schorske, *op. cit.*, p. 208.

40 John Neubauer, *The Fin-de-Siècle Culture of Adolescence* (New Haven, CT: Yale University Press, 1992), p. 2.

The air of unreality was also felt by Czechs as rapid industrialization swept away most of the past. Arthur Breisky described the dandy who "is the knight of todays; he closes his eyes indifferently to all tomorrows."[41]

In Hungary, poet Gyula Reviczky decided that "the world is but a mood,"[42] in step with the hopelessness and flight from society of Decadence in the rest of Europe. But Endre Ady, who started a new epoch in his country's literature, was a fine counter-example. He was a radical anti-feudal social critic who attacked the values of work and efficiency, and advocated simplicity and beauty. A definite non-embrace of the Machine.

And our own period of Decadence? Are we not more "over-civilized" than ever, in greater denial? There is more of the artificial than before, and an even greater indifference to history. Our sense of hopelessness is profound, a techno-industrial fatalism: the inevitability of it all. In 1951 Karl Jaspers wrote of "a dread of life perhaps unparalleled" as modernity's "sinister companion."[43] "As mechanization takes place…man loses his way amid the growth of complexity; he loses the sense of reality, of his own personality."[44] In our own age, Frederic Jameson points to a general "waning of affect,"[45] the cumulative impact of Progress at the expense of affective, or emotional life.

Nothing could be more obvious than that the eco-disasters of Decadence this time are industrially produced. Flattened, bored, deskilled personal lives find their double in the decimated, impoverished physical world. As Jaspers

---

41 Pynsent, *op. cit.*, "Conclusory Essay," p. 177.

42 *Ibid.*, p. 143.

43 Karl Jaspers, *Man in the Modern Age* (London: Routledge & Kegan Paul, 1951), p. 62.

44 *Ibid.*, p. 169.

45 Frederic Jameson, *Postmodernism or the Cultural Logic of Late Capitalism* (New York: Verso, 1991), *passim*.

summed it up, "The machine in its effect upon life and as a model for the whole of existence."[46]

A retreat to aestheticism can be no resolution to what can only be fully faced outside of the aesthetic realm. Freud was right in pointing out that art is not a pleasure but a substitute for pleasure.[47] A complete life would not require the consolation of art.

Edward Carpenter looked at civilization as a kind of disease we have to pass through.[48] This Decadence can be overcome. Confronting the nature of the whole is the inescapable challenge.

---

46 Karl Jaspers, *The Origin and Goal of History* (New Haven, CT: Yale University Press, 1953), p. 144.

47 Sypher, *op. cit.*, p. 203.

48 Carpenter, *op. cit.*, p. 1.

14

SOCIAL AND CULTURAL MOVEMENTS
MEET WORLD WAR I

IT WAS SOON after the years of Decadence in Europe that contestation arose, in a variety of ways, rising in strength until the outbreak of war.

World War I, in Jan Patocka's words, "that tremendous and, in a sense, cosmic event," was a watershed in the history of the West and the major influence on the twentieth century. Regarding its causes, nearly all discussion has concerned the degree of responsibility of the various governments, in particular the alliance system (ultimately, the Triple Entente of England, France, and Russia and the Triple Alliance of Austria-Hungary, Germany, and Italy), which, it is alleged, had to eventuate in worldwide war. The other major

focus is the Marxist theory of imperialism, which contends that international rivalry caused by the need for markets and sources of raw material made a world war inevitable. Domestic causes have received remarkably little attention, and when the internal or social dynamics have been explored at all, several mistaken notions have been introduced.

The war's genesis is examined here in light of the social question and its dynamics. The thesis entertained is that a rapidly developing challenge to domination was destroyed by the onset of war—the most significant stroke of counterrevolution in modern world history. If the real movement was somehow canceled by the outbreak of war in

August 1914, it is clear that the usual reference (in this case, Debord's) to "the profound social upheaval which arose with the first world war" is profoundly in error.

Some observers have noted in passing the prevalence of uncontrolled, unpredictable violence throughout Europe before the war—perhaps the most telling sign of the haunting dissatisfaction within an unanchored society. This could be seen in the major nations, and in many other regions. For example, Halévy was surprised by the 1913 general strikes in South Africa and Dublin, which "so strangely and unexpectedly cut across the feud between English and Dutch overseas, between Protestant and Catholic in Ireland." Berghahn saw that both Turkey and Austria Hungary "were threatened in their existence by both social and national revolutionary movements." Sazanov's *Reminiscences* refer to sudden outbreaks of rioting in Constantinople, and to the Dashnaktzutium, Armenian radicals, of whom it was "difficult to discern" if they were more directed against Turkey or intent on fomenting a revolution at home. And Pierre van Paasen's memoirs tell of social peace disintegrating in prewar Holland. "A new spirit invaded the community. For one thing, the shipyard workers no longer drifted home at nights in small groups or singles. They came marching home...all of them singing, singing as if they wanted to burst their lungs, so that the windows rattled. What had come over these fellows?"

Instead of analysis of this telling background, the coming of war is typically trivialized by a concentration on the assassination of the Austrian Archduke Franz Ferdinand. The nature and duration of the ensuing carnage is falsified as a surprise development. In fact, neither of these approaches to the meaning of the war hold up under scrutiny.

The Serbian militant who shot the Hapsburg archduke did not immediately plunge Europe into hostilities. As Zeman writes, "In all the capitals of Europe, the reaction to the assassination of the heir to the Hapsburg throne was calm to the point of indifference. The people took little notice; the stock exchange registered barely a tremor." In fact, six weeks passed between the June assassination and the August mobilizations.

As for the "surprise" as to the length and design of the war, trench warfare (the hallmark of World War I, to many historians) was anything but new. It had been integral to the American Civil War; in the Crimea, at Plevna (1877–78); and in the Russo-Japanese War of 1904–05. It is little wonder that military authorities predicted it would be used again. Ivan Bloch's six-volume *The Future of War* (1898) emphasized trench warfare and the totality of modern war; this work was discussed in ruling circles.

An alternative thesis views war as a needed discharge of accumulated tensions, requiring war in a form and duration equal to the task of extinguishing radical possibilities. L.T. Hobhouse viewed domestic problems in Europe as successively more clamorous, creating a crescendo of urgency: "Thus the catastrophe of 1914 was...the climax of a time of stress and strain." Similarly, Stefan Zweig wrote of the outbreak of war: "I cannot explain it otherwise than by this surplus force, a tragic consequence of their internal dynamism that had accumulated...and now sought violent release." The scale and conditions of war had to be equal to the force straining against society, in order to replace this challenge with the horror and despair that spread from the battlefields to darken the mind of the twentieth century West.

Beyond the initial value of war in promoting centralization and acceptance of authority, a far larger objective can be seen. In Wells' words, "greater happiness, and a continual enlargement of life, has been checked violently and perhaps arrested altogether." A vibrant desire and expectation of significant change before the war was put paid by four years of death. This longing for change was quite different from the bourgeois ideology of positivism, ossified and insipid, which was being directly challenged in popular life before the war.

The monotonous, uniform present of industrial society was ~~indeed~~ becoming more and more miserably palpable. As Max Weber had forecast, its bureaucracy could only increase. Leftist ideology seemed just as threadbare, measured against a worsening reality. War provided both an escape from daily life and the chance of its transcendence. By 1914, whatever emancipatory visions Marxism might once have represented were moribund; anarchism, which Laurence Lafore described as "imposingly vigorous" before the war, was also demolished by the conflict.

A survey of European countries—beginning with the less developed and ending with Germany and England—offers illuminating details of a generalized internal crisis throughout the continent, and its deflection and destruction by World War I.

Austria-Hungary

The act that eliminated the would-have-been Emperor of Austria-Hungary was by no means atypical of its time. Russia's Prime Minister Stolypin was assassinated in 1911, Spain's Premier Canalejas in 1912, and King George of Greece in 1913. Several attempts were made on the lives of Hapsburg royalty during the prewar years, including more than one against Archduke Franz Ferdinand. All the more suggestive, then, that the Archduke made his state visit to Serbia, the restive vassal nation of the Hapsburgs, on a Serbian church holiday that commemorated Serbian martyrs. Similar in provocation would have been a visit by a British royal to Dublin on Easter Sunday in say, 1917.

For most historians, the agreed-upon villain of this and other Balkan dramas has been the nationalist (or the nationalist student). This may be a case of typecasting. Valiani noted the revival of anarchist affiliation and influence in Serbia and Bosnia, and it is well established that Franz Ferdinand's assassins were not exclusively nationalist. Of course, war always requires a good excuse, especially when the state's enemies are, more clearly than usual, its own citizenry. The Sarajevo outrage was tailor-made for the needs of the ailing regime.

The latifundist system of feudal rule on the land, allied with a high-interest brand of capitalism, spurred a potent social revolutionary dynamic that outweighed even the nationalist-separatist stresses of the polyglot empire. In the ancient capital, a descending lassitude mirrored the crumbling rule; the literary leitmotif of the period is Vienna's strange atmosphere of "something coming visibly to an end." Hofsthmannthal's Elektra cries, "Can one decay like a rotten corpse?" His striking drama is the perfect artifact of imperial Vienna: a vision of disaster. *Elektra* is also an apt allegory of Europe, portraying the obsessive need for bloodletting out of a terror of death. In Gottfried Benn's words, "1910, that is indeed the year when all scaffolds began to crack."

As Norman Stone put it, "Official circles in Austria-Hungary calculated general conflict in Europe was their only alternative to civil war." The ultimatum served on Serbia following the assassination of Franz Ferdinand (a set of humiliating demands amounting to abasement to Austria-Hungary) was merely a pretext for war with Russia that would lead to a more general conflict. Despite Serbia's capitulation, war was declared, with the corresponding involvement of Russia. The ultimatum, widely hailed as Austria's "brilliant diplomatic coup," meant nothing. The immensity of Austria's internal problems demanded war, with a more complete reliance on its perennial school of civic virtues, the Hapsburg army.

Critical to the success of this tactic was the organizational sway of the Marxian mass party over the working classes.

The Austrian Social Democratic Party, most degenerate of the European left, was actually committed to the maintenance (and reform) of the monarchy.

When war came, it was billed as an unavoidable defense against the menacing eastern behemoth, Russia. The left, of course, cast its parliamentary votes for war, and followed with measures against work stoppages and other forms of insubordination. Although some Czechs threw down their arms upon being ordered against Russia, hostilities were initiated without serious resistance. But in the words of Arthur May, "Disaffection and discontent among the rank and file" were such that within months, the prosecution of the war was "seriously affected."

Food riots were common by 1915, and had spread to the heart of Vienna by 1916. Professor Josef Redlich's journal recorded that the populace seemed pleased when a renegade socialist assassinated Prime Minister Strugkh in October 1916. The Social Democratic Party, dedicated to the "cooperation of all classes," organized scores of peace meetings—not against war, but to restrain the masses from breaches of the "domestic peace."

By 1918 people of all classes were weary and bled dry. Following the Hapsburg collapse, rule was preserved by the remaining servants of power. The Social Democrats continued their basic role, along with the equally anti-revolutionary Christian Democrats. Together, they would govern Austria for fifteen years, paralleling Germany's prelude to National Socialism, the Weimar Republic. In Hungary, six months of Social Democratic rule was followed by the bureaucratic-totalitarian efforts of Bela Kun's Hungarian Soviet Republic (with Gyorgy Lukacs as Minister of Culture). Four months of this Leninist failure were enough to usher in the Horthy regime, which would administer a quarter-century of reaction.

Russia

War did not prevent a revolution from occurring in Russia, but its mammoth ravages dictated the deformation of that revolution and ensured the victory of the Bolshevik project. The class structure of Romanov society was too bankrupt to avoid demise. Z.A.B. Zeman wrote, for example, of the "amazing ease of the dynastic collapse in Russia." But the unparalleled destruction and suffering of millions of combatants and civilians rendered a whole, breathing revolution impossible.

Austria-Hungary's declaration of war on Slavic Serbia enabled a barely sufficient response to the Kremlin's consequent call to arms. Pan-Slavism, not Czarism, was the last pro-war chord that could be successfully struck by a doomed regime. Russia's war with Japan had been a transparent attempt to direct internal ferment into patriotic channels; defeat set off an abortive revolution in 1905. In 1914, only a victorious war could offer any hope for the status quo. Barring war, "within a short time," as Germany's Prince von Bulow observed, "revolution would have broken out in Russia, where it was ripe since the death of Alexander III in 1894."

Beginning in 1909, a series of international incidents and crises—mainly in North Africa and the Balkans—diverted popular attention from the gathering social crisis. Throughout Europe, authority was continually on the defensive in this prewar period. In Russia, state weakness was a glaring constant. Memories of the post-1905 repression were fading, and "the temper of the factory workers was turning revolutionary again," according to Taylor. And discontent rose even faster when the regime's policies became more reactionary, following Stolypin's assassination in 1911. When troops attacked workers in the Lena gold fields in April 1912, this act of savagery failed to cow the oppressed. Instead, it aroused workers all over Russia to a new wave of challenges. In the two years before the war, the curve of social disorder mounted steadily. Another year of peace would surely have brought new and even more serious domestic upheavals.

Edmund Wilson observed that "by 1913 and 1914 there was a strike wave even bigger than that of 1905." By spring and early summer 1914, Baku oil workers, St. Petersburg women factory operatives, and others initiated a movement that brought "the proletariat again to the barricades." As Arno Mayer summarized, "during the first seven months of 1914, industrial unrest reached unparalleled intensity, much of it politically and socially motivated." Thus the guns of August roared, the timing all but unavoidable.

The war to save oppressed and threatened Slavdom, launched with momentary enthusiasm, was soon flagging. Meriel Buchanan's biography of her father, the British ambassador to Russia, bemoaned "how brief and frail was that spirit of devotion and self-sacrifice, how soon doubt and despair, impatience, lassitude, and discontent crept in." By 1915, the lament of state ministers was widely recounted: "Poor Russia! Even her army, which in past ages filled the world with the thunder of its victories...turns out to consist only of cowards and deserters!" By January/February 1916, widespread mass strikes broke the civil truce.

The anarchist tide rose swiftly for a time during the war, despite the general draining effect of battlefield carnage, and disillusionment with the pro-war position of Russia's best-known anarchist, Prince Pyotr Alexeyevich Kropotkin. His accommodation to state power, widely seen as a betrayal of principle, was in fact shared by most Russian anarchist ideologues, especially in Moscow. Kropotkin's capitulation led many anti-authoritarians to opt for syndicalism, as a more practical, less utopian ideology. Another moment of the dimming of radical perspectives.

For Kropotkin, competition for markets and the quest for colonies had led to war. Like the Marxists, he ignored the overarching domestic dynamic in favor of an external, mechanistic etiology. With his untiring efforts to urge on the troops of the Entente to greater victories over the Central Powers, Kropotkin evokes Marx and Engels, who could always be counted on to support the more "progressive" state in any given war.

The collapse of the Romanov autocracy in March 1917 demonstrated that the proletariat were far from spiritually exhausted; their uprisings ensured the regime would run out of borrowed time. Lenin had been surprised by every revolutionary outbreak in Russia, because Marxist theory predicted revolution would begin in industrialized settings. But even he could see, in mid-1917, that disintegration of the provisional government would soon be a reality. His victory, the authoritarian Bolshevik counterrevolution, is an all too familiar tale.

Italy

Turbulent through the 1890s and the first decade of the twentieth century, Italy arrived at the prewar years in a volatile state. Propaganda in favor of conquest and expansion had failed to distract the submerged classes; in 1913 only three Nationalists were elected to the chamber of deputies

The months preceding the war were marked by widespread rioting and strikes, culminating in the "Red Week" in June 1914. During demonstrations by anarchists and republicans, violence broke out on the Adriatic coast; nationwide rioting and a general strike followed. F.L. Carsten provides particulars: "In the Romagna and the Marches of Central Italy there were violent revolutionary outbreaks. Local republics were set up in many smaller towns, and the red flag was hoisted on the town hall of Bologna. Officers were disarmed; the military barracks were besieged in many places."

In outlook and methods, the populace displayed an anarchic, autonomous temper—reflected by the anti-war position of the left as a whole. An overwhelming sentiment for neutrality led Italy to cancel its alliance with Austria-Hungary and Germany. War was far too dangerous a card to be played in hopes of defusing class war—for the time being. It seemed unthinkable that only a year later, syndicalists would discover and promulgate a nationalist myth.

By spring 1915, every major European nation had been at war for more than half a year. Italy was being steadily drawn toward the abyss, despite popular resistance. A friend told von Bulow how "the Minister of the Interior had said to him that if there were a plebiscite there would be no war." Zeman observed that in May 1915, "Rome came to the verge of civil war." Using paid demonstrators, foreign elements engineered pro-interventionist riots against the neutralists, who received no police protection and were viciously attacked by the pro-war press.

In mid-May the Turin workers declared a general strike, while the Socialist Party debated its position regarding Italy's apparently imminent participation in the war. "All the factories were closed, all public services completely paralyzed. The strike was total among all categories of workers," according to Mario Montagna's memoirs. "The entire working force of the city gathered before the Chamber of Labor, and then slowly marched—without the urging of speeches—toward the Prefecture to protest the war." Fighting ensued, but the strike came to an end on May 19, mostly because of isolation and demoralization brought on by the Party's refusal of support. Meanwhile, the "revolutionary" syndicalists had become the first section of the Italian left to advocate war, arguing that reactionary Austria must not be allowed to defeat progressive France. Italy entered the war on May 23.

Mussolini's radical rightward shift, in full swing at this time, is a symptom of the intense frustration caused by the left's inaction and betrayals. The young Gramsci even showed a passing sympathy for Mussolini's new pro-war position and his disgust with the passivity forced on the proletariat. When oppositional ideology and its arbiters renounce a popular movement, they prepare the way for steadily more backward forms of thwarted class energies. Forward avenues seemed completely blocked, with no apparent alternative to the avenue and dictates of war.

Giampero Carocci, among others, noted that after three-and-a-half years of war, "the majority of workers and some of the peasants (particularly in the Po Valley, in Tuscany, and in Umbria)" still "longed for revolution." But the pervasive postwar discontent was of an anxious, pessimistic kind.

The occupation of the factories in fall 1920 bears the imprint of a proletariat cheated and blocked by the left, and battered by war. Despite the enormous scale of the takeovers, both industrialists and government let the neutered movement take its course, without state interference. The apparent conquests provoked some alarm early on, but the ever wearier and more confused workers stayed politely in the factories under control of the unions and the left. "Community leaders refrained from every initiative," reported Angelo Tasca. The restless, anxious occupiers saw neither an outlet to expand their action nor the energies to forge new ones. The seizure of most of Italy's industrial infrastructure, along with extensive land takeovers, simply died away, leaving a feeling of total defeat. Mussolini's assumption of power followed this fiasco by less than two years.

A. James Gregor and other historians have demonstrated the substantive continuity between Italy's most militant socialism—syndicalism—and fascism, with the war serving as the essential mode of transition. Mussolini's trajectory, from activist and theoretician of syndicalism to activist and architect of fascism, by way of World War I, is only one connection. Syndicalism, then national syndicalism, provided the core social and economic content of ascendant fascism. Mass mobilization and industrialism set the stage for this transition; but the essentials of nascent fascism, in Gregor's words, were "the product of syndicalist lucubrations, syndicalist sentiment, and syndicalist convictions."

France

At the end of the nineteenth century, French socialists and anarchists were swept into the mainstream of controversy over the legal treatment of Alfred Dreyfus, a Jewish army officer wrongly convicted of espionage. Republicans embraced new causes, outside the sphere of proletarian work; the Dreyfusards were an early version of the popular front, the recuperative answer to reaction, real or otherwise. A socialist, Alexandre Millerand, became the first of his ideological brand to enter a government. He joined a regime that had recently been disgraced by the Panama Canal finance scandal. The outgoing minister of war was General Gallifet, butcher of the Commune. Millerand, his replacement, would be the most chauvinist of prewar officials, later joined by his socialist colleague Albert Thomas, wartime minister of munitions.

Unsurprisingly, this de-radicalizing of the left led many socialists and anarchists to nationalism. Their opportunistic electoral methods alienated the oppressed classes, leading to a widespread turning away from politics. Clemenceau's seventeen-point social reform program of 1906, for example, was greeted with indifference. An acute Cabinet instability emerged, in part because the enragés of the far left made it hard for Marxists to cooperate with the center left. Oron Hale noted that the working class movement drifted from parliamentarianism toward radicalism in the five years before 1914. Just before this period, revolutionary theorist Georges Sorel had warned, "A proletarian violence which escapes all valuation, all measurement, and all opportunism may jeopardize everything and rule socialistic diplomacy."

But even within orthodox political maneuvering there were unprecedented threats to the existing order. Persistent financial scandals were signs of its decay. In March 1914, the shocking murder of the editor of *Figaro* by the wife of the finance minister revealed the disorder among the most conservative sectors of society. In April, elections centered around a 1913 law prescribing three years' military service. Nationalist-rightist candidates were soundly defeated as voters returned "the most pacific chamber the country had ever known," in the words of Alfred Cobban. The conscription law had been roundly repudiated.

Albrecht-Carre, Taylor, and others have written of this shift away from militarism at a time when France, according to von Bulow, "was the only European country in which in certain influential quarters, not in the people, it was justified to talk of 'war fever.'" Prince Lichnowski, German ambassador to England, provided a still more complete picture in a diary note of April 27; he described the French people's calm and "thoroughly pacific mood," while noting the difficulties which internal affairs presented to the government.

The April polling "proved that even in the existing state of international tension French opinion was profoundly pacific and non-aggressive," according to Cobban. In June, President Poincaré was forced to appoint a left-wing regime under Viviani. Reversal of the conscription law was the first order of business; but radical and socialist deputies agreed not to press the issue, in exchange for vague promises concerning future passage of an income tax law—a clear betrayal.

As the war crisis heightened, Jean Jaurès, dean of the left, was assassinated by a chauvinist fanatic on July 31. Viviani then issued the left's call for national unity. In the face of spontaneous anti-war demonstrations, he announced that "in the serious circumstances through which our country is passing, the government counts on the patriotism of the working class."

Both right and left feared the increasingly militant proletariat. In the 1890s there had been hundreds of small, local strikes. There were 1,073 strikes in 1913 alone, involving a quarter of a million workers. The scale and persistence of these strikes generated a good deal of alarm; many saw them as "symptoms of a profound unrest and social sickness," as David Thomson noted. Strikes of Parisian postal and telegraph workers called the loyalty of state employees into question, while agricultural workers' strikes often led to riots and the burning of farm owners' houses.

Syndicalism was not a causal factor. Although syndicalist ideology appealed to some workers, revulsed as they were by the dogma of socialist reformism, there was no apparent positive correlation between syndicalist leadership and strike violence. ~~In fact~~ Syndicalist leaders had to combat violence and spontaneous strikes like any other brokers of organized labor. Syndicalist unions served the same integrative function as the others and showed the same movement toward bureaucratization. It is not surprising that after 1910 there was growing talk of a "crisis of syndicalism."

During the first decade of the twentieth century, Gustave Hervé's doctrine of total military insurrection against the officer class became quite popular. Elie Halévy saw that "no sooner conceived, it spread like wildfire to many countries outside France." He added that on the eve of war it was "still rampant in the rank and file of the French army."

Hervé, editor of *La Guerre Sociale*, had called for revolution in response to mobilization for war. But he changed his tune; when war came he begged to be allowed to serve in the army. As with Viviani's pro-war speech over the coffin of Juarès, internationalist sentiments evaporated, showing how thin the anti-war rhetoric had been all along. France's young men marched, relieved to abandon the debasing contradictions of the left.

But by the end of 1916, desertions were estimated at 30,000 a year. By spring 1917, wholesale desertions gave way to outright mutiny, causing overt panic among the military high command. Whole divisions from the Champagne front cheered for world revolution, and called for firing on the officers and marching on Paris. But exhaustion and a sense of futility, built from prewar disillusionments and compounded by the war's all-encompassing violence, took a toll. The universal united front of unions and the left held firm, keeping the war going and shoring up class society. France was the grand mutilé of the war: 1,400,000 dead—one of every twenty-four citizens. And out of all this, not a hint of postwar revolution was felt in France.

United States

Although the United States stood apart in many ways from Europe's traditions and conditions, many features paralleling prewar Europe are discernible in the American situation. Henry May found that "During the prewar years, passion and violence seemed to many observers to be rising to the surface in all sorts of inexplicable ways." As in Europe, organized ideology could not gain traction from this upsurge. The tame Socialist Party was ebbing after having reached its peak in 1912. The IWW, a syndicalist alternative, got a lot of press, but failed to have much impact.

The Federal Commission on Industrial Relations, sitting between 1910 and 1915, concluded that unionization was the answer to the violence "which threatened the structure of society," in Graham Adams' words. This recommendation, hailed by moderate and radical unionists alike, brings to mind the advice of a few that the IWW's industrial unionism was the specific brand best suited to stabilize American capital relations. Government-sponsored unions established the control apparatus of scientific management, under the War Industries Board, and survived long enough to administer fatal blows in 1919 to the three major postwar strikes: coal, steel, and the Seattle general strike.

John Dewey had predicted that the war would introduce "the beginnings of a public control," and defended it as a needed agency of socialization. But America's entry was far from popular. Ellul concluded that U.S. participation "could be produced only by the enormous pressure of advertising and total propaganda on the human psyche." Zeman quotes a far from typical, if anonymous historian: "We still don't know, at any level that really matters, why Wilson took the fateful decision to bring the U.S. into the First World War." John Higham provides a plausible, if understated reply: "Perhaps a vigorous assertion of American rights functioned...to submerge the drift and clash of purpose in domestic affairs."

Culture pushes the limits

Before examining the two most industrially developed countries, Germany and England, it is useful to understand something of the depth of the turmoil, and its pacification, as seen in radical cultural movements that reverberated internationally in the prewar period.

Stravinsky, whose *Sacre du Printemps* heralded the promise of a new age, exemplifies the supranational composition and appeal of the new music. Nationalism receded as a force in music between 1910 and 1914. In painting, the movement toward pure abstraction emerged simultaneously and independently in several countries during the five years preceding the war. Cubism, with its urgent re-examination of reality, was the most important element of the modern school and the most audacious to date—notwithstanding the frequent and entertaining accusation, in Roger Shattuck's words, that it was "an enormous hoax dreamed up by the hashish-smoking, pistol-carrying, half-starved inhabitants of Montmartre."

Alfred Jarry's nihilistic anarchism, especially in his Ubu plays, constituted a one-man demolition squad, over a decade before Dada. In Apollinaire, the new freedom and urgency in poetry—especially French poetry—is obvious. Apollinaire can also be viewed as an art-historical metaphor: having reached his poetic height from 1912 to 1914, he volunteered in 1914 and was wounded in 1916. His passion and spontaneity drained away, replaced by patriotism and artistic discipline. He died of his head wound in November 1918, the last month of the war. (Hemingway's character Jake, in *The Sun Also Rises*, has been emasculated by the war—an echo of Apollinaire's condition.)

Shortly before the war, a group of young chess players, eventually known as the "hypermodern" school, revivified the game in practice and principle, as exemplified most brazenly by Breyer's "After 1. P-K4, White's game is in the last throes." This arcane case is symptomatic of a time when throughout culture, in every area, an unmistakably daring straining at limits was underway. "More freedom, more frankness, more spontaneity had been regained [in the decade before 1914] than in the previous hundred years," recalled Stefan Zweig.

The war drew a terrible dividing line across the advance of these exuberant cultural movements. The first battle cry of Dada in 1916 was already really the end of it, and the modernist movement of the 1920s acted out a drama conceived, dedicated, and developed before the war. The most anti-bourgeois moments of futurism, all prewar, prefigured Dada in content and also stylistically, as in the issuing of incendiary manifestos. "In postwar Dada, the Futurist enthusiasm had been pacified, ironized, and introverted," according to R.W. Flint.

Shattuck mentions the "disintegrating social order" and a "sporty proletarian truculence" inspired by the avant-garde. Most lines of inspiration and energy were probably flowing in the other direction, but the connection itself is valid.

In H.G. Wells' *Joan and Peter*, the younger working-class generation is described as "bored by the everlasting dullness and humbug of it all." Paul Ricoeur's question of more than fifty years later fits this earlier time perfectly: "if there is not, in the present-day unrest of culture, something which answers correlatively to the fundamental unrest in contemporary work?" This unrest had its origins in the technological speedup of 1914–1918; the "struggle against idiosyncracy," toward completely standardized tools and tasks, received its final, critical impulse from the war. The groundwork was laid for "the time of full mechanization, 1918–1939," in Siegfried Giedion's definition.

Among artists, a revolution of forms gave clear testimony to the social crisis—not that the revolt against the rule of forms was always confined there. German expressionism, a pinnacle of prewar cultural revolt, aimed not only at shattering conventions but also at construction of a "utopian order, or disorder, believed to be freer and more life-enhancing than any to be found in the advanced industrial world just then approaching a new height of development," wrote critic Hilton Kramer. The aspirations and innocence of these revolutionary artists were cruelly destroyed by the war. In its aftermath, the bitter expressionist protests of Georg Grosz, Otto Dix, and Kathe Kollwitz conveyed shock and disillusionment, as with Dali's surrealist nightmares. Literature echoes this trend: Eliot, Joyce, Pound, Yeats, and so many others were prophets of decay and death.

Germany

Bismarck's authoritarian welfare state, several decades old by the time of the prewar years, enforced a state of affairs in Germany that was far from secure. A scandal in the Kaiser's immediate circle (the Eulenberg affair, 1970–1909) aired intrigue, blackmail, and rottenness at the highest levels, tarnishing the state's prestige. A Hamburg capitalist expressed his concern in 1908 about "the growing domestic crisis," hoping that a tax decrease might help defuse it. As early as 1909, war was proposed as a solution. The chief of Germany's military cabinet considered an "external conflict desirable" to move the nation out of "internal difficulties."

Prince von Bulow recalled "a general disgruntlement": "If in Bismarck's day people talked of 'disgust with the Empire,' it was now a case of 'disgust with the government'—a disgust which gained ground every day." More portentous was this high-placed opinion, also recorded in von Bulow's memoirs: "At the end of 1912, I heard from Dusseldorf that Kirdorf, one of the biggest Rhenish industrialists,...had declared that if this goes on another three years Germany will have landed in war or revolution."

In late 1913 and early 1914, the arrogant gestures of German officers against civilians in Alsace constituted the "Zabern incidents," and aroused, in Carolyn Playne's words, "general indignation." A great outcry went up, and the Reichstag voted, albeit impotently, a 293-54 no-confidence resolution. James Gerard saw this as evidence of waning government power; he wrote that the German people seemed "to be almost ready to demilitarize themselves." For John Flynn, the Zabern hubbub merely contributed to a deepening domestic split that had already paralyzed the country. "There was a spirit—and a growing one—of resistance to arbitrary tendencies," he wrote. In this context the naval indiscipline aboard the S.S. *Vaterland* at Auxhaven in spring

1914 is similarly revealing. The bold, spontaneous action of 1,300 crewmen forced immediate, unconditional acceptance of their demands.

Arthur Rosenberg described the political and social tension in Germany as "typical of a prerevolutionary period," concluding that without war in 1914, "the conflict between the Imperial government and the majority of the German nation would have continued to intensify to a point at which a revolutionary situation would have been created." On the eve of war, Chancellor Bethmann-Hollweg complained about the absence of nationalist fortitude, lamenting this as a "decline of values" and a "spiritual degeneration." Bemoaning what he saw as the ruling classes' "solicitude for every current of public opinion," he defined his war policy as a necessary "leap into the dark and the heaviest duty."

This rising crisis was not the work of the left. Despite its millions of adherents, the Social Democrat party was hollow at the core. D.A. Smart wrote of the "widely felt stagnation in the party." In his introduction to *Decline of the West*, Spengler noted both the approaching world war and a "great crisis...in Socialism." It makes sense that rulers feared the breakdown of formerly dependable official adversaries, the party and the unions, that were no longer able to control the workers. Industrial anger in the shipyards was on the upswing and was most often directly fought by the unions. Alienation of workers from trade union membership was strongly developing, with local groups breaking away from the central confederations in textiles, paints, and metals.

The Social Democratic Party was a function of the unions and a loyal handmaiden of the state. Its support of government tax bills made the military alternative possible, alienating workers in the process. As Austin Harrison observed with irony in 1914, "All kinds of men, German bankers, for example, often voted for the Socialists." Workers' penchant for "sudden, unorganized strikes," which has puzzled many commentators, underlined the contradiction and its threat.

In July 1914, Socialist Party leaders met with Beth-mann-Hollweg, enabling him to reassure the Prussian ministry of state of the left's abject loyalty: "there would be no talk of a general strike or sabotage." Following the socialist tradition of defending war by "progressive" powers against reactionary ones, the government and the loyal opposition agreed on anti-czarism as the effective public banner.

While laying plans to preserve the Party machinery, Social Democrats voted unanimously for war credits on August 4. The accompanying statement stressed that imperialism was the cause of war, and explicitly refused any responsibility. Robert Looker aptly termed this "a depth of political and moral bankruptcy...of such enormity that it went far beyond the crimes of particular leaders or parties."

Rosa Luxemberg wrote in early 1915, "The collapse itself is without precedent in the history of all times." She herself upheld the war for years (as legitimized by its enemy, autocratic Russia), until public pressure was overwhelmingly against it. After the rising of November 1918 released her from prison, she grudgingly backed the Spartacist revolt. The Social Democrats and the unions co-managed the war effort with the army. Their police role, most importantly, was to infuse the military authorities' security measures with a fading aura of socialism, to prevent popular uprisings. When Luxemberg wrote in 1916 that "the world war has decimated the results of 40 years' work of European socialism," it would have been more accurate to say that war revealed those results.

The Social Democrats drowned the abortive postwar rebellions in blood. Of course, the road to new horrors was wide open. As Lukacs recorded, "I witnessed the rise of fascism in Germany and I know very well that very many young people at that time adhered to fascism out of a sincere indignation at the capitalist system."

An equally sincere indignation reigned in Germany at the onset of war. Part of this was a nihilist dissatisfaction by many from ruling-class backgrounds. Hannah Arendt detected a common absorption among those most permeated with the ideological outlook and standards of the bourgeoisie: "the desire to see the ruin of this whole world of fake security, fake culture, and fake life." Ernst Junger expressed an exuberant hope that everything the elite knew, the whole culture and texture of life, might go down in "storms of steel."

On the brink of war there was a certain relief caused by the decision to proceed. War gave a release to exhausted nerves caused by the tension of weeks of waiting—a release captured unforgettably by Thomas Mann in ending of *The Magic Mountain*. But release was followed soon afterward, for most, by a confused despair.

In October 1914, the diary of Rudolf Bindung, a young cavalry officer, contained the war's essential lessons: "An endless reproach to mankind...everything becomes senseless, a lunacy, a horrible bad joke of peoples and their history.... It was the end of happy endings in life as in art."

Great Britain

Never before, and nowhere more so than in England, had economic, political, administrative, and military power achieved such a high degree of consolidation. Yet its fragility was becoming palpable, as unfettered, unpredictable mass opposition emerged, in England and elsewhere in Europe. The existence of a widespread challenge to the cohesion and integrity of nationalist states was unmistakable.

Foreign affairs entered a new relationship with domestic upheavals. The 1911 crisis in Agadir, Morocco, is a case in point. A strike by English seamen and dockworkers was marked by unprecedented violence, especially in the ports of Liverpool and London. During the strike, a German gunboat, the *Panther*, arrived in Agadir, provoking furor among English officials. When railway workers joined the strike, troops were called out and fighting ensued. The clash at home was settled on emergency terms, thanks to the Moroccan situation. Thereafter, domestic industrial warfare and foreign crises seemed to grow with equal intensity.

Another area of outbreak in England was a reaction to prejudice against women, as seen in the unrestrained physical fury of the votes for women cause. The fearlessness exhibited by feminists in the period 1910–1914 included pitched battles with police; arson of cricket grounds, racetrack grandstands, and resort hotels; and an attempt to attach a flag to the King's horse at the Derby that ended in death for suffragette Emily Davison. These methods stood in contrast to the movement's professed aim of being able to vote. Many characterized the movement as an outlet for suppressed energy. Reverend Joseph Bibby wrote of suffragettes "who set fire to our ancient churches and noble mansions, and who go about our art galleries with hammers up their sleeves to destroy valuable works of art." Having felt this explosion and the growing proletarian resolve, Bibby in 1915 welcomed the "chastening" effects of the war on these passions.

The prewar Edwardian epoch was an age of violence, when "fires long smoldering in the English spirit suddenly flared, so that by the end of 1913, Liberal England was reduced to ashes." Emanuel Shinwell's memoirs testify to this quickening time: "The discontent of the masses spread, the expression of millions of ordinary people who had gained little or nothing from the Victorian age of industrial expansion and grandiose imperialism."

The seeding time of 1914, in its ferment and fertility, seemed more than ripe for increasingly radical directions.

R.C.K. Ensor felt that an undistracted concentration on home issues may well have brought a revolution, especially, he thought, as reflected by the "prewar loss of balance about home rule." The social and parliamentary impasse over self-determination for Ireland—whether home rule should encompass the whole country or exclude Ulster in the north—boiled over in summer 1914. The south was ready to fight for a united Ireland, the loyalty of English troops was crumbling, and it looked "as if Britain was at last breaking up through her own weakness and dissension," in the words of R.J. Evans.

Colin Cross wrote, apropos of the Irish crisis, industrial strife, and suffrage violence, "Had there been no European war in Summer 1914, Britain might well have lapsed into... anarchy." As Irish workers and peasants moved toward revolt, a divided England appeared "nearer to civil war than at any time since the 16th century," according to Cross. The English party system began to founder, weakened by the split in the army over the Irish dilemma. As James Cameron summed up the situation, "From a hundred obscure places in Britain, from small-time barbers and ice-cream dealers and Diplomatic Secretaries the message went back to the European foreign offices: the United Kingdom, if you could call it such, is riddled with dissension; indeed, there is the considerable likelihood of civil war."

Harold Nicolson saw the industrial upheavals of 1910–1914, with their unfolding "revolutionary spirit," as creating veritable panic among the upper classes; this "incessant labor unrest" plus the home rule clash brought the country, in his view, "to the brink of civil war."

Class tensions were becoming unbearable, "too great to be contained in the existing social and world setting," in the words of Arthur Marwick. In 1911 William Archer had conjectured that some "great catastrophe might be necessary for a new, viable world social order." For England, as elsewhere, the whirlpool of contestation had grown critically turbulent over the four years leading up to mid-summer 1914. "The cry of civil war is on the lips of the most responsible and sober-minded of my people," George V warned participants in a Buckingham Palace conference on July 21, 1914.

It can be argued that viewed close up, the attitudes behind the social crisis amounted to a nascent refusal of modern organizational mediation as a whole. For example, a major social welfare measure, the National Insurance Act of 1911, only increased the discontent of the laboring classes. This act accounted for growth in the trade unions, whose bureaucracies provided functionaries needed for its administration; more distance from the workers, greater closeness between unions and government. A 1912 bill proposing to greatly extend the franchise met with universal indifference.

The Labour Party, voice of the unions and proponent of social legislation, likewise struck no chord with the populace; largely because of the repulsion its bureaucratic nature evoked, it engendered no enthusiasm at all among young people. But the voracious appetites at large could be seen in many major labor battles from 1910 on: in workers' propensity for arson, looting, and violence, and the strong preponderance of unauthorized, anti-contract wildcat work stoppages. Halévy saw the unrest as "verging at times on anarchy," and determined that it was a "revolt not only against the authority of capital but against the discipline of trade unions," as if union discipline were not an essential element of capital's authority.

By 1912 syndicalism and its close cousin, guild socialism, were attracting much attention. But popular excitement was lacking. These projections, staffed by union officials and based on union structures, were indistinguishable from industrial unionism.

Although English unions were strengthened by the war, worker rebellions managed to continue, against great odds. Summer 1916 featured much resistance outside London and along the Clyde in the north. These struggles were not only against the state and the employers, but especially in opposition to union administrations. New mediation was provided by the shop steward movement of union reform, a diversion essential to the containment of workers. The Whitely Councils, a form of co-determination that increasingly emphasized the role of unions, was another wartime development aimed against proletarian autonomy. The parliamentary committees at work on a council formula recognized that ongoing strife was the doing of the "undisciplined," not the unions. They "wanted to find a cure for the malaise that, before the war, had every year weighted more heavily on industry, and in consequence, on all of English politics."

A "Triple Alliance" among the miners', transport workers', and railwaymen's unions was formed during spring and summer 1914. Many thought that a general strike would have occurred in fall, as a culmination of a wave of strikes, had the war not intervened. This thesis confuses the official enemies of domination with its real ones. In fact, strikes were not initiated by union leaders (architects of the Alliance), but in every case broke out locally and unofficially. According to G.A. Phillips, the Alliance was not "a concession to the pressures of rank and file militancy; on the contrary, it was designed specifically to control and discipline such militancy." Union officials forged the new structure out of an immediate and overriding need to avert workers' actions, not facilitate them. Its constitution proclaimed: "Every effort shall proceed among the three sections to create effective and complete control of the respective bodies."

Concerning the actual arrival of war, even as the axe began to fall, "Nobody was 'for' the war, or cared at least to be expressly held to be so, and great numbers were urgently and articulately against it," in Cameron's judgment. Reginald Pound grasped the groundwork for the event: "Probably for a considerable part of the male population the war came, above all, as a relief from pointless labor, one of the major and possibly most dangerous discontents of 20th-century civilization."

World War I canonized the daily misery of the modern world, presenting its apotheosis of authority and technology most precisely in terms of work. Carl Zuckmayer's experience as a soldier summed up power's universal message that work is all: "The monstrous boredom, the exhaustion, the unheroic, mechanical day-to-day of war in which terror, fear, and death are inserted like the striking of a timeclock in an endless industrial process."

Author's note: This chapter was written for a publication that did not want endnotes.

15

CIVILIZATION'S PATHOLOGICAL
ENDGAME

SOMEWHERE GEORG Simmel noted that in the history of philosophy there are only extremely rare references to the story of human suffering. Even more strikingly, history itself also avoids such references. Can this continue to be the case?

There now exists only one civilization, a single global domestication machine. Modernity's continuing efforts to disenchant and instrumentalize the non-cultural natural world have produced a reality in which there is virtually nothing left outside the system. This trajectory was already visible by the time of the first urbanites. Since those Neolithic times we have moved ever closer to the complete de-realization

of nature, culminating in a state of world emergency today. Approaching ruin is the commonplace vista, our obvious non-future.

It's hardly necessary to point out that none of the claims of modernity/Enlightenment (regarding freedom, reason, the individual) are valid. Modernity is inherently globalizing, massifying, standardizing. The self-evident conclusion that an indefinite expansion of productive forces will be fatal deals the final blow to belief in progress. As China's and India's industrialization efforts go into hyper-drive, the environmental, social, and psychological ill effects make near-daily headlines.

Since the Neolithic, there has been a steadily increasing dependence on technology, civilization's material culture. As Horkheimer and Adorno pointed out, the history of civilization is the history of renunciation. One gets less than one puts in. This is the fraud of technoculture, and the hidden core of domestication: the growing impoverishment of self, society, and Earth. Meanwhile, modern subjects hope that somehow the promise of yet more modernity will heal the wounds that afflict them.

A defining feature of the present world is built-in disaster, now announcing itself on a daily basis. But the crisis facing the biosphere is arguably less noticeable and compelling, in the First World at least, than everyday alienation, despair, and entrapment in a routinized, meaningless control grid.

Influence over even the smallest event or circumstance drains steadily away, as global systems of production and exchange destroy local particularity, distinctiveness, and custom. Gone is an earlier pre-eminence of place, increasingly replaced by what Pico Iyer calls "airport culture"—rootless, urban, homogenized, identical.

Modernity finds its original basis in colonialism, just as civilization itself is founded on domination—at an ever more basic level. Some would like to forget this pivotal element of conquest, or else "transcend" it, as in Enrique Dussel's facile "new trans-modernity" pseudo-resolution (*The Invention of the Americas*, 1995). Scott Lash employs somewhat similar sleight-of-hand in *Another Modernity: A Different Rationality* (1999), a feeble nonsense title given his affirmation of the world of technoculture. One more tortuous failure is *Alternative Modernity* (1995), in which Andrew Feenberg sagely observes that "technology is not a particular value one must choose for or against, but a challenge to evolve and multiply worlds without end." The triumphant world of technicized civilization—known to us as modernization, globalization, or capitalism—has nothing to fear from such empty evasiveness.

Some, of course, absolutely glory in the alleged promise of globalization. Matthew Weinert, for example, counsels in his aptly titled *Making Human: World Order and the Global Governance of Human Dignity* (2015) that the individual is best served by politicizing globalization.

Paradoxically, most contemporary works of social analysis provide grounds for an indictment of the modern world, yet fail to confront the consequences of the context they develop. David Abrams' *The Spell of the Sensuous* (1995), for example, provides a very critical overview of the roots of the anti-life totality, only to conclude on an absurd note. Ducking the logical conclusion of his entire book (which should be a call to oppose the horrific contours of techno-civilization), Abrams decides that this movement toward the abyss is, after all, earth-based and "organic." Thus "sooner or later [it] must accept the invitation of gravity and settle back into the land." An astoundingly passive way to conclude his analysis.

Richard Stivers has studied the dominant contemporary ethos of loneliness, boredom, mental illness, etc., especially in his *Shades of Loneliness: Pathologies of Technological Society* (1998). But this work fizzles out into quietism, just as his critique in *Technology as Magic* ends with a similar avoidance: "the struggle is not against technology, which is a simplistic understanding of the problem, but against a technological system that is now our life-milieu."

The Enigma of Health (1996) by Hans Georg Gadamer advises us to bring "the achievements of modern society, with all of its automated, bureaucratic and technological apparatus, back into the service of that fundamental rhythm which sustains the proper order of bodily life." Nine pages earlier, Gadamer observes that it is precisely this apparatus of objectification that produces our "violent estrangement from ourselves."

The list of examples could fill a small library—and the horror show goes on. One datum among thousands is this society's staggering level of dependence on drug technology. Work, sleep, recreation, non-anxiety/depression, sexual function, sports performance—what is exempt? Anti-depressant use among preschoolers—*preschoolers*—is surging, for example (*New York Times*, April 2, 2004).

Aside from the double-talk of countless semi-critical "theorists," however, is the simple weight of unapologetic inertia: the countless voices who counsel that modernity is simply inescapable and we should desist from questioning it. It's clear that there is no escaping modernization anywhere in the world, they say, and that is unalterable. Such fatalism is well captured by the title of Michel Dertourzos' *What Will Be: How the New World of Information Will Change Our Lives* (1997).

Small wonder that nostalgia is so prevalent, that passionate yearning for all that has been stripped from our lives. Ubiquitous loss mounts, along with protest against our uprootedness, and calls for a return home. As ever, partisans of deepening domestication tell us to abandon our desires and grow up. Norman Jacobson ("Escape from Alienation: Challenges to the Nation-State," *Representations* 84: 2004) warns that nostalgia becomes dangerous, a hazard to the State, if it leaves the world of art or legend. This craven leftist counsels "realism," not fantasies: "Learning to live with alienation is the equivalent in the political sphere of the relinquishment of the security blanket of our infancy."

Civilization, as Freud knew, must be defended against the individual; all of its institutions are part of that defense.

But how do we get out of here—off this death ship? Nostalgia alone is hardly adequate to the project of emancipation. The biggest obstacle to taking the first step is as obvious as it is profound. If understanding comes first, it should be clear that one cannot accept the totality and also formulate an authentic critique and a qualitatively different vision of that totality. This fundamental inconsistency results in the glaring incoherence of some of the works cited above.

There was a time when nature was not an adversary to be conquered and tamed into everything that is barren and ersatz. But we've been traveling at increasing speed, with rising gusts of progress at our backs, to even further disenchantment, whose impoverished totality now severely imperils both life and health.

Systematic complexity fragments, colonizes, debases daily life. Division of labor, its motor, diminishes humanness in its very depths, dis-abling and pacifying us. This de-skilling specialization, which gives us the illusion of competence, is a key, enabling predicate of domestication.

Before domestication, Ernest Gellner (*Sword, Plow and Book*, 1989) noted, "there simply was no possibility of a growth in scale and in complexity of the division of labour and social differentiation." Of course, there is still an enforced consensus that a "regression" from civilization would entail too high a cost—bolstered by fictitious scary scenarios, most of them resembling nothing so much as the current products of modernity.

People have begun to interrogate modernity. Already a specter is haunting its now crumbling façade. In the 1980s, Jurgen Habermas feared that the "ideas of antimodernity, together with an additional touch of premodernity," had already attained some popularity. A great tide of such thinking seems all but inevitable, and is beginning to resonate in popular films, novels, music, zines, TV shows, etc.

And it is also a sad fact that accumulated damage has caused a widespread loss of optimism and hope. Refusal to break with the totality crowns and solidifies this suicide-inducing pessimism. Only visions completely undefined by the current reality constitute our first steps to liberation. We cannot allow ourselves to continue to operate on the enemy's terms. (This position may appear extreme; nineteenth-century abolitionism also appeared extreme when its adherents declared that only an end to slavery was acceptable, and that reforms were pro-slavery.)

Marx understood modern society as a state of "permanent revolution," in perpetual, innovating movement. Postmodernity brings more of the same, as accelerating change renders everything human (such as our closest relationships) frail and undone. The reality of this motion and fluidity has been raised to a virtue by postmodern thinkers, who celebrate undecidability as a universal condition. All is in flux, and context-free; every image or viewpoint is as ephemeral and as valid as any other.

This outlook is the postmodern totality, the position from which postmodernists condemn all other viewpoints. Postmodernism's historic ground is unknown to itself, because of a founding aversion to overviews and totalities.

Shrinking from any grasp of the logic of the system as a whole, via a host of forbidden areas of thought, the anti-totality stance of such embarrassing frauds as postmodernism is ridiculed by a reality that is more totalized and global than ever. The surrender of the anti-totality stance is an exact reflection of feelings of helplessness that pervade the culture. Ethical indifference and aesthetic self-absorption join hands with moral paralysis, in the postmodern rejection of resistance. It is no surprise that a non-Westerner such as Ziauddin Sardan (*Postmodernism and the Other*, 1998) judges that postmodernism "preserves—indeed enhances—all the classical and modern structures of oppression and domination."

This still prevailing fashion of culture may not enjoy much more of a shelf life. It is, after all, only the latest retail offering in the marketplace of representation. By its very nature, symbolic culture generates distance and mediation, supposedly inescapable burdens of the human condition. The self has always only been a trick of language, says Althusser. We are sentenced to be no more than the modes through which language autonomously passes, Derrida informs us.

The outcome of the imperialism of the symbolic is the sad commonplace that human embodiment plays no essential role in the functions of mind or reason. Conversely, it's vital to rule out the possibility that things have ever been different. Postmodernism resolutely banned the subject of origins, the notion that we were not always defined and reified by symbolic culture. Computer simulation is the latest advance in representation, its disembodied power fantasies exactly paralleling modernity's central essence.

The postmodernist stance refused to admit stark reality, with discernible roots and essential dynamics. Endless aesthetic-textual evasions amount to rank cowardice. Thomas Lamarre serves up a typical postmodern apologetic on the subject: "Modernity appears as a process of rupture and re-inscription; alternative modernities entail an opening of otherness within Western modernity, in the very process of repeating or reinscribing it. It is as if modernity itself is deconstruction." (*Impacts of Modernities*, 2004).

Except that it isn't. Alas, deconstruction and detotalization have nothing in common. Deconstruction plays its role in keeping the whole system going, which is a real catastrophe, the actual, ongoing one.

The era of virtual communication coincides with an overall abdication, in an age of enfeebled symbolic culture. Weakened and cheapened connectivity finds its analogue in the fetishization of ever-shifting, debased textual "meaning." Swallowed in an environment that is more and more one immense aggregate of symbols, deconstruction embraces this prison and declares it to be the only possible world. But the depreciation of the symbolic, including illiteracy and a cynicism about narrative in general, may lead in the direction of bringing the whole civilizational project into question. Civilization's failure at this most fundamental level is becoming as clear as its deadly and multiplying personal, social, and environmental effects.

"Sentences will be confined to museums if the emptiness of writing persists," predicted Georges Bataille. Language and the symbolic are the conditions for the possibility of knowledge, according to Derrida and the rest. Yet we see at the same time an ever-diminishing vista of understanding. The seeming paradox of an engulfing dimension of representation and a shrinking amount of meaning finally causes the former to become susceptible—first to doubt, then to subversion.

Husserl tried to establish an approach to meaning based on respecting experience/ phenomena just as it is delivered to us, before it is re-presented by the logic of symbolism. Small surprise that this effort has been a central target of postmodernists, who have understood the need to extirpate such a vision. Jean-Luc Nancy expresses this opposition succinctly, decreeing that "We have no idea, no memory, no presentiment of a world that holds man [sic] in its bosom" (*The Birth to Presence*, 1993). How desperately do those who collaborate with the reigning nightmare resist the fact that during the two million years before civilization, this earth was precisely a place that did not abandon us and did hold us to its bosom.

Beset with information sickness and time fever, our challenge is to explode the continuum of history, as Benjamin realized in his final and best thinking. Empty, homogenous, uniform time must give way to the singularity of the non-exchangeable present. Historical progress is made of time, which has steadily become a monstrous materiality, ruling and measuring life. The "time" of non-domestication, of non-time, will allow each moment to be full of awareness, feeling, wisdom, and re-enchantment. The true duration of things can be restored when time and the other mediations of the symbolic are put to flight. Derrida, sworn enemy of such a possibility, grounds his refusal of a rupture on the nature and allegedly eternal existence of symbolic culture: history *cannot* end, because the constant play of symbolic movement cannot end. This auto-da-fé is a pledge against presence, authenticity, and all that is direct, embodied, particular, unique, and free. To be trapped in the symbolic is only our current condition, not an eternal sentence.

It is language that speaks, in Heidegger's phrase. But was it always so? This world is over-full of images, simulations—a result of choices that may seem irreversible. A species has, in a few thousand years, destroyed community and created a ruin. A ruin called culture. The bonds of closeness to the earth and to each other—outside of domestication, cities, war, etc.—have been sundered, but can they not heal?

Under the sign of a unitary civilization, the possibly fatal onslaught against anything alive and distinctive has been fully unleashed for all to see. Globalization has in fact only intensified what was underway well before modernity. The tirelessly systematized colonization and uniformity, first set in motion by the decision to control and tame, now has enemies who see it for what it is and for the ending it will surely bring, unless it is defeated. The choice at the beginning of history was, as now, that of presence versus representation.

As mass society is introduced everywhere, the meaning of its accelerating and fatal history has become tragically clear. The rampage shootings, worsening drug epidemics, rising suicide rates, and so much else trumpet the fact that in late civilization community is simply gone. Pathologies abound in a state defined by its defining pathology: civilization.

Once and for such a very long time, we walked on this earth with all the skills we needed, in community, in healthy numbers. The destruction of the planet was as unneeded as history.

History commences ruin, the story of every civilization. Time to end this story.

Author's note: This chapter was written for a publication that did not want endnotes.

16

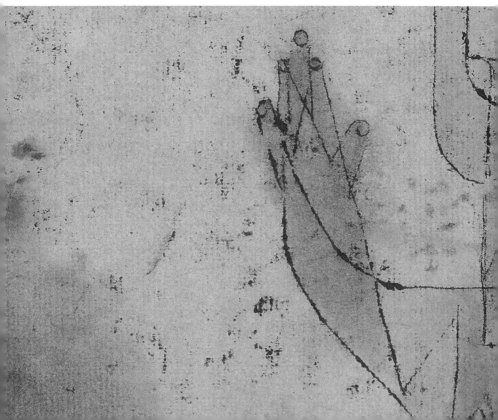

CONCLUDING ANTI-HISTORY
POSTSCRIPT

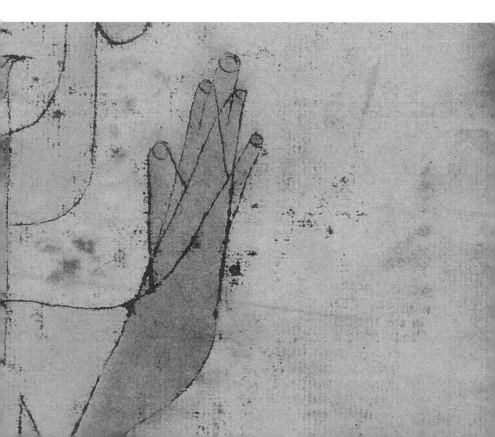

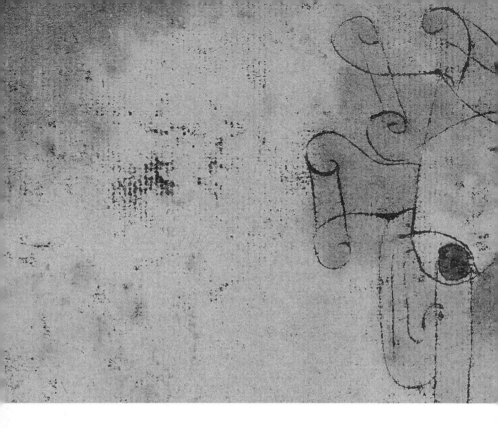

WE KNOW THAT the past is always molded to sanction the approved order, its government and social institutions. History is written by the victors. The story of civilization is not told by those who lost to the domesticators, the civilizers. But as we have seen, recurring transitions and crises are proof that civilization never enjoys a long, untroubled sleep.

Its ideologues have always presented a different picture, one of stability and pacification. A famous somewhat recent example is Francis Fukuyama's *The End of History and the Last Man* (1992), announcing the victorious end to the evolution of civilization. The world system of capital and technology is

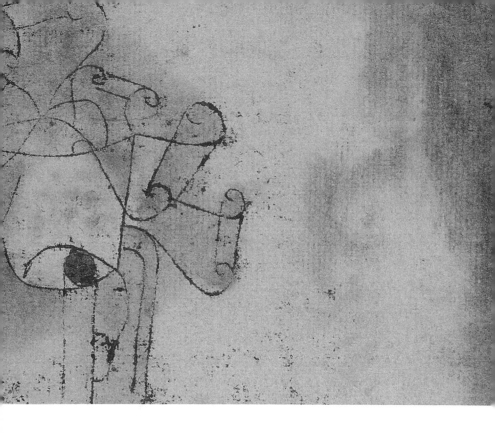

complete, upon the end of the Cold War; no further rough seas to cross. But in less than a decade the Anti-Globalization movement (1999–2001) provided a strong challenge to that hegemony in North America and Europe.

There's a lot more to history than questions of accuracy, of fidelity to events and currents. The most basic question would seem to be: What is history? In James Joyce's *Ulysses*, Stephan Dedalus says, "History is a nightmare from which I am trying to awake." Theodor Adorno referred to "the infernal machine that is history," pointing to its continuum of suffering. Everything has a history, and history has everything. Domestication requires storage; history is a form of storage.

Walter Benjamin counseled that we must go against the historical movement. The limits of history are increasingly being revealed to us. The historic dimension wears the mask of death. If the past is somehow to be redeemed, that redemption will occur outside of history.

Historiography, the study of history, does not concern itself with time. But the nature of history is very deeply tied to the question of time, the regime of time, its ever-greater materiality and oppressiveness. The continuity of history—and time—is imposed and alienating. Time is more than a medium; like technology, it is far from neutral.

In the 1980s I came upon a passage in Walter Benjamin's "Theses on the Philosophy of History," and was immediately intrigued by this now well-known piece. It is his meditation on a 1920 painting by Paul Klee, *Angelus Novus*:

> Where we perceive a chain of events, he sees one single catastrophe which keeps piling wreckage upon wreckage and hurls it in front of his feet. The angel would like to stay, awaken the dead, and make whole what has been smashed. But a storm is blowing from Paradise; it has got caught in his wings with such violence that the angel can no longer close them. This storm irresistibly propels him into the future to which his back is turned, while the pile of debris before him grows skyward. This storm is what we call progress.
>
> —Walter Benjamin, *Theses on the Philosophy of History* (1940)

Benjamin's interpretation of Klee's angel seems to me profoundly insightful. The storm blowing from Paradise is time, which becomes history and progress. The pile of debris is the course of civilization, growing skyward.

The book you are now finishing is a testimony to the need for historical awareness; but Benjamin points us further. A messianic dimension is needed if history is to be redeemed, if a part of the happiness our ancestors could not have is to be validated. To "awaken the dead, and make whole what has been smashed." To unmask the paradigm of history and its fundamentally legitimating enterprise.

Outside the symbolic system, beyond representation; what Lacan calls the encounter with the Real. Time and history ceaselessly advance all-encompassing domination; so a rupture, a break is needed. Only then could humanity realize a past, citable in all its lived moments, un-reified.

This vision is the opposite of Hegel's totalizing notion of history as the process by which the principle of freedom actualizes itself. Breaking the spell in a frankly apocalyptic way is Benjamin's counter-offer. A glimpse of this was presented in 1830, when radicals fired at clock towers.

Benjamin provides a striking contrast with the promise of historical advancement:

> Marx says that revolutions are the locomotive of world history. But perhaps it is quite otherwise. Perhaps revolutions are [or should be] an attempt by passengers on this train—namely, the human race—to activate the emergency brake.

The brake is a break with history. We were conscripted into history and we must make our exit from it.